The Inklings, the Victorians, and the Moderns

The Inklings, the Victorians, and the Moderns

Reconciling Tradition in the Modern Age

Christopher Butynskyi

FAIRLEIGH DICKINSON UNIVERSITY PRESS
Vancouver • Madison • Teaneck • Wroxton

Published by Fairleigh Dickinson University Press
Copublished by The Rowman & Littlefield Publishing Group, Inc.
4501 Forbes Boulevard, Suite 200, Lanham, Maryland 20706
www.rowman.com

6 Tinworth Street, London SE11 5AL

Copyright © 2020 by Christopher Butynskyi

All rights reserved. No part of this book may be reproduced in any form or by any electronic or mechanical means, including information storage and retrieval systems, without written permission from the publisher, except by a reviewer who may quote passages in a review.

Fairleigh Dickinson University Press gratefully acknowledges the support received for scholarly publishing from the Friends of FDU Press.

British Library Cataloguing in Publication Information Available

Library of Congress Cataloging-in-Publication Data

Names: Butynskyi, Christopher, 1978– author.
Title: The Inklings, the Victorians, and the Moderns : reconciling tradition in the Modern age / Christopher Butynskyi.
Description: Lanham : Fairleigh Dickinson University Press, 2020. | Includes bibliographical references and index. | Summary: "The Inklings, the Victorians, and the Moderns examines a small group of twentieth-century traditionalists in their quest to reconcile and translate conservative traditional ideas within a progressive modern scientific context. The method of reconciliation derives from their continued value of myth, religion, liberal education, and ancient texts"—Provided by publisher.
Identifiers: LCCN 2019050690 (print) | LCCN 2019050691 (ebook) | ISBN 9781683932277 (cloth) | ISBN 9781683932284 (epub) | ISBN 9781683932291 (pbk)
Subjects: LCSH: Inklings (Group of writers) | English literature—20th century—History and criticism. | Ancients and moderns, Quarrel of. | Great Britain—Intellectual life—20th century. | Modernism (Literature)—Great Britain.
Classification: LCC PR478.I54 B88 2020 (print) | LCC PR478.I54 (ebook) | DDC 820.9/00912—dc23
LC record available at https://lccn.loc.gov/2019050690
LC ebook record available at https://lccn.loc.gov/2019050691

Contents

Acknowledgments	vii
Introduction: Instruments of Tradition in the March of Progress	1
1 Ink and Parchment: A Historiographical Review	17
2 Tradition: More than Custom and Convention	37
3 G. K. Chesterton: Mouthpiece of Tradition	63
4 Raising the Temple of Science: A New Marketplace	77
5 Fellowship of Tradition	107
6 The Broader Conspiracy	133
7 Not All Books Are Created Equal	153
Epilogue: Passing the Torch	175
Bibliography	183
Index	193
About the Author	197

Acknowledgments

I have spent the majority of my academic career in the dark about the Great Conversation, its ideas, and contributors. I am enlightened by those who know what it means to discuss and dialogue in hope of reconciliation despite our perceived individualism and disunity. This book is my humble attempt to participate in the ongoing conversation of the Western tradition. I have done this by highlighting a well-known group of intellectuals who were not received favorably by popular culture given the parlance of their time. They faced scrutiny as do all who swim against the current. It appears that humanity moves in the direction of change, progress, and self-reliance. During this movement a necessity exists for men and women to keep the past relevant and translate it to their contemporaries—to reconcile the past with the present. The group I highlight in these pages, their intellectual counterparts as well, did just that and to them I am indebted. Whether I agree with them or not is neither here nor there. They have taught me what it means to read widely, converse collegially, and evaluate philosophically through a variety of disciplines.

I would like to thank those who have provided assistance with this project. My wife, Tricia, you continue to support me on a number of different levels. Thanks for the push. My mentor, friend, and colleague Professor Gary Jenkins, who discovered the wonderful program at Faulkner University, thus giving birth to the conversation found within this project. You encouraged me to continue my education because another degree "would really tie the room together." Doug Cornelius, iron truly sharpens iron; our friendship is priceless. To my friends and family who continued to ask when was I going to be "done this thing." Thank you for enduring my often lengthy discussions on the benefits of academic rigor, liberal learning, conservatism, myth, and many more subjects that caused you to glaze over. Although this was not your cup of tea, you helped me to brew it anyway. Cheers. My most humble thanks go to Tim Austen, my grammar and formatting lackey—without you these ideas would not have the clarity and eloquence they deserve. My thanks to the staff at the Wade Center of Wheaton College, you were most hospitable and helpful to a lowly junior scholar. A hearty thank you is in order to *The Chesterton Review, Journal of Faith and the Academy, The University Bookman*, and Apocryphile Press for publishing portions of this book while in its infancy. Your acceptance of my work led to a more complete vision. To the mediators of conversation in the Great Books Honors College at Faulkner University you are fighting the good fight as educators and humanists. We are all in your debt for the wealth of knowledge you have imparted and inspired us to seek out in hope of worthwhile participation in the Great Conversation. Thank you especially, professors Jason Jewell, Robert Woods, Ben Lockerd, and Brad Birzer for your insight and wisdom into my attempt to join in the conversation of the humanities. Your guidance and kind words will stay with me even if fame should befall me. I dedicate this book to my children, Chase and Molly—yes, Daddy can play now.

C. A. Butynskyi

Parts of the following chapters appeared in an earlier form in the following articles/book chapters:

Chapters 3 and 6: Originally published under the title, "The Reconciliation of Tradition in the Modern Age." *The Chesterton Review*, Vol. XLI, No. 1/2 (Spring/Summer, 2015): 147–58.

Chapters 4 and 5: Originally published under the title, "Spiritual Quest in a Scientific Age." Co-authored with Jason Jewell. In *The Inklings and King Arthur: J.R.R. Tolkien, Charles Williams, C.S. Lewis and Owen Barfield On the Matter of Britain.* Edited by Sørina Higgins. Berkeley, CA: Apocryphile Press, 2018: 213–38.

Chapter 6: Originally published under the title, "Babbitt and Belloc: Two Peas, Different Pods." *The University Bookman*, September 29, 2014. http://www.kirkcenter.org/index.php/bookman/article/babbitt-and-belloc-two-peas-different-pods/.

Chapter 7: Originally published under the title, "Not All Books Are Created Equal: In Defense of Liberal Studies." *Journal of Faith and the Academy*, Vol. VII, No. 1 (Spring 2014): 58–74.

Introduction

Instruments of Tradition in the March of Progress

Intellectual (or perhaps cultural) history characterizes the research on the traditionalists found within these pages. The intention of this book is not to challenge the existing scholarship and its recognizable depth regarding certain intellectuals from the late Victorian and Modernist eras, but rather to point out, perhaps obviously, the overarching connection between these individuals and the culture of the twentieth-century West. A book covering the overarching connections of a particular period will come off, regrettably, as broad and sweeping. It will most likely seem shallow or leave out other important figures. My intention, however, is not to create a metanarrative, but rather highlight ten to twelve key figures within the context presented in order to show evidence that something reactionary was indeed afoot—a common mind. This book draws on these ten to twelve authors to make a specific critical intervention: traditionalists did not want to see destroyed in a new image what Western civilization had built and raised. These traditionalists are often described, in the words of Edward Shils and Michael Polyani, respectively, as "active continuators and modifiers of the inherited stock of knowledge which changes as it passes onward"[1]—a form of "apostolic succession."[2]

Admittedly, this study is heavy on the Oxford literary group the Inklings, specifically C. S. Lewis, J. R. R. Tolkien, Charles Williams, and Owen Barfield, as they are the most popular and prolific. However, a shared camaraderie persists, at times directly, with a number of other traditionally minded contemporaries, namely Russell Kirk, Christopher Dawson, Irving Babbitt and Paul Elmer More, Josef Pieper, G. K. Chesterton and Hilaire Belloc, and T. S. Eliot. Despite their differences in academic discipline, religious conviction, political platforms, and cultural critique, a common mind deeply united these figures as they relied on the shared endeavors of those who came before. These particular connections are typically acknowledged on a specified level, but nothing has been compiled that suggests that tradition, conservatism, fantasy, myth, and liberal learning are somehow all tied to a small Christian renaissance found in the first half of the twentieth century. This book is focused on the perspective of traditionally minded intellectuals and their reactions.

They were all part of serious and scholarly endeavors to change the world for the better. In an age that saw them as regressive due to their hesitancy toward modern progressivism and ideologies, traditionally minded intellectuals echoed other champions of tradition. There were also a few select female intellectuals, namely Willa Cather, Dorothy Sayers, and Flannery O'Connor who shared similar, often Catholic, views on tradition. The lack of their presence has nothing to do with their gender. Instead, it is a reflection of the imperfect mindset of nineteenth- and twentieth-century traditionally minded intellectuals showing that these women were not given their due. They were perceived as not as widely read as their male counterparts (yet significant in their own fields) in the discussion of modernity, tradition, and scientism; yet persisted without shared influential end until much later in their careers. Perhaps this lack of focus leaves room for the opportunity to address their intellectual prowess in another setting. For most traditionalists, the idea of history as the narrative of humanity is one that reflects history as a record of God's activity and humanity's participation in that activity. Traditionally minded individuals were careful to avoid what they deemed the heresies of modernity (i.e., rationalism). It only makes sense to examine this particular group in a similar light in order to translate their ideas to the modern reader as they wished to do for their contemporaries.

Aristotle begins his seminal work, *Metaphysics*, with the statement, "All human beings by nature desire to know."[3] For most of Western history, the search for knowledge has been conducted within a system that incorporates metaphysical and transcendent characteristics as plausible and necessary components toward a complete knowledge of mankind. Since the dawn of the early Modern Age in the late fourteenth century, Western culture has slowly, yet deliberately, reordered the systematic understanding of the universe.[4] The ancient Greeks and Romans had provided their own versions of various systems of cosmology, philosophy, science, and mathematics. After the establishment of Christianity through the Roman Catholic Church, a Christian influence of these systems characterized the Western world for the next eighteen hundred years. Since the eighteenth-century Enlightenment, the deconstruction of the Christian universe has been at the forefront of modernity.[5] The nineteenth and twentieth centuries reflected the fruits of modern civilization's labors through the setting aside of tradition for the sake of progressivism.

It can be argued that Western civilization's commitment to progress led to its enhanced capabilities and success, namely the scientific and technological. Along with the West's desire for new knowledge about the physical universe, its obsession with progress increased exponentially. The focus on empirical knowledge largely was beneficial, but according to twentieth-century traditionalists, some of the success came at a price. The once prominent metaphysical or immaterial component to knowledge had slowly become less and less relevant. For twentieth-century German philosopher Josef Pieper (1904–1997), this signified the attempt of Western civilization to divorce itself from tradition and authority, which, according to Pieper, would eliminate basic structures of belief: "Accepting tradition has the basic structure of belief, i.e., relying on someone else. This amounts to saying that we cannot think of tradition without authority."[6] As modern thought promoted more individualized and subjective philosophies, the authority of tradition and the institutions associated with it endured an increased level of scrutiny.

F. C. S. Schiller (1864–1937) offered a simple explanation for the loss of the metaphysical in *Studies in Humanism* (1907). According to Schiller, when "making reality," rather than receiving it, the relationship between the physical and metaphysical are indeterminable, thus proving difficult to assess the immaterial existence or effect on knowledge: "It seemed possible that our so-called making of reality would not in the end amount to a revelation of the ultimate essence of the cosmic process, and that the analogies between the two would finally prove fallacious or insufficient."[7] The embrace of a secular understanding of the universe and humanity was not Schiller's alone and led to a more material understanding of things as well as a small but strong defense of tradition in the face of the changing tides of modernity. However, the unencumbered pursuit of "progress" led the West to act like a promiscuous honey bee flitting about from flower to flower in search of the nectar of truth. This nectar was, in the Modern Age, of a new and specific type and only came from those flowers deemed worthy of visiting. Truth, for the modern thinker, was seen through an empirical lens that homes in on hard facts. It seeks a specific kind of truth, and is therefore unconcerned with the nectar of those flowers which offer metaphysical, transcendent, religious, or imaginative insights as these were fraught with foolish and unfounded ideas.

The idiom of the modern scientific age reflected the redefinition of humanity through the lens of scientific, most often empirical, data. The justification of new knowledge originated through the modern idea that humanity, like the rest of the universe, was in a constant state of development toward an ultimate version of civilization. However, there were those who did not abide the modern definition of humanity, and although they did not decry a sense of development, they did not believe that all of the West's activity could be categorized as progress. Oxford's literary group the Inklings, American and British intellectuals known as the New Humanists, and other traditionally minded intellectuals (referred to collectively throughout as "traditionalists") provided a response to progressive ideologies of the modern scientific age in the twentieth century.[8]

A number of scholars recognize connections to the "Old West," the premodern, and tradition. A number of academics have touched on the relationships between the tradition of these authors, the reality of the twentieth-century intellectual climate, and their responses—political, literary, and historical. Some even talk about their service to the preservation of tradition and the permanent things (Benjamin Lockerd). The work at hand draws connections in order to show that a shared identity or common mind was conveyed over time through tradition, by means of a Western canon (*Great Books*), and more often than not attached to Christianity. Traditionalists were on a quest to reconcile tradition within the realities of their own age, one that was increasingly incompatible. The individuals themselves are not simply connected by their disciplines, religious beliefs, or political affiliation; they all felt cultural and intellectual crisis could be averted if tradition remained present. They held out hope, but tradition did not need to be supreme in order to be preserved.

The conception of some progressives is that tradition has become obsolete and no one, especially intellectuals, should accept an authority not of their own making. Traditionalists want to show that finding authority of another's making is not only a relevant desire, but an innately human desire. The hope here is to place the traditionalists in this book accurately within the movements of intellectual history, showing that they were their own robust and notable response to progressivism and scientism. They were not simply zealots, auctioneers of religion, or polemicists, but intellectuals with a deep concern for the well-being of their fellow man. The subsequent chapters explain the connections between the issues of tradition, modernity, imagination, progress, et cetera, which, in some ways, are left unexplained through the lens of intellectual history. The discussion is merely a continuation of a centuries-old conversation regarding the advent of modernity, in which key ideas will be examined in order to draw out and define their greater significance to the Western individual's desire to know himself or herself.

Whether through Christian humanism or secular humanism, the subject of the humane necessitated preservation. Those in opposition to the subjects of this study leaned toward secular humanism, but even they faced a decrease in popularity to the industrialized and scientific turn of the twentieth century. Lament, woe, and a tendency to pen jeremiads and eulogies are often associated with the study of these intellectuals—traditional and religious dinosaurs aware of their own extinction who scratch with tooth and claw to remain relevant. However, there are those in the progressive and secular camp that recognize the same concerns. Granted, each group sees the value of the humanities for different reasons and therefore possess different courses of action, but nonetheless, the direction of modern Western civilization warrants concern.

There are three authors I wish to highlight in order to cast the direction and conclusions of this book in a more discursive manner. Martha C. Nussbaum, Anthony T. Kronman, and John M. Ellis examine the corruption and loss of the humanities within liberal arts education. Many intellectuals and academics see the university as a crucial tool to convey the ideas that shape culture and move society toward progress and a better end. The diagnosis from these three in particular shows that Western society has reached a unique, perhaps even pivotal, moment in its history—one seen on the horizon in the early twentieth century and come to fruition only a hundred years later in the early twenty-first century. No matter the discourse of examination, the concerns and state of modernity (e.g., culture, politics, education) resonate through numerous authors and their perspectives.

Martha Nussbaum's *Not for Profit: Why Democracy Needs the Humanities* (2010) is an obvious foil to the traditionalists in this book. She sees the arts and humanities as a way out from under the yoke of blind tradition and authority—thus their importance to maintaining a democratic society. For Nussbaum, there are two major concerns that go largely unnoticed: the insistence on making college students financially literate and competitive; incentivizing STEM over humane studies. Nussbaum's argument examines the healthy relationship between a strong economy and the requirement "to draw on the humanities and arts, in order to promote a climate of responsible and watchful stewardship and a culture of creative innovation."[9] The traditionalists in this book and Nussbaum see the world very differently. However, they both reflect a deep concern for the cultivation of the technical over the humanity of the individual. Traditionalists and progressives alike are impacted by the effects of what Nussbaum describes as "obtuseness," claiming that "moral obtuseness is necessary to carry out programs of economic development that ignore inequality."[10] Chesterton and Nussbaum have different ideas on the definitions of social, political, and economic equality, but their overarching concerns align—the cultivation of imagination through a humanistic pedagogy. Chesterton, the Inklings et al. discovered profound beauty in the pagan and secular literature of the past, something that can be reconciled with the poiesis of the Modern Age.

Anthony Kronman's *Education's End: Why Our Colleges and Universities Have Given Up on the Meaning of Life* (2007) reaches similar conclusions. However, Kronman is focused more on the impact of science and technology, namely the detachment from the bigger questions of what it means to be human (e.g., the meaning of life). Kronman argues that one of the obvious issues with the relationship between the sciences and humanities is what they ask of the individual—detachment and attachment, respectively. Due to the contentious nature of the relationship, Kronman, like Nussbaum, sees a solution in the secular humanities, saying:

> Secular humanism neither reaffirmed the religious dogmas of the old order nor embraced the most radical doubts of the new one. It refused to endorse the idea that human life has meaning only in a world created by God and directed toward His ends. But it also rejected the notion that we are able to create for ourselves, as individuals, whatever structures of meaning our lives require in order to have purpose and value.[11]

Kronman's perspective and the perspective of the *Great Books* approach of traditionalists are extremely similar. Both approaches rely on the tradition of arts and letters derived from classical studies paired with the continuity of an ever-expanding canon in order to participate in what twentieth-century philosopher Michael Oakeshott calls a "great conversation."[12] Neither Kronman nor traditionalists wish to rely solely on contemporary works, but instead find value in the discussion between the past and present: "The expansion of arts and letters to include vernacular works of the modern period necessarily gave their study a living historical significance the classics alone can never possess."[13] The aspects of interpretation and uncertainty are prevalent in this approach, one that Kronman and traditionalists recognize does not translate well into the objective certainty of the modern scientific age.

At this point it may seem redundant, but John Ellis's *Literature Lost: Social Agendas and the Corruption of the Humanities* (1997) is yet another example of someone within the ranks of the literati who feels something is amiss. Ellis is writing at a pivotal moment in academic discourse and one could argue that his diagnosis is less egregious than the current state of literature departments. All three examples here insist the humanities are at the center of very real cultural crisis—one that no longer seeks to cultivate imagination. While the traditionalists of the twentieth century witnessed the germination, the authors of the present experience the bloom. The majority of the concerns is a reaction to the relationship between the arts and sciences in Western culture and society—specifically the preference of science and technology over the arts and humanities. Ellis focuses on the impact this mentality has on theories of academic discourse, something not specifically in full effect during the time of most of the authors in this book, but they certainly would have noticed new seeds being sown. Social agendas have a significant effect in any age and intellectuals diagnose and deal with them in relation to their own context. However, there are ideas that translate to different eras even if they manifest themselves in unique ways. For Ellis, race-gender-class theory has corrupted the study of literature. The connection between Ellis and the traditionalists is one that recognizes the symptoms of something larger—the influence of the social sciences on the arts and humanities and the growing intrigue of cultural relativism due to living in an age concerned with objective reality through empirical facts. The curricula and focus in literary programs began to shift in the late nineteenth and early twentieth centuries. Ellis points out that literature began, and has increasingly become seen, as "a kind of forum in which the members of society reflect together and brood upon the many issues that arise in their lives. Inevitably, the thoughts of those who offer the most insight into the most interesting and most enduring issues—that is, those with an unusual gift for doing so, great writers—float to the top and get the most attention."[14] The study of great writers of the past is crucial to the traditional ethos, thus the perspectives of Nussbaum, Kronman, and Ellis are helpful in order to create dialogue that speaks to the concerns, however different in scope, of traditionalists and progressives. My hope is that each chapter explains the perspective of the traditionalist with the intention of both sides finding common ground.

The chapters are broken up to address the nuances of twentieth-century Western intellectual thought and spotlight a small but influential group of traditionalists and their reactions within a new marketplace of ideas. Although the discussion is anchored in the discipline of intellectual history, the interdisciplinary style of the *Great Books*[15] has greatly influenced the following study in order that it may include and draw insights from various disciplines beyond history (e.g., literature, sociology). Intellectual historian Donald R. Kelley notes the complex task intellectual and cultural historians face in recreating the past: "Intellectual history is closely related to cultural history, being analogous to the polar modes of inquiry commonly known as internalist and externalist—or the 'intellectualist' (or even 'spiritualist') and the 'contextualist'—approaches."[16] The use of literature, social sciences, and historical discourse aid in seeing the ideas of the past, not only in their own context, but also as they translate from age to age.[17] Kelley points out that there are those who "look on literary works as philosophical surrogates and seek ideas,"[18] while others see it as a philistine practice. The authors in this book were largely from the literary class; it is only fitting to use their works, fiction and nonfiction alike, in attempt to see and understand their attempts at reconciliation. As German Romantic poet Novalis (1772–1801) wrote, "Therefore we have a duty to think of the dead. It is the only way to remain in communion with them."[19]

Undeniably, the spirit of the Modern Age is drastically different from that of its ancestors. It could be the result of a number of different reasons: secularization, advancements in science and technology, humanity's self-reliance, evolution of species or what Owen Barfield, in *Saving the Appearances* (1957), saw as an evolution in consciousness and C. S. Lewis shared, at least in part, in *Mere Christianity* (1952).[20] Whatever began the course of Western history is no longer relevant in its original form, but conservative thinkers have primarily looked to tradition to guide them in their development. A significant portion of twentieth-century intellectuals, influenced by individuals such as Alfred North Whitehead and Friedrich Nietzsche, saw tradition as the enemy of progress, unable to adjust its forms within Western culture. Donald Kelley explains the climate of influence saying:

> Yet change there is; and I seem to detect, among historians, a significant turn away from the spiritual world of ideas to the human condition of language, interpretation, communication, and cultural construction. As Whitehead remarked, "Ideas won't keep." For twenty-four centuries "ideas" have served to locate the elements of human experience and reflection (and indeed still serve as a useful shorthand), but successive waves of skepticism have cast shadows over the bright and avowedly "real" world of Plato's devising. For Nietzsche this is illusory, if not mendacious; for in his view humanity has remained confined to the cave, and the dream of escaping into a spiritual world belongs to the hope of religion and philosophy, not the experience of history.[21]

Granted, Kelley examines the state of history from a twenty-first-century perspective, but one that would have resonated with the early to mid-twentieth century. Tradition is the result of a gradual and long process of historical evolution and therefore it may be difficult to convince those born to the "virtues" of progress. Instead of lamenting the bygone ways of the past, traditional twentieth-century Western intellectuals committed themselves to the rehabilitation, revitalization, rediscovery, reclaiming of, relocation, or recovery of the ideas that the Western world held as foundational.[22] The chapters that follow also examine the realities of the modern scientific age and the attempts of traditionalists to reconcile the tradition of the Western canon to the new spirit of the age. In *Tradition: Concept and Claim* (1970), Josef Pieper provides an anecdote about discussing Western philosophy with Japanese academics in search of a similar stamp on human thought. His conclusion speaks to the unique discourse of the Western canon, saying: "All of Western philosophy maintains its vitality by nourishing itself on the conversation . . . with the sacred tradition of Christendom that precedes it. . . . Even when this sacred partnership is thoroughly understood, it cannot be simply transported to the soil of a fundamentally different culture."[23] A classical definition of liberal learning provided a platform from which traditionalists evaluated progressivism and practiced a life of the mind. It led them to see the conversation within the *Great Books* as one that elevated the humane in the face of modernity's attempt to redefine centuries-old concepts.

In light of the growing popularity of progressivism, these intellectuals relied on tradition in order to understand and discuss the ideas and concepts necessary for the comprehension of the purpose and meaning behind humanity and civilization during significant periods of change. The definition of progressivism is difficult because of its manifold implications and contextual realities—pragmatism, nationalism, scientism, et cetera. For example, during the early twentieth century, there were two different types of progressivism between America and Britain—American nationalist progressives and British socialist pluralists. According to historian Marc Stears, this is clearly defined by American progressives who "wished to construct a new central state machine in the United States, one capable of overcoming the obstacles of localism and sectionalism and imposing a nationwide political agenda and social identity across the several States."[24] On the other side of the pond, the British "celebrated diversity, social difference, and group autonomy, and argued for a radical decentralization of authority in all aspects of social, economic, and political life."[25] The variations of progressivism possess numerous perspectives on how to address the different issues of societal life. As nuanced as each version is, there is a common definition running through all of them—the desire to develop a new coherent and stable social order, indeed, an ideal society for the future to bring about larger and improved measures of human fulfillment. The intellectuals of this study were not against this premise, but were deeply concerned with some of the paths used to achieve this ideal—particularly suspicion toward the State, science, materialist definitions of humanity and spirit, and the growing concerns of the average person.[26] Factors regarding modern ideology, the non-bias nature of empirical data, and the methodology of religion and the humanities created friction from each camp's position on civil rights, misogyny, and antisemitism—progressives finding fault with traditional views and vice versa.[27]

One of the most obvious points of conflict is between the sciences and humanities. Early twentieth-century traditionalists were not anti-science, but they were hesitant at placing their faith in it at the levels of their contemporaries and the growing public demand (something discussed more specifically in chapters 4 and 5). The authority of science is tied to technology and its ability to increase the power of humanity exponentially—something that the twentieth century saw in ways never imagined before. Historian Max Hastings notes: "Between 1900 and 1914, technological, social, and political advances swept Europe and America on a scale unknown in any such previous timespan, the blink of an eye in human experience."[28] One of the concerns of traditionalists was the self-reliance of humanity brought about by scientific innovation—one that may disturb morality and spirituality. One of the goals of this book is to examine the dynamic of reconciling a humanities focused tradition within a scientific age. Due to the dilemma of authority, Kronman sees this as a difficult task for anyone:

> Culture, by contrast, is neither uniform or progressive. It tends to be a force of separation more often than one of convergence. It sets us apart, according to taste and tradition, and however meaningful its products, however much enjoyment they afford, the claim that some cultural object or activity reveals in a

decisive way the universal and incontestable truth . . . culture lacks the authority that science possesses, and the humanities . . . lack such authority too.[29]

In many ways, the authority to assert was stripped of traditionalists simply because the age recognized a new modernized authority.

Both traditionalists and progressives endured the pains that came with defense and growth. These were not reduced to the emergence itself, but were rather reduced according to the emergence of modern ideas. It was a purpose and meaning reduced according to new ideas without roots that were so frequently emerging. Classical scholar J. B. Bury (1861–1927) sought to foretell the demise of progress in his 1920 work *The Idea of Progress*: "A new idea will usurp its place as the directing idea of humanity. . . . Does not Progress itself suggest that its value as a doctrine is only relative, corresponding to a certain not very advanced stage of civilization?"[30] The purpose of the discussion here is to study points of reconciliation between tradition and progressivism as viewed through the eyes of those who desired to maintain the high standards of Western culture in the Modern Age. Even a cursory evaluation of the evidence demonstrates that there are pros and cons to any movement or shift in the course of human history. Instead, historical discourse provides an emphasis on the interaction between the concepts of modernity and tradition, as seen in the conscious efforts of traditionalists. To examine tradition as a response to the progressive changes of the twentieth century provides evidence that the spirit of tradition did not go gently into that good night.

Tradition, to modern progressives, appears to be the enemy of modern progress in the twentieth century and so it calls for a twentieth-century definition based on the relationship between custom, convention, and good habits of mind.[31] With maybe the exception of the Hobbit-esque Tolkien, traditionalists have shown they were not out to create Luddite revival societies who renounced the modern world and its influence.[32] Those who adhered to more traditional ideas were often chastised for their criticism of relativity and plurality. One such bulwark, G. K. Chesterton (1874–1936), is the subject of his own chapter due to his influence on the context for what it meant to defend tradition in the twentieth century. His ideas directly affected the traditionalists who claimed their perspectives mounted a defense of the permanent things.[33]

Ultimately, the quest for empirical truth was the driving desire of the Modern Age, one that altered its perspective from the promises of the Christian religion.[34] Traditionalists are better categorized as individuals unwilling to see things without the value of the past and its historical evaluation. It was only in the last few hundred years that a new definition of humanity became widely preached.[35] It is important to understand that tradition did not disappear from Western dialogue, but rather was privatized, something traditionalists saw as a matter of concern. The *Great Books* tradition provides opportunities to dialogue with a number of disciplines across decades of time from multiple perspectives. It is with this attitude that the following examination of twentieth-century studies will reflect. The discourse of reconciliation allows one to read traditionalists alongside modern progressives. Nussbaum desires to make "citizens of the world," yet does recognize the value in more traditional approaches, saying: "For this reason, I have argued that all colleges and universities should follow the lead of America's Catholic colleges and universities, which require at least two semesters of philosophy, in addition to whatever theology or religious courses are required."[36] Many of the points brought up in this book are not necessarily new perspectives. The focal points are an attempt to see the subject of Western historiography in the context of what many have deemed as "grand narrative."[37] Tradition did not perish with the inception of modernity. On the contrary, it was alive and well in the hearts and minds of these groups of twentieth-century authors. The traditionalists' commitment led to the survival of tradition in a skewed battle during an era of ongoing changes. The greatest fear resides in a trend of relegating tradition to a place without influence or voice if it shows any resistance to the new status quo. While many of their contemporaries saw their fears as alarmist in the early twentieth century, both progressives and conservatives have recognized a shared reality in this group's examination of Western culture.

Trends of nineteenth and twentieth-century historiography caused a shift toward more empirical and scientific methods. For some, it was demonstrated by the desire to see history through class struggle, the eyes of the common person, or the feminist perspective. Each of these methods contains valuable insights, but the study of the past is not one of single causes. In Jacques Barzun's *The Culture We Deserve* (1989), he warns against the trap of examining the past in search of a single cause in sacrifice of the narrative:

> Narrative history presupposes men and women whose motives lead to action and result in events. But we no longer believe in the importance of reality, of active men and women; we think they are moved by other forces, of which they are not conscious—by economic, dialectic, material determinism; by a thing called "their society"; by unconscious, individual or collective; or . . . by the environment.[38]

The interdisciplinary examination of a subject provides a way to avoid this fallacy. A multifaceted methodology also reflects the desire of the traditionally minded with regard to avoiding a purely scientific understanding of humanity. Barzun quotes Woodrow Wilson as an example of those who did not forsake a more classical approach; "by the time a man was old enough to have a son at college, he had become so immersed in some one special interest that he no longer comprehended the country and age in which he was living."³⁹ Historical discourse demands the discussion of not only the ideas, but the individuals who created and expanded the ideas in their respective fields.

Catholic historian John Lukacs (1924–2019) critiques the claim of current trends that want history to provide some level of utility and profitability, otherwise it should be cast off for the sake of progress:

> For instance, even those professional historians who by now refuse the categorical assumption of history being a Science still tend to write and teach as if human history were largely determined. Also, even those professional intellectuals who by now tend to react against the dominations of neo-positivism feel somehow compelled to express themselves in a language which is abstract, reflecting not only the intellectual temptation of substituting vocabulary for thought but also the inroads on their mentality of their colleagues' prestige in the natural sciences.⁴⁰

The modern era of history has concerned itself more with the public appetite of history and its causality, rather than the accuracy of the consciousness. The modern scientific age of the twentieth century was unique in that it allowed for certain egregious uses of science to flourish for the sake of progress, while at the same time there existed a well-informed group that warned of the dangers of fully realized progressivism. Traditionalists sought guidance in the liberal arts to build a bridge from the past to the present, so that the traditional definition of the permanent things of humanity could maintain a substantive presence despite their lack of pragmatic utility. The movement of materialism spoke much louder and promised more immediate results through the inception of many modern ideologies, essentially solidifying its popularity amid public opinion. The place for metaphysics, or the immaterial, slowly became an untrustworthy epistemology in the modern canon of empirical knowledge.

The reaction of traditionalists to the progressivism of the modern scientific age is a subject suited to the theory that the past is not the start to a series of improvements. The resistance to these proceedings did not wish to stunt progress, but rather keep such advancements within a reasoned and humane perspective. Geoffrey Elton's explanation of knowledge of the past closely resembles the views of the Inklings et al.: "If knowledge of the past is to entitle the historian to speak to his own day, it must not be so organized as to satisfy that day's whim; if it is to teach usefully about mankind and the human condition, it must be understood for itself and in all its variety, undermined by the predilections of the present and unruled by it at a time when the present did not yet exist."⁴¹ The tendency exists for anyone in the present to unleash a hermeneutic assault on the past for the sake of relevancy or spurious religious claims. Most level-headed traditionalists sought truth and understanding through various modes in order to evaluate a healthy culture in pursuit of a better future—something that could not occur through the annihilation of some ideas for the sake of progress. In order to maintain a sense of narrative, history must possess a record of victories and flaws and support a consistent theme where new stories do not simply emerge with no reference to past events.

The significance of the intellectual ventures of the twentieth century has not gone unnoticed. The chapters that follow will examine the idea that the moderns have attributed all rationality to the present, which is a denial of logic, in that syllogisms are linear. Modernity operates under the assumption of a privileged present which had then nothing against which to judge it. Simply, the past has no context and the future has yet to exist. Thus, the twentieth century petitioned science as its final arbiter in response to its view of reality—one built heavily on existence and experience. They sought a more modernized place, mode, and object of reverence, around which they built their own temples. The advent of modernity gave way to the principles of individualism, secularization, and pluralism. The effect is an ahistorical discussion that measures and relates objects in space, either organic or inorganic, but does little about objects through time, like ideas, beauty, or truth. To show themselves as "modern," the majority of the West attempted to use scientific methods to connect humanity to history, literary theory, et cetera. This mentality relegated history to nothing more than a chronicle of human agency. Traditionalists provided a small but significant foil to the enthusiasm of twentieth-century progressive ventures.

Tradition explained as part of this context has led to Western society's ability to recognize its own historical consciousness and location in the narrative of history. In so doing, this type of study reflects the belief that history indeed can "talk sense."[42] According to John Lukacs, the Western world possesses a unique ability to avoid past mistakes because the West has the ability to think historically.[43] The philosophy of history reveals different methods to tell the story of humanity, but the methods are not always the problem. Lukacs states, "the West has involved not merely a deficiency of a method, but differences in mentality: not only insufficiency of 'records' but distinct differences in the way in which different cultures have remembered their past."[44] The differences in mentality have caused the study of history to become bogged down by bureaucratic notions of universal history as opposed to defining a distinct historical consciousness for the period under review. Whether or not the process is objectively scientific or professional has become more important than humanity's discovery of *what is*.

The language of tradition as it relates to conservative ideas, typically, is perpetuated by the liberal arts. Terms associated with tradition, such as New Humanists or conservatism, should not be confused with the current political ideology of Neo-Conservatives[45] who are often assumed to denote traditionalists. One can find traditionalist intellectuals, during the twentieth-century, in opposition to the trends within their academic circles, as well as a burgeoning modern mindset because of religious affiliation and a glaring critique of progressivism and the secularization of Western society. Yet the connection proposed here runs deeper than political and religious affiliations. Their camaraderie will be explained through what they as individuals valued within the more general concepts of liberal learning, the reaction to progressivism, and their individual attempts to reconcile or translate tradition in the context of the twentieth century. Whether they consciously intended to or not they acted as living stones who continued to preserve and build on a Western foundation established by defined permanent ideas.

NOTES

1. Edward Shils, *Tradition* (Chicago: University of Chicago Press, 1981), p. 117.
2. Michael Polyani, *Science, Faith, and Society* (Chicago: University of Chicago Press, 1964), p. 40.
3. Aristotle, *Metaphysics* I.1, 980a21, *Classics of Western Philosophy Seventh Edition*, ed. Stephen Cahn (Indianapolis: Hackett Publishing, 2006), p. 228.
4. See Vincent Pecora, "The Modernist Movement: Virginia Woolf Voyages Out," in *Secularization and Cultural Criticism: Religion, Nation, and Modernity* (Chicago: University of Chicago Press, 2006): 157–94.
5. The reaction to "modernity" is based on the commonly held definition from Charles Baudelaire that views the post-traditional, post-medieval intellectual movement that roughly began around the Renaissance and continued into the twentieth century. Its tenets include, but are not limited to: industrialization, secularization, rationalization, existentialism, et cetera.
6. Josef Pieper, *Tradition: Concept and Claim* (Wilmington: ISI Books, 2008), p. 23.
7. F. C. S. Schiller, *Studies in Humanism* (New York: The Macmillan Co. 1907), pp. 426–7.
8. The Inklings is in reference to Oxford's literary group. The big four (C. S. Lewis, J. R. R. Tolkien, Owen Barfield, and Charles Williams) are the focus of this research, but the following is a more complete and revolving list: Tolkien's son, Lewis's elder brother Warren, Roger Lancelyn Green, Adam Fox, Hugo Dyson, R. A. Havard, J. A. W. Bennett, Lord David Cecil, Nevill Coghill, and John Wain. New Humanism refers to a theory of literary criticism, together with its consequences for culture and political thought. It was developed around 1900 by Irving Babbitt and Paul Elmer More. They were focused, from a conservative perspective, on the relationship between the liberal arts and university education.
9. Martha C. Nussbaum, *Not for Profit: Why Democracy Needs the Humanities* (Princeton: Princeton University Press, 2010), p. 10.
10. *Ibid.*, p. 22.
11. Anthony T. Kronman, *Education's End: Why Our Colleges and Universities Have Given Up on the Meaning of Life* (New Haven: Yale University Press, 2007), p. 81.
12. Michael Oakeshott, "The Voice of Poetry in the Conversation of Mankind," in *Rationalism and Politics and Other Essays* (Indianapolis: Liberty Fund, 1991), pp. 351–59.
13. Kronman, *Education's End*, p. 84.
14. John M. Ellis, *Literature Lost: Social Agendas and the Corruption of the Humanities* (New Haven: Yale University Press, 1997), p. 42.
15. The *Great Books* refers to certain classics of literature, philosophy, history, and science that are believed to contain the basic ideas of Western culture as compiled by Mortimer Adler and Robert Hutchins.
16. Donald R. Kelley, *The Descent of Ideas: The History of Intellectual Ideas* (Burlington: Ashgate, 2002), p. 2.

17. This is a widely known debate among historians. For example, postmodern theorists like Quentin Skinner contend that "love" to Aristotle does not possess the same meaning as "love" to the present; whereas Alfred Lovejoy sees ideas as a "great chain of being" one that exists in an ideal form and is tapped into across the ages.

18. Kelley, *Descent of Ideas*, p. 186.

19. Novalis, *Philosophical Writings*, trans. Margaret Mahony Stoljar (Albany: SUNY Press, 1997), p. 29.

20. Barfield holds that more primitive peoples practiced what he calls "original participation" with the natural world—one that incorporated practices and beliefs of the physical and metaphysical world. Over time, the consciousness of man had evolved away from this participation into a new stage—one that sufficiently lacked a level of mysticism and completeness. However, Barfield did believe that a form of "final participation" was alive and well in those who practiced Christianity—thus giving to a more mystical union between Creator and creation. Owen Barfield, *Saving the Appearances: A Study in Idolatry* (Middletown, CT: Wesleyan University Press, 1988). Lewis discussed similar ideas in terms of the relativity of behavior and whether or not there was a universal definition within natural law. C. S. Lewis, *Mere Christianity* (San Francisco: HarperOne, 1980).

21. Kelley, *Descent of Ideas*, pp. 7–8.

22. All of these words are used to reference what the Inklings, New Humanists, and other traditionalists were doing through their fictional, nonfictional, and political work.

23. Pieper, *Tradition*, p. 64.

24. Marc Stears, *Progressives, Pluralists, and the Problems of the State: Ideologies of reform in the United States and Britain, 1909–1926* (Oxford: Oxford University Press, 2002), p. 260.

25. *Ibid.*

26. Walter Nugent, *Progressivism: A Very Short Introduction* (Oxford: Oxford University Press, 2010), pp. 2–4.

27. Examples of dissonance and friction are well documented in the life of Margaret Thatcher—a woman in a man's world of politics, but also the leader and life-long member of the Conservative Party. See Robin Harris, *Not for Turning: The Life of Margaret Thatcher* (New York: Thomas Dunne Books, 2013) and Meredith Veldman, *Margaret Thatcher: Shaping the New Conservatism* (Oxford: Oxford University Press, 2015).

28. Max Hastings, *Catastrophe 1914: Europe Goes to War* (New York: Alfred A. Knopf, 2013), p. 2.

29. Kronman, *Education's End*, p. 228.

30. J. B. Bury, *The Idea of Progress* (New York: Dover Publications, Inc., 1955), p. 352.

31. See Doug Rossinow, "Introduction" and "The Emergence of the New Liberalism" in *Visions of Progress: The Left-Liberal Traditions in America* (Philadelphia: University of Pennsylvania Press, 2008): 13–58. Edward Shils, "Introduction" in *Tradition* (Chicago: University of Chicago Press, 1981): 1–33.

32. The legendary Thursday evening conversations were not devoid of scientific perspectives as evidenced by the presence of Dr. Havard. See J. T. Noetzel and M. R. Bardowell, "The Inklings Remembered: A Conversation with Colin Havard." *Mythlore* 31. 1 / 2 (#119/120) (2012): 29–46.

33. See Maisie Ward, "A Circle of Friends" and "The Distributist League and Distributism" in *Gilbert Keith Chesterton* (Jefferson Publication, 2015): 90–95 and 165–69, respectively.

34. See Paul Johnson, "A Relativistic World" in *Modern Times: The World from the Twenties to the Eighties* (New York: Harper & Row Publishers, 1983): 1–48.

35. See Patrick J. Deneen, "Science and the Decline of the Liberal Arts," *The New Atlantis*, Number 26, (Fall 2009/Winter 2010): 60–68.

36. Nussbaum, *Not for Profit*, p. 55.

37. An example of this assessment would be Johan Huizinga's seminal piece *The Waning of the Middle Ages* (1919).

38. Jacques Barzun, *The Culture We Deserve* (Hanover: Wesleyan University Press, 1989), pp. 135–36.

39. *Ibid.*, p. 112.

40. John Lukacs, *Historical Consciousness: The Remembered Past* (New Brunswick: Transaction Publishers, 2009), p. 21.

41. G. R. Elton, *Return to Essentials: Some Reflections on the Present State of Historical Study* (Cambridge: Cambridge University Press, 1991), p. 9.

42. Gertrude Himmelfarb, *The New History and the Old* (Cambridge: The Belknap Press of Harvard University Press, 2004), p. 171–84.

43. Lukacs, *Historical Consciousness*, pp. 23–25.

44. *Ibid.*, p. 24.

45. A political movement beginning in the 1960s toward the promotion of democracy, the elimination of radical leftist ideology and the preservation of American interests both domestic and international. Its biggest critics point out that more often than not it does not condemn the use of military force. Some of the more notable names are Irving Kristol, Daniel Bell, Daniel Patrick Moynihan, Jeane Kirkpatrick, and Norman Podhoretz.

Chapter One

Ink and Parchment

A Historiographical Review

Certainly, one cannot weigh in on, much less catalogue, the full corpus of Western historiography to date. One can, however, point out some connections that have not yet been explained, and thereby reveal a conscious resistance to the trends that characterize twentieth-century thought and beyond. A quick search through an archive of journals yields broad conceptual articles on anything from "Tradition versus Modernity," "Science as Progress," "Empire in Britain," anti-intellectualism, and a greater, more specified, number of race, gender, ethnicity, and sexuality studies.[1] Mainstream journals scarcely publish articles on the Inklings and other traditionalists, the impact of Western European thought, and the relevancy of classical liberal arts. It is something John Ellis perceives as a failing gap between ideals and performance, which does not recognize periods of transition, stating: "A period of transition is, of necessity, one of inconsistency, in which parts of the old and the new exist side by side. Change will occur more quickly in some regions than in others, but even in regions that lead, there will be ambivalence. The form that this inconsistency takes among Europeans is interesting but hardly surprising. The Enlightenment gives them a new view of humanity and also advances their scientific and technological knowledge."[2] In order to find such studies, one has to bypass the mainstream of research in the Western tradition to find relevant boutique sources. There is a small trend in both secular and religious circles that, despite differences in desired outcome or definition, see similar connections in the problematic relationships between traditional liberal arts programs, traditionalists, the humanities, and culture.

The scholarship surrounding these topics focuses on one group or another, but does not typically make the connection beyond Catholicism, or the political leanings of British and American traditionalists. Those who have made connections have not done so with the same discourse in mind. Patrick Allitt comes close to making such a connection when he draws lines from American traditionalists to the Europeans through an intellectual genealogy. He traces a common descent of ideas from Edmund Burke, to John Henry Newman, to Alexis de Tocqueville, to Jose Ortega y Gasset, to G. K. Chesterton and Hilaire Belloc.[3] These particular traditionalists embodied a significant enough movement and intellectual debate of the time that led to the founding of two journals, namely, *The National Review* and *Modern Age*. The success of an independent conservative journal was no small feat. There are numerous journals that have maintained a solid following on account of their early success, namely *The American Conservative*, *The Imaginative Conservative*, and *The University Bookman*. Tolkien, Chesterton, and Belloc were interested in precisely the types of issues discussed in the aforementioned journals/publications. Their discontent involved not only the secularization of Western society, but also the encroachment of liberalism on a Christianity that sought to identify itself as orthodox. The central conflict was the democratization of traditional standards in order to incorporate more and more exceptions to the rule, amounting to a conscious effort to make Christianity more "mainstream" and "relevant."[4]

The preservation of influential and permanent characteristics of Western culture was of utmost importance. It is becoming more recognizable now that this can be done through points of reconciliation between secular and Christian humanism. However, the twentieth century was in a time of transition that shadowed this possibility—a possibility that became dimmer with the passage of time and movement into the postmodern. The idea that the West could not be studied or understood without the inclusion of the Church reflects the beliefs championed by the historical inquiries of British historian Christopher Dawson (1889–1970). He states, "For the existence of the Catholic Church is one of the great objective realities of history. It is impossible to write the history of Christianity without it, and it is equally impossible to understand the history of our own civilization."[5] A Modern Age devoted to progress would covet such proceedings as they held firmly to the belief that Western society was in a perpetual state of evolution. Progressivism's desired evolution departed from the tenets defended by twentieth-century traditionalists because it could not abide the idea that humanity was in a fixed and universal state. However, not all were attracted to progressive ideologies.

Christopher Dawson wrote a number of books on the Modern Age's belief that it was the most evolved human civilization at that point. Dawson's books were histories of the Western world, but they also dealt with the implications of progress, the loss of tradition, secularization, and the spiritual, cultural, and intellectual conditions of Western society. Dawson described the activity of the Modern Age as a process of tearing down the accumulation of tradition in order to rebuild on newly discovered tenets, stating: "The traditional European polity, with its semi-divine royalty, its state Churches and its hereditary aristocratic hierarchy, was swept away and its place was taken by the liberal bourgeois state of the nineteenth century, which aimed, above all, at industrial prosperity and commercial expansion."[6] Dawson's position reveals a very real dilemma in the discourse of the twentieth-century historian—the transition from traditional methodology (Arthur O. Lovejoy, 1873–1962) to new methodology (Michel Foucault, 1926–1984). Donald Kelley explains Lovejoy's agenda as ambitious in its reflection of interdisciplinary orientation and use of ideas and their effect on Western culture and intellectual history, while recognizing Foucault's contribution of unveiling "power relations concealed by ideology" through the "unities of discourse," for whose conceptual value it is impossible to mount much of a defense, at least when they are divorced from the historical materials that might give them meaning.[7] It is difficult to write scholarship from a perspective that is often seen as counterintuitive to the current movements of the field, especially if the proponents of said methodology are also subjects of the study itself.

Adam Schwartz's *The Third Spring* gives evidence to the fact that Dawson's language aligns closely with that of the traditionally minded: "Finally he charged that academic overspecialization and capitulations to scientism had hindered both the interdisciplinary approach he favored, and the use of analytical paradigms that accented nonempirical evidence like literature and religion."[8] Dawson considered a society without spiritual roots—a key part of tradition—as a dying culture. He posited that the death of society was a direct result of secularization and its obsession with progress.

All societies have practiced some form of religion, and Dawson suspected that the Modern Age's insistence on moving away from religion and the metaphysical would be problematic. The perspective of this discussion hinges on concurrence with Dawson that without the preservation of tradition and its ancillary characteristics, traditionally minded intellectuals felt that they would be lost in what they perceived as a vapid abyss of a society with no hope in a greater purpose or meaning. Modernity reacted to the fact that Christianity once was a dominant force in Western society, and led to the public belief that Christianity did not stand on its own, but was a servant of the established order.[9] Tradition became synonymous with the established order, and all of its societal and structural flaws were out of step with the pace and direction of the modern world.[10] Society demanded measured results and empirical certainty in moving forward. Tradition appeared to lumber at a pace unconcerned with making leaps and bounds, and at times resisted change. Christianity's association with these principles led many to believe that the Church was antiquated and out of touch with the needs of society and the common individual. Because of this attitude, Western society sought other avenues of deliverance—namely, something more keenly recognized by ideologies such as John Dewey (1859–1952) and William James' (1842–1910) pragmatism.[11] Secularization negated faith, science disproved religion, and progressivism outran tradition.

The authors discontented with the trajectory of the modern world buttressed tradition with the hope that society would return to its roots. Instead, they found themselves surrounded by a society concerned with a material knowledge of how things worked and marked by an emotional attachment to equality, freedom, and Social Gospel.[12] Present scholarship reflects similar concerns as well. Beyond the subject matter, the methodology is one founded on empirical pillars—i.e., without the record, history is suspect. Traditionalists believed the path of progress was one that maintained its previous commitment to the discussion and evaluation of itself through a conversation with the authorship of the past.

The scholarship on the twentieth century typically addresses the monumental and drastic changes of Western civilization from the advancements of science to the decreased value of religion. Ultimately, historians are careful when evaluating the past; some even avoid evaluation by writing systematic and "factual" histories devoid of narrative. In spite of the alleged nostalgic proclivity toward antiquarianism of many traditionalists, they are for the most part not anti-progress. However, this effort has entailed a long and gradual process of development within an age of increasing pluralism and scientific influence, in which the most basic assumptions of traditionalists about reality receive scorn as outmoded and outdated. Twentieth-century traditionalists were of the opinion that the Western world had, like Tolkien's Middle-earth in the days of the ring, arrived at a new age—one that must be accepted without any intention of returning to what the world once was.

In light of the relationship twentieth-century traditionalists had with the past, those who study traditionalists, tradition, conservatism, and Christianity have of late been using words like "rehabilitation," "rediscovery," "recovery," and "bearer."[13] These words call to mind an accessible living past, not one entombed by its own context.[14] The Modern Age is distinct in that it was concerned with "remaking." Can two distinct perspectives on the past reach a point of reconciliation? Education, one of the catalysts of both the traditional and progressive movements, introduces subsequent generations to the slalom of the diametrically opposed perspectives of tradition and modernity. But what if one of these perspectives on Western civilization is phased out completely by a conscious effort on the part of the academy? There are those who see John Dewey's pragmatism in education as a guilty party. However, Martha Nussbaum applauds Dewey's progressive mind-set and attempts at accessibility within the cultural shifts of the twentieth century. The disparity of opinion regarding the goals of the twentieth century could lead to opportunities for reconciliation between tradition and modernity—even if those involved at the time did not see it that way.

Dawson, in *Understanding Europe* (1952), declared that the dialogue had indeed become one-sided due to the shift in purpose and value of education:

> Now from the modern point of view this traditional education was shockingly narrow and pedantic. It was also useless, since it had no direct bearing on the life of the modern world, on the world's work and on the techniques of modern civilization. Therefore, the nineteenth-century reformers insisted first that education should be widened to include the whole realm of modern knowledge, and secondly that it should be made practically useful in order to produce skilled technicians and trained specialists or research workers.[15]

Dawson is decrying the vast amount of universal knowledge and the impossibility of the mastery by the individual alongside an obsession with specialization. Current scholarship has not offered many solutions to this problem. The hope is to flesh out the possible solutions, if plausible, held by traditionalists.

While it is true that the Western world, to a large degree, was the result of a unique, religious belief in the Incarnation of the Christian God, the goal is not to promote a strictly Catholic, or even a specifically Christian agenda, but rather to encourage renewed devotion to a more holistic and complete knowledge of Western humane traditions—a benefit to both secular and Christian humanists. Many traditionalists are not ashamed of their devotion to Christ, but they do recognize that the preservation of the permanent things cannot rest solely in the pages of Scripture or the doctrines of the Church. Take for example C. S. Lewis' idea that divorce laws force a Christian view of marriage on the rest of the community and therefore could be conceived as injustice.[16] This made him unpopular with fellow believers and was a point of contention with friend and colleague J. R. R. Tolkien. In order to dialogue about such issues, Christian humanists embrace the liberal arts, which provide a platform of common mere humanity, on which candid but charitable interaction with the past may take place. Even though the Modern Age has changed the West at the core, Dawson argues that some things cannot be forgotten: "The vital thing was not the conversion of the Empire and the union of church and state, but the gradual penetration of culture by the Christian tradition, until that tradition embraced the whole of the life of Western man in all its historic diversity and left no human activity and no social tradition unconsecrated."[17] The majority of historians typically recognize the significance of spiritual and metaphysical elements in the narrative of Western civilization only as it reflects the dominant beliefs of a premodern world.[18] This perspective is dominant enough that in 2009, president of the American Historical Association, Gabrielle Spiegel, explained the task of the historian and urged her colleagues to move beyond the "cultural turn."[19] The position of the Poststructuralist movement rooted itself in the discourse of history. The history produced within this discourse was grounded in a more social scientific approach,[20] one that did not incorporate metaphysics into a twenty-first-century study of the past. This was not an invention of postmodernity, but rather something recognized by Auguste Comte in the nineteenth century and set in motion by his logical positivism. Nonetheless, there is a small contingent of historians who continue to produce work that values metaphysics as something more than an episode in the past. They carry on the conversation of tradition in a number of disciplines. There are historians, biographers, and novelists who continue to recognize the contributions of authors like the Inklings, the New Humanists, and even earlier examples who are often treated as individuals manipulated by their time and place. The work being done currently may not be consumed at a high volume, but it still has a significant impact.

Upon the review of Inklings scholarship, the reader is immediately overwhelmed by the abundance of work. The range of perspectives regarding the Inklings fluctuates from highly favorable to extremely hostile. It is the middle ground where one finds quality work written about these literary luminaries. Names like Humphrey Carpenter, Walter Hooper, George Sayer, Tom Shippey, Bradley Birzer, Stratford Caldecott, Malcolm Guite, and Alister McGrath provide priceless insights into the world of the Inklings and its supporting cast. In recent years Patrick Curry and Colin Duriez were added to the list of noted Inklings scholars. Philip and Carol Zaleski have also added their insights to the growing field. Time will tell if they share a place with the elites mentioned above.

The Inklings can be viewed as polarizing because of their devotion to tradition, conservatism, and a common mind—mostly influenced by medieval principles. André Gushurst-Moore defines the common mind as: "the mind at various levels of thoughts, feeling and understanding, embracing the ordinary person, and the man of genius in whom the human may be seen to an unusually rich or developed degree, recognizes a common human nature subsisting in all the vagaries of time and place."[21] Many writers and thinkers return to the idea of common mind, thus making it a form of common sense (not practical thinking), but a sense of what is understood and shared to be true. This is something that exists pervasively in the Middle Ages and has declined since, thus making it more and more alien a concept with the approach of the present day—especially if by nature it is in opposition (relative to the time) to the spirit of the age. It is exactly why these twentieth-century authors orbited around such ideas. They wished to communicate the inheritance of the common mind from the medieval and translate it into their contemporary vernacular. The reflection of their opposition can also be seen in the fact that their fans and critics are generally opposed to one another in matters of epistemology or progressivism. Oddly enough, they do maintain a peculiar relevance and popularity, especially Lewis and Tolkien. It should be noted that popularity does not necessarily mean that their Christianity and academic scholarship reflected the sentiments of the twentieth-century

West.[22] There are any number of reasons for the longevity of their popularity. Tolkien's *The Hobbit* (1937) and *The Lord of the Rings* (1954) have both witnessed a revival through their conversion into major motion pictures at the hands of Peter Jackson. Lewis's *The Chronicles of Narnia* (1950–1956) has seen some renewed exposure as well, but not to the level of Tolkien. Typically, adolescents come into contact with these books either through a Christian influence or the love of the fantasy genre. Due to their new popularity, the modes of interaction have expanded and the dream of the Inklings is being realized, even if some of the audience does not yet understand that the stories with which they have become familiar were books before they were CGI-laden action films.

The widespread consumption of their books is interesting given the fact that they were not bashful about their Christianity. In relation to their time, Christianity was sidelined in the sense of mass consumption, yet some of these authors saw significant sales of their publications. They were quoted as saying that Christianity is a fighting religion, and they meant to fight to preserve it.[23] Their staunch defense of Christianity is a shared characteristic in most biographies as well as a target for their harshest critics. The Nazi incursion and subsequent occupation of Western Europe halted whatever resurgence of religion associated as a result of World War II. The characteristically Christian identity of Britain continued a trend of reduced participation, one that has not slowed in recent times. The British Humanist Association (BHA) claims that at least 57 percent of Brits identify with secular or atheistic beliefs.[24] Historians have produced countless works on the distinct change of the twentieth-century Western world which support the data and the attitude that most appear to be in favor of this shift.

British historian Niall Ferguson (1964–) claims that the de-Christianization of Britain is a relatively new development. He points out in *Civilization* (2011) that as recently as 1917, G. K. Chesterton's *Short History of England* saw Christianity as synonymous with civilization.[25] Quoting Sigmund Freud, Ferguson offers insight into the drastic shift from a character of tradition founded on religion with progress founded in science: "[Religion] also reconciled men to 'the cruelty of fate, particularly as shown in death' and the 'sufferings and privations' of daily life."[26] There was an obvious recognition of the efforts of figures like Freud to deconstruct traditional ideas of civilization and provide new "scientific" meaning for human behavior. Ferguson describes the commonly held ideas surrounding the recent, yet rapid, change in both the American and British mindset.[27] Ferguson creates a narrative on the concerns of Christian intellectuals who are not looking to repress and control Western humanity through the institutions of tradition. Instead, he notes that the changes brought on by the modern scientific age were perceived as a drastic decline in Christian faith bordering on crisis.[28]

The narrative throughout the following chapters provides insight into the relationship between tradition and modernity as it was carried out in certain twentieth-century circles. The idea of the secularization of the West is not a revelation. However, the individuals highlighted here created a unique bridge between the tradition in the past and the realities of their contemporary modern world. Since at least the mid-nineteenth century, numerous thinkers have proposed variations on what has come to be known as the "secularization thesis," which predicts that as a society makes scientific and technological progress and modernizes in other ways, religiosity in that society will decline. Throughout much of the twentieth century, the secularization thesis was widely accepted among Western intellectuals, even among those who deplored declining religiosity, including some of the Inklings themselves. However, in recent years the secularization thesis has come under attack from various quarters. In 2003, syndicated columnist David Brooks, describing himself as a "recovering secularist," wrote in *The Atlantic*, "It's now clear that the secularization theory is untrue. . . . We are living through one of the great periods of scientific progress and the creation of wealth. At the same time, we are in the midst of a religious boom."[29] Some scholars such as Mark Morrisson and Robert Whalen have begun the process of reexamining the nineteenth and twentieth centuries and have uncovered a religious energy not recognized by an earlier generation of scholars for whose research agenda and secularization theory may have created blind spots.[30]

Though they may not have recognized it at the time, the success of the Inklings' writings is itself further evidence against the facile picture of secularization that twentieth-century intellectuals often accepted. It is this idea that is often underestimated or seen as a residual effect of tradition. Traditionalists urge their contemporaries to explore the plausible significance of tradition, according to which the Inklings and others ought to be considered as a plausible link between modernization and traditionalism. The Inklings saw themselves as carrying the torch through an age that wished to dim the light of metaphysical reality. Both popular and scholarly interest in their work, which is laden with spiritual themes, continues unabated and perhaps even has increased in the twenty-first century. Nevertheless, even at the height of their literary careers in the middle decades of the twentieth century, they still justifiably considered themselves out of step with the *zeitgeist*, that of scientific secularism.

The Inklings have maintained a sense of cult following. There are numerous journals, societies, festivals, online communities, blogs, and conferences dedicated to all things Inklings.[31] One should not mistake dedication for simple fanfare. Many of these outlets are dedicated to the integrity of peer-reviewed scholarship. The topics are either general in nature or extremely specific.[32] The exploration into their fictional and nonfictional work, especially the crossover between the two, favors an interaction with the subjects of mysticism, mythopoeia, King Arthur, Christian apologetics, philology, and the medieval.

The majority of the work done on the Inklings has kept to the previously mentioned themes. There is also work that addresses ideas and ancillary themes. They are not necessarily in opposition to or in favor of, but are important pieces of a greater whole. As it pertains to the overall conversation of tradition and modernity, one may find different concerns from the typical picture through a narrative of twentieth-century intellectualism. To date there is very little mainstream scholarship in regard to the intellectual history of traditionalists.[33] The central theme of "tradition" led to articles and books on heritage, but not in reference to progressivism and the like. In one sense, the task of adding to the field is unencumbered. However, the reality may be that these journals do not identify this subject matter as historical or significant enough to devote to academic query.

Despite the mainstream unpopularity of an intellectual or cultural history of the traditionalist perspective, the review of a wider sample of scholarship reveals an existing recognition, however small, toward a greater narrative beyond a solely nuanced treatment of the subject. The field is predominantly literary in nature and focused on: character studies, imagery, impact on fictional writing, political implications, memoirs, romanticism, and literary theory.[34] In both the historical and literary community there does not appear to be an exposition on the relationship between tradition, conservatism, classical liberal learning, and modernity using traditionalists to study the reality of twentieth-century reaction to what some have called a period of crisis. Although not an indictment of the present work, one does recognize the lacunae provides a justification for a new perspective. For example, Patrick Curry's *Defending Middle-Earth* and Jay Corrin's *G.K. Chesterton and Hilaire Belloc: The Battle Against Modernity* address the dynamic of the rejection of myth and tradition in the Modern Age, respectively.[35] Their subjects of study believed they were under attack for their mere conservatism. In this sense, their recognition of traditionalist detractors has a place in the annals of twentieth-century history. Arguably, these perspectives, at times, are subjugated to a more esoteric base of readers, and yet their theses generate an appropriate discussion of the two topics side by side.

A handful of historians have contributed extensively to the subjects found within this book. The focus of their work, typically, is biographical or concentrated on one factor or theme.[36] Biographies serve this topic well as they flesh out the reality of the subjects' Christianity, conversion (literary and religious), their responses to contemporaries, and the self-awareness of their own milieu. The historians who address such issues often come to similar conclusions found in this book. For example, in *Catholic Converts*, Patrick Allitt is struck by the common issues each of these intellectuals faced, despite their colorful differences.[37] The common task to provide a strong alternative to modern secularism led to a renewed vitality in the Catholic Church. Joseph Pearce's *Literary Converts* echoes similar claims through the study of the effects of religious conversion on literary figures and their immediate circles. My treatment does not dispute the conclusions of Allitt and Pearce, but rather seeks to examine a few characteristics that inform the activity of traditionalists recognized in the field of study. The study of progressives yields, perhaps unsurprisingly, an abundant amount of study as well. As their treatments are of progressives and their respective ideologies, the traditionalists studied here rarely if ever show up in their pages, thus necessitating a study of the opposition.

The work of three more scholars is worth mentioning in regard to the subject of influential literary Catholics in the twentieth century—Adam Schwartz, Meredith Veldman, and James Lothian. All three are instrumental in advancing the field of scholarship. This book supports a number of their conclusions, namely evidence of a clear defense of religious belief among certain literary intelligentsia. Schwartz refers to the renewed popularity of British Catholicism during a time of great hostility and empty intellectual trends as the third spring—a reference to the revival of British culture through Catholicism following John Henry Newman's own references to a second spring. Meredith Veldman examines the relationship between science and fantasy in the twentieth century, specifically the British dynamic. Her focus on fantasy provides substantive evidence that a "romantic resistance" to the modern age existed amid literary circles, namely Tolkien and Lewis. The scope of Veldman's book examines the link between fantasy, the protest of the nuclear bomb, and environmentalism created by the "romantic resistance." Fantasy is a significant element to the figures mentioned in this book as it informs their pre-modern tendencies. For Veldman, Lewis and Tolkien protest the seduction of technological progress, scientism, and secular rationalism through fantasy and its romance with the pre-modern world.[38] James Lothian for his part is concerned specifically with the nuances of the English Catholic intellectual community. He examines the making and unmaking of this community through the examination of key figures such as Chesterton, Belloc, and Dawson. While Lothian's assessment of the tension within the English Catholic intellectual community between engagement with contemporary society and the impulse to turn away is accurate,[39] his focus mainly centers on the political implications and the creation or undoing of generations of Catholics influenced by the intellectual community of the twentieth century.

Alister McGrath has done the same for Inklings scholarship, even if he has primarily focused his work on C. S. Lewis. The important contribution from McGrath is his attempt to "set Lewis in the greater context of Western literary and theological tradition, exploring how he appropriated and modified its narratives, ideas, and images . . . [stating] Lewis's work is not embedded within a Christian sub-culture . . . but within the Western intellectual tradition as a whole."[40] McGrath's work extends credibility to the ideas that the Inklings, as evidenced through Lewis, are not beholden to Christian culture alone. Instead, they are connected to the Western canon and, therefore, necessitate more in-depth scrutiny.

Medieval historian Norman Cantor points out that the Inklings made it their life's work to convey or possibly translate these ideas to modern audiences with the hope of "impart[ing] a sense of medieval myth to the widest audience possible. They wanted to represent to the public the impress of the kind of traditional ethic they derived from their devotion to conservative Christianity."[41] Cantor's line of thought has been used to aid in the explanation of the context of twentieth-century traditionalists. In Cantor's *Inventing the Middle Ages* (1991) he argued that Tolkien and Lewis were two of the great medievalists of the twentieth century. The ability to embody the spirit of the Middle Ages is something characteristic of a handful of authors. Cantor puts Lewis and Tolkien in league with prominent contributors in the field of medieval studies such as Etienne Gilson, R. W. Southern, and Johan Huizinga. Veldman echoes the perception that Tolkien and Lewis made lengths to bridge the divide between modern English culture and the lost natural and spiritual worlds of the Middle Ages.[42] They are primarily known for their work in the genre of fantasy, but they were formidable scholars in the language and subject matter of the Middle Ages, even if the vast majority has never read it.

Robert Boenig's *C.S. Lewis and the Middle Ages* even goes so far as to call Lewis an actual medieval.[43] He did not simply study and love the Middle Ages, but embodied its sentiments in a way that allowed him to translate seemingly foreign concepts to his contemporaries. Boenig is focused on the medieval identity of Lewis, rather than the dialogue between tradition and modernity. That Lewis saw himself in this light is evidenced by his inaugural speech to the Medieval and Renaissance Literature chair at Cambridge in 1954 where he referred to himself as both a "native of the Middle Ages" and a "dinosaur."[44] Boenig's recognition of the group's medieval character is similar to Cantor's. Their insights are a platform in which to build a stronger case for the Inklings' defense of tradition in the scope of twentieth-century thought. They mention the invaluable contribution made by Lewis and Tolkien, but their identity as a formidable force in twentieth-century Britain is usually underestimated. Even though, by 1943, "Lewis was the best-known Christian polemicist in Britain."[45]

Carpenter insists that there are certain aspects of the Inklings' relationship that cannot be explained or expressed accurately.[46] The boys' club mentality, at times, has been misconstrued to explain the intensity of the group through the possible latent homosexuality or sadomasochism of Lewis, Tolkien, Barfield, or Williams. Perhaps even the hobbits are subject to similar ridicule, in an attempt to spur some controversy.[47] It is possible that moderns cannot remove Freudian exposition from a world that defined medieval traditions of friendship and camaraderie between males differently.[48] Examples such as this serve in the sense that they establish both the unique character that was the Oxford Circle and the flurry of misconception that surrounds their intentions. Such positions cater to a predictable and recycled Freudian sexuality that emphasizes the power of the unconscious.[49] A good deal of the work on the Inklings points to matters of tradition, imagination, and the like, but although a few scholars have hinted around the connections made here between the reconciliation of tradition in the Modern Age, the pages that follow mean to press the issue further.

There are three biographies representative of the general sentiments behind Inklings studies—Humphrey Carpenter's *The Inklings* (1978), Colin Duriez's *The Oxford Inklings* (2015), and Philip and Carol Zaleski's *The Fellowship* (2015). Each book has its own identity and character regardless of the overlap in anecdotes and notable major themes. All three are well researched and possess writing styles that engage the mind of the reader. Much of their information comes from the two large storehouses of Inklings information: Marion O. Wade Center at Wheaton College and the Bodleian Library at Oxford University. Details with sensible assumptions on the talk of pub meetings, smoky offices, and long walks create an accurate portrayal of the group. The depth of the research is obvious and in Carpenter's and Duriez's case, proximity creates a number of connections that are not necessarily obvious to those who do not understand the context.

All three biographies are mindful of the complexity of the literary group. At any one time there were roughly twelve members, some more influential and consistent than others. For example, R. E. Havard was not a group regular, but was nonetheless important in his role. The core of the group, C. S. Lewis, J. R. R. Tolkien, Owen Barfield, and Charles Williams, were bound to one another, despite a noticeable rift between Lewis and Tolkien,[50] until death bade them farewell. The strength of their relationships is a necessary characteristic in the establishment of the Inklings as a group committed to the preservation of the permanent things. It is appropriate to begin with the first and still highly praised book by Humphrey Carpenter. Each book will not be reviewed in its entirety, but in a capacity appropriate to the overall theme of the subject matter.

Humphrey Carpenter's *The Inklings: C.S. Lewis, J.R.R. Tolkien, Charles Williams and Their Friends* has long been the seminal biography on the Inklings. Of the five main points of Carpenter's work, the symptoms of the Modern Age and the moniker the "Oxford Christians" inspired the idea to look at the dialogue between tradition and modernity through the eyes of traditionally minded authors. The expansion into understanding the larger significance of this one aspect creates helpful parameters. The main topics of

Carpenter's book have set the stage for other biographies as well. The recognition from the group itself on these matters has become an important debate within present scholarship. Personal letters, remembered conversations, and minutes of meetings are judiciously studied in an attempt to figure out if the Inklings were a self-aware phenomenon, or if they were imposing their own notions from the present onto a past with which they were often enamored.

Carpenter explains the significance to the question of whether the Inklings possessed a conscious agenda. Carpenter saw two links, namely the love of myth and C. S. "Jack" Lewis. His study and personal interaction with the Inklings led him to believe that all of the discussions of a common attitude were founded on nothing. The contention here is that he underestimated the importance of the group and its larger effect on the dialogue of modernity, as well as the strength of their arguments for tradition. The group's love of myth (used in different ways) was a bridge that united them in that they were all unique individuals: "What remains that can be called a 'common Inklings attitude'? Certainly it seems a significant link that Tolkien, Lewis and Williams all wrote stories in which myth plays an important part."[51] Myth, for the Inklings,[52] was not just a thing written about or a tool used in writing, it reflected deep realities of the human story and led to the use of imagination to understand metaphysical reality.

Carpenter's other link, Lewis, acted as a proverbial St. Peter for the Inklings—he indeed was the fox.[53] Lewis undoubtedly possessed a gravitational force akin to Jupiter. He was loud, jovial, sharp, witty, and charismatic. Carpenter's assessment is accurate, but incomplete. While the Inklings gravitated to Lewis in different capacities, their individual success did not depend on his. In his chapter "A fox that isn't there,"[54] Carpenter dispels the idea that the Inklings agreed with or even recognized a unified front: "So 'The Oxford Christians' does not seem to be a term which holds much real meaning. Nor does the idea that there was an *academic* viewpoint common to Lewis and his friends stand up at all well to examination."[55] The combination of their individual influence was not a mere audience for Jack, but something more important. Their open criticisms of one another speak to a desire to sharpen and hone the skills needed to respond to what they saw as the darker forces of modernity. The collective effect on twentieth-century Britain and a more recent revival of the Inklings' popularity calls Carpenter's assessment into question.[56]

Carpenter's biography of the Inklings was published in the late 1970s. Its narrow view of the Inklings can be attributed to the lack of confirmation from the actual group regarding certain distinctions and assumptions. In 1966 Warnie Lewis was quoted as saying, "[the name 'Oxford Christians'] strikes the wrong note . . . by suggesting an organized group for the propagation of Christianity, while in fact the title is justified only in the most literal sense, i.e. that we nearly all lived in Oxford and were all believers."[57]

The connection between Carpenter and Colin Duriez's *The Oxford Inklings: Lewis, Tolkien, and Their Circle* is unavoidable. Duriez's conclusion departs from Carpenter's conclusion, and in so doing, it complements the atmosphere and hunch within the pages of this discussion. He states, "I've come to the conclusion that it is equally mistaken to see the literary club simply as a group of friends, or as a doctrinaire group driven by a highly defined common purpose."[58] Although there is no hard evidence surrounding the intentions of the Inklings, Duriez is willing to provide a new line of thought—"Romantic Religion." This idea was influenced by something Barfield said in 1969 about the different names given to the group by others (e.g., the Oxford Christians, Romantic Theology, School of Romantic Religion): "I found it rather amusing when I first began to hear people talking about this, and found that they were writing dissertations and so forth, but I have been beginning to wonder, to put it crudely, whether there isn't something in it!"[59]

There is no need to go into too much detail on Duriez's idea of "Romantic Religion," but it does speak to the possibility that there was something going on in this group. The difficulty is a result of the group's unwillingness to label themselves. In a letter to William Luther White, Tolkien mentioned the origin of the name: "I called the name a 'jest', because it was a pleasantly ingenious pun in its way, suggesting people with vague or half-formed intimations and ideas plus those who dabble in ink."[60] Due to the difficulty of creating an empirical assessment of the group's self-awareness, the employment of a more interdisciplinary approach is in order to study the intellectual climate of the twentieth-century with the hope of drawing clearer connections of the Inklings' interaction with modern foils. Their humility is quite possibly a resistance to the modern desire to categorize literary and historical movements (e.g., Classical-Medieval, Renaissance, British Marxists, *Annales*, Historicism). By refusing to label themselves, they do not claim a grandiose sense of significance. Despite how they saw themselves, an argument can be made that they were a part of something significant during the height of modern progressivism. The Inklings are called a great number of names and defined as one movement or another, but later member and novelist John Wain saw them clearly as "a circle of instigators, almost of incendiaries, meeting to urge one another on in the task of redirecting the whole current of contemporary art and life."[61] The quote from Wain best explains the idea of connecting the Inklings to the greater importance of tradition, traditionalists, and the preservation of the permanent things.

Duriez does not fabricate the significance of the Inklings. By examining the different eras of the group—1920s, 1930s, War Years, Golden Age—and their reactions to the world around them, he provides insight to their impact on Britain and beyond. The Inklings' work was generally met with opposition from their academic peers. Duriez points out that they remained a consistent defense of an older wisdom and a minor Christian renaissance.[62] The consistency of the group leads Duriez and others to see the Inklings as a refuge in an intellectual wasteland.[63] Meaning appeared lost in the scuffle of modern forms of specified criticism such as linguistic studies, historicism, and individualism. The discussion within Western tradition possessed a generalist disposition in hope of a complete knowledge of humanity. For the cadre of traditionalists, the worship of progress, mainly through science and technology, could not provide salvation. Granted, many of them meant salvation through the acceptance of Christ, but there was also a desire for the redemption of society through humanism. The Inklings and traditional allies were a living rebuttal of an age that actively sought to redefine Christianity, spirituality, and the meaning of humanity.[64]

The virtue of the Inklings' contribution can be a hard sell at times because it is stuck between a modern scientific rock and a religious hard place. In recent scholarship, "The C.S. Lewis you never knew," a blog post on CNN's "Belief Blog," presented a more private side of Lewis. It included anecdotes of Lewis's "fascination" with sadomasochism, his smoking, his drinking, and the acceptance of long-time friend Arthur Greeves' homosexuality.[65] The premise of the blog cites the difficulty in selling C. S. Lewis to a religious audience even though he is seen as one of the most prolific Christian apologists of the twentieth century. It is by no means desirable to re-enchant the Inklings by garbing them in an aura of antiquarianism and the spirit of tradition, for the Inklings themselves would have abhorred such an approach. Rather, trends in scholarship have resulted in an unfortunate lack of intellectual history of the Inklings, and surrounding traditionalists. The void is in need of being filled.

The reality of these conscious efforts is visible beyond the realm of Inklings studies as well. The shift in the values of Western intellectuals was due to the transition from the pre-modern to the modern. It is generally assumed that interest in religion, as anything more than a relic of the past, has been reserved for "believers." As Roger Luckhurst and Jed Etsy respectively point out, there is scholarship both in literary and historical studies that reacts to the current academic climate: "These sweeping statements are often the result of an allergy to the Christian conservatism of J.R.R. Tolkien and C.S. Lewis."[66] "It has become conventional to think of [T. S.] Eliot's later work as the product of either a simple-minded Tory retreat into traditionalism or an exhausted personal retreat into Christianity, both taken as inevitable expressions of Eliot's latent and rigid conservatism."[67]

Generally, religious conviction in academia is scarce, but that does not remove it from its important relationship with certain disciplines. Philosophy has always been seen as a sibling of religion and continues to be so in some capacity in the Modern Age. The change in character was mentioned earlier as a result of the shift from a religious or metaphysically dominant culture to a more empirically dominated culture. In *Modern British Philosophy* (1971), British philosopher Bryan Magee published a number of interviews based on conversations with prominent scholars across a diverse sample of disciplines. In his tenth conversation with professor of religious studies Ninian Smart, he learned that the philosophy of religion was alive and well and was enjoying a revival.[68] Forty or fifty years later, this does not seem to be the case, but it is hard to measure the influence of such movements. To speak of subjects in this light without addressing the flaws of the age is unorthodox by today's standards. Smart points out that it is indeed a revival because epistemology is influenced by the dominant science of a given age.[69] Nonetheless, examples of a respected Christian perspective do exist. One such example is Alvin Plantinga and his contribution to the field of philosophy through a Christian perspective.

There are also historians who are concerned with the important aspects of traditionally minded intellectuals. Bradley Birzer is one historian who has studied the world of the traditionalists, namely the Inklings and New Humanists. Birzer examines the links between influential twentieth-century intellectuals who valued tradition and the liberal arts as a catalyst for the education of subsequent generations in the heritage of Western ideas. Birzer directs curious readers to a 1939 *New York Times* article that openly recognized the philosophy of Christian humanists: "'This is the theme recurring in much of the writings of some of the foremost thinkers of our day, such as the late Irving Babbitt and Paul Elmer More, and [Nikolai] Berdyaev, Christopher Dawson, and T.S. Eliot.' The newspaper of record might have added others: C.S. Lewis, J.R.R. Tolkien, and their circles in Britain, as well as philosophers Jacques Maritain and Etienne Gilson in France."[70]

Unfortunately, many prominent traditional intellectuals were separated by insurmountable personal and intellectual differences. Birzer has revealed the tip of the iceberg in his accurate portrayals of the period. Although his subjects were typically devout Christians, he did not avoid their flaws. Birzer does not focus on the flaws alone, but merely recognizes their presence as a hindrance of what could be a large and significant Christian renaissance. Birzer's vein of scholarship has inspired this book's particular explanation of the different components of twentieth-century Christian humanism, specifically the reconciliation of tradition in the Modern Age, the reaction to scientism in a new marketplace, classical liberal learning, and the dialogues that have preserved Western tradition (i.e., the *Great Books*), with the intent to convey what many of these authors claimed was a crisis of Western civilization.

Birzer's work stands in contrast to Inklings' critics Germaine Greer and Harold Bloom, who focus heavily on the narrow perspective of Tolkien.[71] Instead, he is focused on what the Inklings did accomplish and more importantly what they were doing for the rest of Western humanity. The Inklings,

New Humanists, and other traditionalists were aware of one another, but they were fragmented. Barfield lamented the absence of a group mentality. He wrote in 1940, "One should pursue the sober effort to build up and maintain a common stock of thought rather than to startle with a series of sparkling individual contributions." To promote truth and defend the ideals of the West, Barfield continued, a group of men should create "a commonwealth of the spirit, in which there is no copyright."[72] They all knew the enemy and worked at sharpening their weapons of defense. The impact of the Inklings and other Christian humanists cannot be overlooked or seen as the last dying gasp of an old way of life. Traditionalists of the twentieth century did not pretend to have the answers, but knew what questions needed to be raised: What is man? What is God? And in what way do God and man relate to one another?[73] No matter how technologically advanced or progressive Western civilization becomes, a dialogue of what is human will always maintain relevance. Historians like Birzer have taken it upon themselves to be vanguards of the dialogue's continuation. The preservation of tradition is not the province of dead men who spoke dead languages, but lives in the interdisciplinary humanities of the liberal arts.[74]

NOTES

1. Here is but a sample: Reinhard Bendix, "Tradition and Modernity Reconsidered," *Comparative Studies in Society and History* 9, no. 3 (April, 1967): 292–346. L. E. Shiner, "Tradition/Modernity: An Ideal Type Gone Astray," *Comparative Studies in Society and History* 17, no. 2 (April, 1975): 245–52. Nadia L. Alhasani, "Tradition vs. Modernity: The Quest for a Cultural Identity," *Traditional Dwellings and Settlements Review* 7, no. 2 (Spring, 1996): 35–41. Thomas William Heyck, "Myths and Meanings of Intellectuals in Twentieth-Century British National Identity," *Journal of British Studies* 37, no. 2 (Apr., 1998): 192–221. Frank Trentmann, "Civilization and Its Discontents: English Neo-Romanticism and the Transformation of Anti-Modernism in Twentieth-Century Western Culture," *Journal of Contemporary History* 29, no. 4 (October, 1994): 583–625.

2. Ellis, *Literature Lost*, pp. 103–4.

3. Patrick Allitt, *Catholic Intellectuals and Conservative Politics in America, 1950–85* (Ithaca: Cornell University Press, 1993), p. 2.

4. *Ibid.*, p. 13.

5. Christopher Dawson, *The Formation of Christendom* (New York: Sheed & Ward, 1967), pp. 4–5.

6. Christopher Dawson, "Enquiries into Religion" in *Sources in Western Civilization: The Twentieth Century, 1914–1964*, ed. Arthur P. Mendel (New York: The Free Press. 1965), p. 212.

7. Kelley, *Descent of Ideas*, p. 297–98.

8. Adam Schwartz, *The Third Spring: G.K. Chesterton, Graham Greene, Christopher Dawson, and David Jones* (Washington, D.C.: The Catholic University of America Press, 2005), p. 262.

9. *Ibid.*, p. 213.

10. Kelley, *Descent of Ideas*, p. 103.

11. Nugent, *Progressivism*, p. 78.

12. *Ibid.*, pp. 59–63.

13. For example, see Philip and Carol Zaleski, *The Fellowship: The Literary Lives of the Inklings: J.R.R. Tolkien, C.S. Lewis, Owen Barfield, Charles Williams* (New York: Farrar, Straus, & Giroux, 2015): revitalize, p. 510; reclaim, p. 511; restore/refresh, p. 512; recovered, p. 508. Norman F. Cantor, *Inventing the Middle Ages: The Lives, Works, and Ideas of the Great Medievalists of the 20th Century* (New York: Quill, William, Morrow, 1991): reestablish, p. 213. Colin Duriez, *The Oxford Inklings: Lewis, Tolkien and their circle* (Oxford: Lion Hudson, 2015): rehabilitate, pp. 221, 227. Humphrey Carpenter, *The Inklings: C.S. Lewis, J.R.R. Tolkien, Charles Williams and their friends* (London: Harper Collins. 2006): reimagine, p. 223. Bradley Birzer, *Russell Kirk: American Conservative* (Lexington: University of Kentucky Press, 2015): bearer, p. 169. R. J. Reilly, *Romantic Religion: A Study of Owen Barfield, C.S. Lewis, Charles Williams, and J.R.R Tolkien* (Great Barrington: Lindisfarne Books, 2006): rediscover, p. 206; reconciling, p. 7.

14. A clearly articulated treatment of this by Kenneth Minogue titled, "Method in intellectual history: Quentin Skinner's *Foundations*," can be found in *Meaning & Context: Quentin Skinner and his Critics* (Princeton: Princeton University Press, 1988): 176–93.

15. Christopher Dawson, *Understanding Europe* (Washington, D.C.: The Catholic University of America Press, 2009), p. 5.

16. Lewis, *Mere Christianity*, p. 102.

17. Christopher Dawson, *The Dynamics of World History*, ed. John J. Mulloy (New York: Sheed and Ward, 1956), p. 278.

18. A recent search of scholarly journals and books with the keywords, "Tolkien and Lewis, tradition, conservatism" yielded roughly ten sources out of seventy-seven that came somewhat close to the context of the topic. Everything else dealt with genre studies, gender, ethnicity, and poststructural commentary.

19. Gabrielle Spiegel, "The Task of the Historian." Presidential Address at 123rd Annual American Historical Association, New York City, 2009. http://www.historians.org/about-aha-and-membership/aha-history-and-archives/presidential-addresses/gabrielle-m-spiegel. For further reading see Keith Windschuttle, *The Killing of History: How Literary Critics and Social Critics are Murdering Our Past* (New York: Encounter Books, 2004); Paul R. Gross and Norman Levitt, *Higher Superstition: The Academic Left and Its Quarrels with Science* (Baltimore: Johns Hopkins University Press, 1997); Peter Novick, *That Noble Dream: That "Objectivity Question" and the American Historical Profession* (Cambridge: Cambridge University Press, 1988); Joyce Appleby, Lynn Hunt, and Margaret Jacob, *Telling the Truth About History* (New York: W.W. Norton & Co., 1995).

20. Statistics show a distinct rise in the amount of certain types of history being done (i.e., environmental, sexuality, gender, and race). This is according to the Robert Townsend article "The Rise and Decline of History Specialization over the Past 40 Years," *Perspectives on History: The Newsmagazine of the AHA* (December 2015). https://www.historians.org/publications-and-directories/perspectives-on-history/december-2015/the-rise-and-decline-of-history-specializations-over-the-past-40-years.

21. André Gushurst-Moore, *The Common Mind: Politics, Society and Christian Humanism from Thomas More to Russell Kirk* (Tacoma: Angelico Press, 2013), p. 9.

22. In the enlarged edition of *Chronology of the Modern World* (1994), only Lewis and Tolkien are mentioned for *The Screwtape Letters* (1942) and the first two installments of *LOTR*, respectively. Chesterton is mentioned for two books as well. The introduction states that there will always be a debate as to who or what should be included in this type of compendium. The goal was to include names, dates, and events that would be found most anywhere and without a narrow philosophy as to how they were chosen.

23. Carpenter, p. 217.

24. See BHA website: https://humanism.org.uk/ for the full scope of their growing influence and agenda.

25. Niall Ferguson, *Civilization: The West and the Rest* (New York: Penguin Books. 2011), p. 268.

26. *Ibid.*, p. 271.

27. The following historians also produce scholarly work on similar topics as well: Christopher Dawson, Paul Johnson, John Carey, George Mosse, Stratford Caldecott.

28. Ferguson, p. 273.
29. David Brooks, "Kicking the Secularist Habit: A Six Step Program," *The Atlantic* (March 3, 2003), www.theatlantic.com.
30. Robert W. Whalen, *Sacred Spring: God and the Birth of Modernism in Fin de Siècle Vienna* (Grand Rapids: Eerdmans, 2007). Mark S. Morrisson, *Modern Alchemy: Occultism and the Emergence of Atomic Theory* (Oxford: Oxford University Press, 2007).
31. For example, Mythcon, *Seven, Journal of Inklings Studies, Mythlore,* Mythgate, The C. S. Lewis Society, among others.
32. For example, Kath Filmer, "Out of the Silent Planet: Reconstructing Wells with a Few Shots at Shaw," *Inklings Jahrbuch fuer Literatur und Aesthetik* 6 (1988): 43–54. Simon J. Bronner, "The Meaning of Tradition: An Introduction," *Western Folklore* 59, no. 2, *The Meaning of Tradition* (Spring 2000): 87–104.
33. A search of *Journal of British Studies* and *Twentieth Century British History* turned up almost nothing. The more general search is referenced in (footnote 17).
34. For example: Glen GoodKnight, "The Social History of the Inklings: J.R.R. Tolkien, C.S. Lewis, Charles Williams 1939–1945," *Mythlore* 2.1, no. 5 (1970)/ *Tolkien Journal* 4.2, no. 12 (1970): 7–9. L. Markos, "Apologist for the Past: The Medieval Vision of C.S. Lewis's *Space Trilogy* and *Chronicles of Narnia,*" *Mythlore* 23.2 (#88) (2001): 24–35. "Tradition": Chris Hopkins, "Tolkien and Englishness," *Mythlore* 21.2, no. 80 (1996): 278:80. Ashley Pfeiffer, "T.H. White and the Lasting Influence of WWI: King Arthur at War," *Baptism of Fire: The Birth of the Modern British Fantastic in WWI,* ed. Janet Brennan Croft (Altadena: Mythlore Press, 2015): 299–310. Eric Schweicher, "Aspects of the Fall in *The Silmarillion,*" *Mythlore* 21.2, no. 80 (1996): 167–71. Chris Seemen, "Tolkien's Revision of the Romantic Tradition," *Mythlore* 21.2, no. 80 (1996): 73–83. Patrick Curry, "'Less Noise and More Green': Tolkien's Ideology for England," *Mythlore* 21.2, no. 80 (1996): 126–38. Steven Yandell, "'A Pattern Which Our Nature Cries Out For': The Medieval Tradition of the Ordered Four in the Fiction of J.R.R. Tolkien," *Mythlore* 21.2, no. 80 (1996): 375–92. "Modernism": A. R. Bossert, "'Surely You Don't Disbelieve': Tolkien and Pius X: Antimodernism in Middle-earth," *Mythlore* 25.1/ 2, no. 95/96 (2006): 53–76. Jon Garrard, "The Conqueror Worm: Eddison, Modernism, and the War to End All Wars," *Baptism of Fire: The Birth of the Modern British Fantastic in WWI,* ed. Janet Brennan Croft (Altadena: Mythlore Press, 2015): 263–78. Sister Pauline, C.S.M., "Mysticism in the Ring," *Tolkien Journal* 3.4, no.10 (1969): 12–14.
35. Patrick Duffy, *Defending Middle-Earth: Tolkien: Myth and Modernity* (New York: Houghton Mifflin, 2004). Jay Corrin, *G.K. Chesterton and Hilaire Belloc: The Battle Against Modernity* (Athens: Ohio University Press, 1981).
36. Ian Ker's extensive work on John Henry Newman has defined the field of study. He has also greatly influenced the study of Chesterton through biography and edited works of essays.
37. Patrick Allitt, *Catholic Converts: British and American Intellectuals Turn to Rome* (Ithaca: Cornell University Press, 1997), p. xi.
38. Meredith Veldman, *Fantasy, the Bomb, and the Greening of Britain: Romantic Protest, 1945–1980* (Cambridge: Cambridge University Press, 1994).
39. James Lothian, *The Making and Unmaking of the English Catholic Intellectual Community, 1910–1950* (Notre Dame: University of Notre Dame Press, 2009), p. xxiii.
40. Alister McGrath, *The Intellectual World of C.S. Lewis* (Oxford: Wiley & Sons, 2014), p. 3.
41. Cantor, pp. 207–8.
42. Veldman, *Fantasy, the Bomb, and the Greening of Britain,* p. 76.
43. Robert Boenig, *C.S. Lewis and the Middle Ages* (Kent: Kent State University Press, 2012), pp. 144–50.
44. C.S. Lewis, "*De Descriptione Temporum,*" Inaugural Lecture from The Chair of Mediaeval and Renaissance Literature at Cambridge University, 1954, p. 6. *Internet Archive.* https://archive.org/stream/DeDescriptioneTemporum/DeDescriptioneTemporum, By C.S. Lewis.
45. Cantor, p. 206.
46. Carpenter, p. 166–67.
47. *Ibid.,* p. 168.

48. See Colin Duriez, *Tolkien and C.S. Lewis: The Gift of Friendship* (Mahwah, NJ: Paulist Press, 2003).

49. For example, see the essays by Brenda Partridge, Nigel Welmsley, and Nick Otty in *J.R.R. Tolkien: This Far Land*, ed. Robert Giddings (Vision Publishers, 1983).

50. In 1963, Tolkien wrote about Lewis's death in a letter to his daughter, saying, "So far I have felt the normal feelings of a man my age—like an old tree that is losing all its leaves one by one: this feels like an axe-blow near the roots."

51. Carpenter, p. 156.

52. When used, the term Inklings will refer to the commonly held core group of Lewis, Tolkien, Williams, and Barfield.

53. Carpenter, p. 171.

54. *Ibid.*, pp. 153–71.

55. *Ibid.*, p. 155.

56. The connections drawn by American historian Brad Birzer (1967–) between the Inklings and other traditionally minded intellectuals will be discussed later in the chapter.

57. Quoted from Charles Moorman, *The Precincts of Felicity: the Augustinian City of the Oxford Christians* (Gainesville: University of Florida Press, 1966) in Clyde S. Kilby and Douglas R. Gilbert, *C.S. Lewis: Images of His World* (Grand Rapids: Eerdmans, 2005), p. 12.

58. Duriez, p. 217.

59. Rand Kuhl, "Owen Barfield in Southern California," *Mythlore*, Issue 4, October 1969, p. 10.

60. Letter to William Luther White, 11 September 1967, in *The Letters of J.R.R. Tolkien*, ed. Humphrey Carpenter with Christopher Tolkien (New York: Houghton Mifflin Co., 2000), p. 388.

61. John Wain, *Sprightly Running: Part of an Autobiography* (New York: St. Martin's Press, 1962), p. 181.

62. Duriez, *Oxford Inklings*, pp. 102, 150–53.

63. *Ibid.*, p. 130. The chapters that follow are meant to expand on an already recognized idea, one that has not been given expansive attention as to the connections between tradition, liberal learning, the *Great Books*, and these specific authors.

64. *Ibid.*, p. 227.

65. John Blake, "The C.S. Lewis you never knew," *CNN* (blog), last modified December 1, 2013 (6:00am), http://religion.blogs.cnn.com/2013/12/01/the-c-s-lewis-you-never-knew/comment-page-3/.

66. Roger Luckhurst, *Gothic Science Fiction: 1980–2010*, eds. Sara Wasson and Emily Alder, first ed. (Liverpool: Liverpool University Press, 2011), p. 22.

67. Jed Etsy, *A Shrinking Island* (Princeton: Princeton University Press, 2004), p. 109.

68. Bryan Magee, *Modern British Philosophy* (New York: St. Martin's Press, 1971), p. 175.

69. *Ibid.*, p. 176.

70. Bradley J. Birzer, "Making Modernity Human: Can Christian Humanism Redeem an Age of Ideology?" *The Imaginative Conservative*, November 8, 2012, http://www.theimaginativeconservative.org/2012/11/making-modernity-human-can-christian.html.

71. Bradley J. Birzer, "How Did Lewis and Tolkien Defend the Old West?" *The Imaginative Conservative*, July 1, 2015, http://www.theimaginativeconservative.org/2015/07/how-did-lewis-and-tolkien-defend-the-old-west.html.

72. Birzer, "Making Modernity Human."

73. *Ibid.*

74. This can be seen in books about friendship in the context of World War I: Joseph Loconte, *A Hobbit, A Wardrobe, and Great War* (Nashville: Nelson Books, 2015); an anthology regarding the matter of Britain: *The Inklings and King Arthur* (San Francisco: Apocryphile Press, 2017); and different Western canons from Mortimer Adler and Robert Hutchins *Great Books of the Western World* (Chicago: University of Chicago Press, 1952) to Harold Bloom's *The Western Canon* (New York: Riverhead Books, 1994).

Chapter Two

Tradition

More than Custom and Convention

Custom and convention are tenets of any civilization, advanced or primitive. The effects of custom and convention often are attributed to habit. Because of this attribute, each age evaluates the past and decides what is worth preservation or removal from their value system. It is a natural occurrence as civilizations move through time. Prior to the Modern Age, the present did not see the need to redefine itself from a completely subjective position. The premoderns upheld a position of unique value in the teachings of the past in order to evaluate their own age. However, the Modern Age, especially the nineteenth and twentieth centuries, began to see nature, humanity, and civilization in a constant state of progressive development and evolution. The modern scientific age of the nineteenth and twentieth centuries was suspicious of anything associated with custom, convention, conservatism, habit, or tradition (much of what was conveyed through classical education). The prominent intellectuals of these two centuries desired strongly to redefine or "update" the ethos of the West through more material and scientific lenses. They championed progress in order to deconstruct a tradition that incorporated pre-modern knowledge, especially the metaphysical, claiming they knew more than their ancestors. T. S. Eliot provided a response saying: "Some one said: 'The dead writers are remote from us because we *know* so much more than they did.' Precisely, and they are that which we know."[1] The following chapter examines the state of tradition in the twentieth century through the definition held by traditionalists, the effects of modern perspectives, and the various explanations of its purpose in society. The explanation of these aspects is derived from the traditionalists' treatment of the ideas there within and provides clarity to the activities of those who sought to preserve the permanent things found within Western ideas while they swam against the current of their own age.

WHAT IS TRADITION?

The standard definition of tradition is "a way of thinking, behaving, or doing something that has been used by the people in a particular group, family, society, etc., for a long time; an inherited, established, or customary pattern of thought, action, or behavior (as a religious practice or a social custom)." There is also a definition that mentions "a belief that is held, but not necessarily verifiable." This particular line is the definitive characteristic as to why the Modern Age is not always comfortable with tradition, so it leans toward progress, specifically verifiable scientific progress. However, traditionalists did not claim their ideas as an unreflective perpetuation of the past.

British essayist T. S. Eliot (1888–1965) and American political theorist Russell Kirk (1918–1994) explain the importance, even for conservative traditionalists, to accept some change. Eliot's problem with progressivism was with its reflection of the extreme idea of individualism, one that needed constant redefinition due to its detachment from any canon or past. This detachment supported the negation of tradition through the position that the present offered the best insights, ideas, et cetera. In "Tradition and the Individual Talent" (1921), Eliot expressed fault in this reasoning, claiming that the present could not escape those who came before, saying: "Whereas if we approach a poet without this prejudice we shall often find that not only the best, but the most individual parts of his work may be those in which the dead poets, his ancestors, assert their immortality most vigorously."[2] The reality of a canon, something akin to the *Great Books*, creates an evaluation of the past because: "Certainly the word is not likely to appear in our appreciations of living or dead writers. Every nation, every race, has not only its own creative, but its own critical turn of mind; and is even more oblivious of the shortcomings and limitations of its critical habits than of those of its creative genius."[3] The definition of tradition outside its specific proponents provides context to its importance in the Western canon. Twentieth-century traditionalists did not give tradition meaning any more than progressives created new meaning. Tradition reflects the permanent and is nominally subject to the will of the present.

Russell Kirk, in *Eliot and His Age* (1971), clarified the significance of the past in his response to Eliot's critics, specifically progressivists, humanitarians, and grim ideologues, stating:

> The Present, Eliot knew, is only a thin film upon the deep well of the Past; the Present was ceasing to exist even as he wrote at Margate or Lausanne; the Present evaporates swiftly into the cloud of Future; and that Future, too, soon

will be the Past. The ideological cult of Modernism is philosophically ridiculous, for the modernity of 1971, say, is very different from the modernity of 1921. Once cannot order his soul, or participate in a public order, merely by applauding the will-o'-the-wisp Present.[4]

For Kirk, true conservatives recognize the reality of change and need for progress, but not through the process of destroying ancient temples to make room for modern architecture. Kirk's perspective unifies diverse intellectual backgrounds under the banner of tradition. Granted, most of our traditionalists were religious, namely Catholic, yet tradition had its defenders that were not religious, and were not orthodox either. More importantly for Kirk is the recognition that conservatism best reflects the characteristics of tradition. The modern West constantly seeks new ways to define itself through education, scientific progress, or individual interpretive literature or philosophy. Traditionalists did not feel as if they were redefining tradition for their age, but reconciling the permanent to the realities of human progress. Kirk described, through the avoidance of modern ideologies, the acceptance of change as a way to mediate reconciliation: "Conservatism never is more admirable than when it accepts changes that it disapproves, with good grace, for the sake of a general conciliation."[5] Tradition asks that the present be aware of the abuse of new knowledge and power for the sake of conservation.

Tradition is defined and evaluated in a number of ways ranging from the transcendent received truths to simple customs and conventions practiced by a given society. In order to understand tradition as was perceived by the traditionalists in this context, one needs to consult Josef Pieper. Pieper's definition defines tradition as something received instead of derived by humanity.[6] While most traditionalists claim the reception from transcendence, namely God, there are a few, individuals of humane letters, who attest similar goals in a reflection of human dignity as a thing beyond the contrivances of naked apes.[7] For Pieper, Knowledge received from the transcendent naturally reflects humanity's relation to tradition. It is the relationship that changes over time, but our focus is the change in the modern scientific age. Pieper saw a structure of authority within tradition, one that reflected the relationship of Creator to creation, saying: "One person transmits, while the other receives something transmitted. This 'something,' which is occasionally also given the name 'tradition.' The partners who confront one another when tradition is taking place are not standing on the same level, although this does not mean that one has to be more intelligent than the other."[8] The difference of modern thought was that it did not accept the authority of the ancients, the past, or tradition. Nonetheless, much of the difficulty is a result of the conversation, often with different linguistic usage, between the past and present. The problem may be one of style of communication and translation. Isaiah Berlin (1909–1997), in *The Proper Study of Mankind: An Anthology of* Essays, notes when discussing Giambattista Vico: "But, Vico maintains, if you read primitive utterances (Latin antiquities, which he knew best, provide him with the majority of his examples) you will soon realise that we call metaphorical speech is the natural mode of expression of these early men."[9]

Other issues arise when terms such as liberal and conservative are part of the conversation of tradition and progressivism. Tradition is typically linked to conservatism, while progressives are seen as liberal. The term "liberal" can be confusing as well because it is also applied to a type of education and learning that tends to be geared toward tradition and free thought at the same time. Conservatism is often defined as: "A philosophy that seeks to maintain and enrich societies characterized by respect for inherited institutions, beliefs, and practices, in which individuals develop good character by cooperating with one another in primary, local associations such as families, churches, and social groups aimed at furthering the common good in a manner pleasing to God."[10] Tradition and conservatism are not the offspring of religion alone. Religion is a major component of a society's custom and convention, thus it is more closely linked to traditions and identity. For example, the Western world owes a debt of knowledge to both pagan and Christian agency alike. The ideas of the Western world largely originate from the pre-Christian societies of the Greeks and early Romans. After the inception of Christianity, the classical "religions" fell by the wayside and were replaced by Christianity for the next eighteen centuries. The key to understanding its effect on Western identity is best described by fifth-century Gallic author St. Vincent of Lérins when he claimed that tradition is "that which has been believed everywhere, always, by everyone." Whether or not this belief contains absolutes or universals is part of the conversation contained within the pages of the *Great Books*.

There is one more issue to address and it is the contextual definition of the key terms during the twentieth century. While tradition can maintain a broad sweeping reference to ideas from ancient Greece to the present, it possesses contextual meanings as well. For twentieth-century Britain, tradition is often tied to the philosophical movement of Idealism.[11] The traditionalists connected to Chesterton, Pieper, and the like would not consider themselves Idealists. The modern scientific age reacted twofold to both groups, as its followers not only valued hard facts, but also they could not justify the idea of objective absolute truth based on the belief that similar meanings could not be possessed by different people in different ages. For nontraditionalists, the context of the past reveals a meaning unique to itself. They abide by the more Poststructural idea that language, idiom, symbols, values, etc., do not transcend periods of time. Those who broke away from Absolute Idealism, most notably Bertrand Russell (1872–1970) and G. E. Moore (1873–1958), developed a system based on the analysis of language and the difficulty of meaning when discussing the philosophical. Empiricism and subjectivism began to dominate intellectual circles and eventually popular culture at a rapid rate. American traditionalists came under similar fire as well. Modernity was not distinctly American or European, but a spirit that characterized the West in its entirety.

In order to provide a clear context of tradition, one should avoid a long political debate about what constitutes the practice of conservative and liberal ideologies. Instead, a combination of the standard definitions of tradition and conservatism can be used to explain the core values of those associated with the preservation of tradition. This serves to define what constitutes tradition in the West as well as determine the new ideas of the modern world. Tradition can be linked to classical liberal learning, one that sees the value of knowledge for the sake of knowledge and not solely for the sake of utility. It values the past as well as the institutions responsible for the preservation and progress of Western society. According to American philosopher Allan Bloom (1930–1992), the reality of the modern individual is that they possess low expectations in what can be learned from old literature.[12] Bloom calls on great literature to combat low expectations, saying: "There is, of course, literature that affects a generation profoundly but has no interest at all for the next generation because its central theme proved ephemeral, whereas the greatest literature addresses the permanent problems of man."[13] The *Great Books* represent an interdisciplinary conversation across the ages that is committed to the discovery of truth, goodness, beauty, and what it means to be human.

The *Great Books* compendium is not limited to classical and Christian treatises and nonfiction. They exist across a wide array of eras, subjects, and genres. The *Great Books* tradition is often criticized because they only contain the ideas of old or dead white men with a narrow and limited perspective.[14] Many critics would strike it from the modern syllabus on account of its alleged Christian bias, bigotry, homophobia, xenophobia, Islamophobia, and antisemitic leanings. The modern world strives for a relativistic and tolerant perspective on humanity, free from judgment and standards that are not freely determined by each individual. In the same vein as sacred texts, the great works of the Western world, if approached in a traditionalist manner, seek to shape and mold its readers, rather than the other way around. The contribution of this collection is focused on the human conversation of the Great Ideas.[15] The Ideas give birth to a dialogue with different perspectives on Western disciplines. The Modern Age claims to be relativistic and in search of truth; yet traditionalists are seen as antiquated, thus limiting the voices who are allowed to participate in the conversation, further limiting the interaction between the Modern Age with the past. The attitude in which traditionalists examined the context of primary sources left room for a narrative that sought an open dialogue between past and present. C. S. Lewis focused on the importance of the past in his 1944 introduction of Athanasius's work *On the Incarnation* titled "On the Reading of Old Books." In it he informs his readers that one of the purposes behind the reading of ancient books is so that the present can evaluate itself within the greater narrative of history in hopes of comprehension of itself and to ameliorate the mistakes of the current age.[16] The representatives of the Modern Age did not view the past in the same light. In a series of lectures (Lowell Lectures of 1925) later published as *Science and the Modern World* (1941), Alfred North Whitehead, explains the problem with tradition as follows: "[n]othing does more harm in unnerving men for their duties in the present, than the attention devoted to the points of excellence in the past as compared with the average failure of the present day."[17] The disdain for tradition was not limited to the sciences. Lytton Strachey's *Eminent Victorians* (1918) contemptuously chronicles the lives of those whom he believed to be the foremost exemplars of Victorian tradition and society/ideals, specifically Cardinal Henry Edward Manning, Florence Nightingale, Dr. Thomas Arnold, and General Charles George Gordon. He refused a dialogue with tradition in favor of criticism and the desire to tear down barbarisms of nineteenth-century British values.

One of the many benefits of dialogue is that any age can evaluate itself against discussions of the concepts of custom and convention. According to the *Great Books' Syntopicon*, custom and convention are defined as follows: "Though customs are not, in the strict sense, made by man, as are works of art, they do grow only as the result of the kind of acts which men perform voluntarily rather than instinctively. Similarly, conventions like contracts, are social arrangements or agreements into which men enter voluntarily."[18] Custom and convention are rather simple to define; their appropriateness, consistency, and necessity to the overall discussion are far more complex. The *Great Books* do not simply provide one perspective with the purposes of indoctrination. Although she does not agree with the goals of traditionalists, Martha Nussbaum does recognize the value of the pedagogy: "This tradition argues that education is not just about passive assimilation of facts and cultural traditions, but about challenging the mind to become active, competent, and thoughtfully critical in a complex world."[19] The attitude of the discussion of tradition in this manner echoes that of J. S. Mill's *On Liberty*: "But on every subject on which difference of opinion is possible, the truth depends on a balance to be struck between two sets of conflicting reasons."[20] It does not, however, descend into relativity as there remains a belief in absolute or universal truth—pursued in different ways by individuals from Euripides to the present. Mill's methodology may be similar, but his conclusions rest solely on the experience of the individual due to the despotic nature of custom.[21] The benefit of this process allows for the interaction with Mill's ideas even though they are in opposition to the tenets of custom. Even though the critics of the Western tradition point it out with disdain, the *Great Books* tradition does pair well with Christianity as the former reflects ideas, institutions, and traditions that have shaped the Western world from its infancy.

Traditionally minded individuals were reticent to adopt new core principles on a regular basis. Custom and convention maintain their importance in society because they exemplify permanence. Those who aligned themselves with the virtues of tradition readily defended its significance and place within Western society. Traditionalists did not see their ideas as a prison for the individual's identity or freedom of thought, but rather as grounds for examination of truth and the rich history of human knowledge over the course of thousands of years. Russell Kirk (1918–1994), in *Prospects for Conservatives* (1954), defended the importance of tradition, stating:

> [It] confers upon change the element of continuity, keeping the alteration of society in a regular train. Everything which the living possess has roots in the spiritual and intellectual achievements of the past. Everything man has—his body, his mind, his social order—is in large part an inheritance from people long dead. The passage of time brings new acquisitions; but unless men know the past, they are unable to understand distinctions between what is permanent and what is transient in their lives. Man always is beset by questions, of which the largest is the question of his own existence. He cannot even begin to think about his existence, and lesser questions, until he has acquired the command of means that come to him from the past, such as the names that people customarily use with reference to modes of being and acting.[22]

This perspective does not deny the reality of change and progress within humanity. Kirk sought to provide society and the individual with a firm foundation to properly evaluate these changes.

Modern progressives do not typically believe that man has a fixed nature, but one that is in a perpetual state of evolution. Hilaire Belloc (1870–1953) was an outspoken figure of the twentieth century and often verbally jousted with progressives in open forums and publications. He maintained that because of the definition of humanity in conjunction with natural law, human beings had a fixed nature; something H. G. Wells (1866–1946) deemed absurd in one of his many responses to Belloc.[23] In *Mr. Belloc Objects to* The Outline of History (1926), Wells quoted Belloc on the claims of natural selection and evolution: "There is no Mind at work in the universe; therefore changes of this sort must come from blind chance or at least *mechanically*. At all costs we must get rid of the idea of design: of a desired end conceived in a Creative Mind. Here is a theory which will make the whole process entirely mechanical and dead, and get rid of the necessity of a Creator."[24] Wells alleged that the problem with Chesterton and Belloc is that they see humans as fallen and not risen. Their dogmatism (often a tenet of tradition) bound them to a doctrine incapable of reform. Unfortunately for Wells, he could not simply write them off as insignificant commentary. As Joseph Pearce puts it,

"Chesterton and Belloc were about to achieve both fame and notoriety as the champions of 'orthodoxy' in the face of the 'heretics.'"[25] For Wells, a reconciliation of the two perspectives (addressed in chapter 6) was not possible either, as it was simply an attempt to put new wine into old bottles.[26] If human nature is not fixed, then the concept of permanence is null and void. If what it means to be human is married only to actions and behavior, then a permanent understanding is impossible because each spirit of the age is different as well as the actions and reactions of individuals and communities within their respective ages. British logical positivist A. J. Ayer (1910–1989) describes the modern perspective of what it means to be human in his essay "The Concept of a Person," noting:

> Can we significantly divorce our thoughts and our emotions from their characteristic expressions in action or in speech? . . . Human behaviour does not present itself to us as a physical process from which we have to make a dubious inference to the thoughts and feelings and purposes which lie "behind" it. It is itself expressive of these thoughts and feelings and purposed; and this is how we actually see it.[27]

The reduction of the human being to the solely physical (experiential) is a modern concept as nearly all of pre-modernity allowed for a metaphysical component to the definition of human nature. Ted McAllister points out that the modern disregard for permanence began as a new idea, but quickly became the status quo, thus forcing the idea of tradition and its defenders to become reactionary.[28]

The idea of tradition and its link to permanence is derived from the classical and typically Catholic understanding of natural law. Classically speaking, natural law refers to the use of reason to analyze human nature and from this analysis create binding morals. The Catholic Church largely agreed with the classical definition, but added the idea that God had determined the universal laws of nature, which echoes Aristotle's concept of teleology. If humanity is a part of nature and is bound by natural law, logically, it would maintain some fixed characteristics. American historian Garry Wills explains the theory of humanity in the Catholic intellectual tradition:

> Catholic thought involves an endless retracing of different strands in the traditional teaching. These strands unite and intertwine, and their entire force cannot be felt if isolated issues are dealt with. The economy of revelation must be considered as a whole; separate moral insights attain validity only as enunciated within this economy, as emerging out of a large and providential pattern, as interdependent with many other moral truths.[29]

Wills argues that secularization of traditional concepts did not bring about intellectual clarity, rather something closer to the claim of Patrick Allitt that it "fostered idolatry and brought forth a plethora of religious surrogates."[30] Secularization did not narrow the path to truth, instead it created a marketplace of variety (explained in chapter 4). For conservative traditionalists, morality, ethics, and the like fell within these parameters. God was viewed as the ultimate lawgiver who created natural laws with specific reasons and purposes in mind—a telos. The core principles of natural law largely remained untested until the sixteenth-century Protestant Reformation and the seventeenth-century Scientific Revolution. Even then, Isaac Newton's conclusions led to the belief that the universe acted in a uniform fashion.

MODERN PERSPECTIVES

The modern scientific age provides the most significant challenges to the established traditions, customs, and conventions of the Western world. Tolkien and Lewis knew there was tension between myth and rational historical knowledge going back to ancient times. Only in the modern world has this been seen as a crisis in knowledge. Before then the tension created great literature.[31] In a series of essays and lectures given under the more general topic of "Why I am not a Christian," Bertrand Russell (1872–1970) challenged the traditional West's hold on meaning and purpose. For Russell, Christianity, as with all religions, is nothing more than a social phenomenon that reflected the reality of the pre-modern understanding of natural laws. He explains, "We now find that a great many things we thought were natural laws are really human conventions. . . . Human laws are behests commanding you to behave a certain way."[32] New knowledge, for moderns like Russell, overturns old customs and conventions rather than clarifies or builds off of them. In the case of the modern individual he saw an unexplored realm of possibilities:

> The modern man, who as yet exists in only a few samples, has a different outlook. The material world is not to him a datum to be accepted with thankfulness or with prayerful supplication; it is raw material for his scientific manipulation. A desert is a place to which water must be brought, a malarial swamp is a place from which water must be taken away. Neither is allowed to maintain its natural hostility to man, so that in our struggles with physical nature we no longer have need of God to help us against Satan.[33]

The modern individual has become an agent of determination, not subject to it as believed in the past.

The debate centered on the reality of two separate cultures is not a new one. English chemist C. P. Snow (1905–1980) gave a lecture which was eventually published as *The Two Cultures* at Cambridge University in 1959. It sparked a heated debate regarding the inherent differences between the scientific and nonscientific cultures in the academy. Twentieth-century Britain (1928 Cambridge Union debates, 1946 BBC, and 1956 Jacob Bronowski lectures) was well aware of the magnitude and effect of the division between the sciences and humanities, dubbed "the challenge of our time."[34] Admittedly, Snow found that both were ignorant of one another, but that the more egregious fault came from the nonscientific camp because of their association with tradition:

> But I believe the pole of total incomprehension of science radiates its influence on all the rest. That total incomprehension gives, much more pervasively than we realise, living in it, an unscientific flavour to the whole "traditional" culture, and that unscientific flavour is often, much more than we admit, on the point of turning anti-scientific. The feelings of one pole become the anti-feelings of the other. If the scientists have the future in their bones, then the traditional culture responds by wishing the future did not exist. It is the traditional culture, to an extent remarkably little diminished by the emergence of the scientific one, which manages the Western world.[35]

Snow was not in praise of this reality, but believed the polarization was a detriment to society. British literary critic, F. R. Leavis (1895–1978) took issue with this critique and responded in kind with *Two Cultures?: The Significance of C.P. Snow* (1962). The lively debate between them was public and concerned both sides of the academy. Observing the virtues of one culture more closely than the other, in any setting, is often detrimental. Reconciliation comes from the ability to see the value of one without the compromise of the other's principles. Quite possibly the problem with Leavis and Snow was their inability to access the other's culture. There are numerous examples of individuals who attempted to straddle both cultures in the attempt to better serve either God or humanity. The discussion between the values of both cultures within the context of twentieth-century Western culture, which had begun to fervently choose science and "progress" over the humanities and "tradition," provides valuable insight.

Those who wish to preserve antiquity, however, can make a case from Francis Bacon's *Advancement in Learning* (1605). He claims that the natural relationship between custom and progress creates a resistance to change and an impediment of progress: "Antiquity envieth there should be new additions and novelty cannot be content to add but it must deface"; however, he goes on to say: "Antiquity deserveth that reverence that men should make a stand thereupon and discover what is the best way; but when the discovery is well taken, then to make progression."[36] Custom allows for progress as long as it is evaluated and judged against the knowledge of the past—an often inconvenient and laboriously slow process. Due to the variability of custom in different civilizations and the belief in a uniform natural law, skepticism regarding tradition is widespread.[37] The growth of modern skepticism aided in the idea that the individual must have a greater responsibility and function evaluating claims of fact, truth, and tradition in order to promote reason and avoid habitual action.

It is the modern camp that warns against the evils of convention as it has led generations to keep slavery as the status quo or imperialism as a form of government policy. Even if what Plato and Aristotle assert is true—"Man's will governs his reason, and convention, or the agreement of individual wills, decides what is acceptable to the group"—this does not remove the possibility of evil or oppressive cultural customs.[38] For the modern agenda to gather force and uphold the dignity of the individual, it often made tradition the enemy in the West. This idea is not unique to the modern scientific age. The *Great Books* incorporate the dissident voices in a number of authors (e.g., J. S. Mill and Michel de Montaigne).

Mill's insistence on the ability of society to recognize the voice of dissent against convention is imperative if the society is to survive as free and civilized—especially if it seeks to avoid the tyranny of the majority.[39] For Mill, custom is an unwelcomed antidote to individuality and free-thought. Montaigne is skeptical of custom, yet the purpose it serves far surpasses the evils it is capable of:

> Society itself can do without our thoughts but the rest—our actions, our work, our fortunes, and our very life—we must lend and abandon to its service and to the common opinions, just as the great and good Socrates refused to save his life by disobedience to the magistrate, even to a very unjust and very iniquitous magistrate. For it is the rule of rules, and the universal law of laws, that each man should observe those of the place he is in.[40]

The range of ideas in Mill and Montaigne speak to the interdisciplinary nature of the *Great Books*. They define tradition based on the conversation through the ages. Peter Kreeft's *Socrates Meets* series imagines the possible dialogue between Socrates and the other major contributors to the heritage of Western thought. Modernity provides the platform for this type of evaluation. Granted, the topic of race, gender studies, and ethnicity are seen as postmodern endeavors; nonetheless, modernity redefined the Western mind in order to leave room for a more diverse compilation of factual insights. If Western thought continues to maintain its tradition, its critics see this as the refusal to progress and evolve into better societies.

Modernity evaluates all claims of truth and fact through the empirical process in order to eliminate any subjective biases. Even if traditions are tested by time, and on occasion exist across different cultures, modernity harbors suspicion based on the evidence of historical atrocities. Canadian philosopher Charles Taylor explains the disposition of the modern person as one living in a "disenchanted world."[41] English composer John Tavener echoes this sentiment in relation to music as a return to the source of human creation. Tavener claims that the Modern Age lacks the ability to return to the source: "The fact that modernism can envisage no source is a very grave and catastrophic state of affairs."[42] Universal morality without dissident perspectives is seen as detrimental. Morality cannot be tested scientifically and therefore remains unviable as a standard of uniformity. Modernity's relativistic leanings are ultimately more popular, in part, due to a new spirit of human mentality, one that does not accept a universal transcendent standard, but it allows for the individual to make and remake his or her own personal standard, in relation to truth—something traditionalists hesitate to accept.

Due to the redefinitions ushered in by the Modern Age, McAllister claims that, "[t]raditionalist conservatives find themselves without much to conserve. Their only real option in these times is to seek recovery rather than conservation."[43] The awareness of "recovery" can be read within the words and passionate response to modernity. Custom and convention possess an enormous power over the individual—one that governs the ideas and beliefs of the individual against the evaluation of standing beliefs. Tradition's power is enough that it elicits the participation of entire civilizations so that they may begin to pass on the identity of their culture. A new sense of pluralistic and frequently revised practices may cause some traditionalists to claim that they do not have much to conserve. The basis for their reaction comes from the fact that modern society moves in a direction against standard forms of definition, which make it easier to find niches—no matter how small—for each individual. Traditionalists argue that despite modernity's best efforts to ignore tradition, the reality of custom will not allow it. In other words, one must accept that all people are inevitably the product of existing customs and accepted norms, regardless of how strong their desire may be to cut ties with their cultural heritage. German philosopher Ernst Cassirer (1874–1945) explains the effect of custom on the individual by saying: "Custom is the abiding, unaltering atmosphere in which he lives and has his being; he can no more remove himself from it than from the air he breathes."[44] One could logically deduce then that individualism never truly exists apart from an established order. In order to further clarify, Pieper thought it necessary to distinguish tradition from cultural progress. The latter is something learned, then passed on, assimilated, verified, or corrected and then passed on again, while the former is something received and handed down again.[45] The inability to completely separate from tradition may be a saving grace for some, but others see it as a dark reality of civilization and therefore take up progressivism in order to sever ties.

There is friction between mainstream relevancy and the traditions of the past. Custom and convention can be a comfort, and can make life easier due to the concept that custom or convention does not require active thought or awareness; it is habitual or automatic. The traditionalists in this study refer to the structure as a means of guidance, where free-thought can coexist as well.

Often, traditions of the past are deemed archaic or old-fashioned and become synonymous with intolerance and antiquated thought, these being the enemies of progress. Traditionalists, however, see custom and convention differently. They see them as tried and tested ideas and methods of understanding humanity, society, and God. There are a number of components needed to complete the knowledge of what it means to be human. If a society begins to devalue certain important components, their fate may be a factual compilation of materials without a teleology beyond the imagination of the individual. If this is the perceived reality of the age, then it is a fitting pathway. However, traditionalists maintain that without a spiritual component to human nature, the derivation of a superficial meaning is inevitable. According to those who resisted the new, modern definition of man, Western tradition reflects a metaphysical necessity. Russian philosopher Nicolas Berdyaev (1874–1948) saw the idea of man without God as a form of dehumanization.

Berdyaev's ideas are consistent with a more traditional definition of what it means to be human. In *The Fate of Man in Modern World* (1935), Berdyaev examines the different aspects of modernity and its secularization of Western life. By reducing the essence of humanity to the material, the Modern Age equates the human being to an organic machine. The insistence that science is the best tool for understanding human beings and society further supports the idea that the human being can be changed and worked on like a machine. Once the proper diagnosis is made through science—not religion—society can create an image of the "perfect individual" in the likeness of the mechanic, rather than the Creator:

> The process of dehumanization attains its climax in the technique of modern war, where human bravery is no longer necessary. Technical civilization demands that man shall fulfil one or another of his functions, but it does not want to reckon with man himself—it knows only his process. . . . When man strives for complete fulfilment of his technical functions, when he tries to be like his new god, the machine.[46]

Berdyaev posits the idea that the technical obsession of the Modern Age, mainly through modern physics, has created a dissonance in modern thought.

Due to the fact that mere function and action cannot provide meaning, modern philosophy has run the gamut from logical positivism, to idealism, and existentialism searching for a systematic understanding of humanity.[47] Berdyaev's ideas on the effects of modernity share similar conclusions with traditionalists, especially Charles Williams and Owen Barfield. There is a cosmic catastrophe implied in the idea that human beings are part of the natural machine of the universe—what Berdyaev calls a "non-humanized, cosmic milieu."[48] The new forces of science have replaced the cosmic authorities of the Old West.

The common perception of moderns is that tradition is without reason due to its relationship, not only with the cosmic, but also with custom and habit. If this is the case, then the ideas typically found in the liberal arts of the Western canon are not useful and therefore do not need to be learned by everyone—only those who choose to do so. Lukacs points out that the Western canon is not devoid of reason, but impervious to the full embodiment of twentieth-century intellectual movements.[49] Often the complaint toward the Western canon is that it does not reflect the progressive mentality of the new West. Lukacs and other Catholic intellectuals defend the value of permanence in the Western canon for its ability to withstand fashionable intellectual movements even if it grows due to significant contribution.[50] The reality is that both American and British universities were dominated by this perspective as secularization became a tool academics used to discount the erroneous ways of the past for the sake of a brave new world.

Catholic philosopher Frederick Wilhelmsen (1923–1996), John Lukacs, and a handful of British intellectuals were part of a movement that believed educators were responsible for imparting tradition to subsequent generations.[51] The attitude of "knowledge for its own sake" characterizes the classical liberal arts and is abrasive to the pragmatic and utilitarian ideals of modern education. At Oxford, Lewis and Tolkien fought against the complete modernization of the English syllabus—something they were able to maintain for a few decades until the voices of opposition became deafening and the English syllabus was pronounced outdated—namely by Cambridge professor of literature I. A. Richards (1893–1979).

Leo Strauss (1899–1973) responded with a challenge to moderns, when he asked how, without tradition, they could know what ethos they wanted to pass on to the future/posterity: "The crisis of modernity reveals itself in the fact, or consists in the fact that modern Western man no longer knows what he wants—that he no longer believes that he can know what is good and bad, what is right and wrong."[52] Strauss represents a humanist response to the problems of modernity—one that originated with literary scholars Irving Babbitt (1865–1933) and Paul Elmer More (1864–1937). They themselves did not see their humanism as new, but more classical in nature.[53] Although Babbitt, More,[54] and Strauss did not espouse any religiosity as an influence of their revolt against modernity, their ideas did resonate with a number of Catholics and Anglo-Catholics. The project of the New Humanists involved a defense of the classical liberal arts in the University which came out of a long custom of conservative traditionalists insistent on the preservation of the "idea" of the University despite the spirit of the age (see chapters 6 and 7). The defense of the University was not the only thing at stake. Western culture's relationship with the metaphysical was also in jeopardy of being phased out by the Modern Age.

The efforts of traditionalists were a reaction to the growing sentiment that metaphysical questions no longer needed to be discussed. C. S. Lewis saw it as the result of the new reality of Western history, saying: "Roughly speaking we may say that whereas all history was for our ancestors divided into two periods, the pre-Christian and the Christian, and two only, for us it falls into three—the pre-Christian, the Christian, and what may reasonably be called the post-Christian."[55] In conjunction with the reality of a new age, metaphysical questions are seen as insignificant for two basic reasons: they are largely unanswerable and the assumed answers ask individuals to judge and align themselves with standards that they themselves did not create.[56] The issue is one of value-free knowledge. As Anthony Kronman points out:

> They [humanities] study human values as they have been expressed in one setting or another and invite—indeed, compel—students to engage these values themselves by asking whether they are sound and attractive. It is not enough for a student of philosophy to know that Plato held one view of justice and John Stuart Mill another. He must consider which, if either, to endorse himself. He must enter the conversation, join the debate, and take sides in it. He cannot put brackets around questions of value in order to preserve his objective detachment. The natural and social sciences require such detachment. Philosophy, literature, art, and other humanities forbid it.[57]

Traditionalists struggled with the demands of custom versus the alteration of the system in order to reflect each individual person in pursuit of objective definition for morality, truth, beauty, or goodness. The Modern Age may not be concerned with the vexation of the unknown as its primary concern is with material knowledge. Traditionalists maintained the custom and convention of the West, despite its obvious flaws, could be a welcome companion to the Modern Age.

The new methodologies (e.g., logical positivism) of the modern scientific age reject the need to consult the humanities in the discussion of human questions.[58] Spirituality waned under the growing trust in human capability and the achievement of certainty. Such a symptom is telling, given the age was marked by terrific innovation and rapid expansion, though in an atmosphere of pessimism brought about by the pivotal events of the twentieth century, namely World War I, the Great Depression, and World War II. Waves of pessimism came from two fronts. The first wave came from German thinkers Friedrich Schopenhauer (1788–1860) and Friedrich Nietzsche (1844–1900), as well as French essayists Jean-Paul Sartre (1905–1980) and Albert Camus (1913–1960). The second wave came from those who lamented the progressives' movement away from tradition.[59] Alongside pessimistic ideology, the increased acceptance of scientism aided in carrying the ideals of the late nineteenth century into the twentieth.

Scientism provided a system that its followers applied to all manners of discourse. It may have even saved modernity from any dying gasps as it developed both an empirical and spiritual form of "worship" (see chapter 4).[60] Regardless of the path, the main concern was for critical reevaluation of Western society without the influence of traditional institutions. The goal was to leave behind anything resembling custom or convention as it may impress its strict interpretations on society and humanity. The shackles of tradition would not be loosed enough for the freedom of progress the twentieth century so desperately craved. Tradition does not equate with a hatred of improvement, but it is unwilling to accept progress through the reduction of humanity to a series of physical properties and functions. Custom finds itself at the center of societal debates with those either seeking to tear it down or those who take up its defense. In either case, custom's greatest application involves the individual and the community. Pre-modern and modern societies differed in perspective. It is not that the ancients and medievals reviled the individual. In fact, a great deal of responsibility is placed on the individual to study and live a virtuous life, one that avoids vice, thus making better citizens.

Through self-awareness and evaluation, the individual can participate in deciding the values of custom and convention as they are discussed in both pre-modern and modern contexts. The purpose is synonymous with that of the humanities: "Critical thinking, appreciation of the arts and humanities and understanding how to relate to society and the natural world are essential characteristics of the educated person. . . . Historically, the liberal arts and humanities have contributed to developing such a person."[61] Both the ancient and the modern world realized that the value of the community was priceless, and both have endeavored to save, improve, and understand civilization for the sake of the species. Custom and convention have always been key participants in the dialogue.

PURPOSE IN SOCIETY

The discussion of the individual and community is a helpful illustration of the ancient and modern differences as they pertain to the influence of custom and convention in society. Customs are a part of everyday life, but they are initiated by groups voluntarily within societies where the individual has the freedom to abide by the customs and conventions of the group.[62] Granted, the participation is voluntary, but the ancients believed the actions originated from an inevitable necessity. In *The Republic*, Plato articulates the notion of common or collective interest as Socrates' belief in the catalyst for the creation of societies:

> A State, I said, arises, as I conceive, out of the needs of mankind; no one is self-sufficing, but all of us have many wants. Can any other origin of a State be imagined? . . . Then as we have many wants, and many persons are needed to supply them, one takes a helper for one purpose and another for another; and when these partners and helpers are gathered together in one habitation the body of inhabitants is termed a State.[63]

Socrates and Plato believe a set of common interests would connect others in the community, thus a vested interest in the virtue and success of the city is created. The "common interest"[64] and embodiment of such ideals in the individual, ideally, should reflect one another; "the good and true City or State, and the good and true man is of the same pattern."[65]

The moderns did not see custom as something entered into voluntarily, as subsequent generations could not possibly share the same goals for the direction of society. In *Beauty for Truth's Sake* (2009), Stratford Caldecott (1953–2014) describes the mentality of the modern construct:

> The stories these writers tell (setting aside various differences in emphasis) is of a philosophical shift, associated not only with a severing of the intimate bond between cosmology and ethics, facts and values, but with a changing sense of the self, and of the relation between self and society. . . . The modern person feels himself to be disengaged from the world around him, rather than intrinsically related to it (by family, tribe, birthplace, vocation, and so forth). He is expected to forge his own destiny by an exercise of choice.[66]

The moderns are not confident that the Good Society can come from custom and tradition. The basis of the Good Society cannot be something subjective; the primitive and mystical interpretation of God is why Sigmund Freud (1856–1939), William James (1842–1910), and Thorstein Veblen (1857–1929) saw the pre-moderns as superstitious and oppressive in their desire to preserve the structure of the ruling class with the influence of the transcendent.

The moderns do not see the pre-modern idea of leadership as benevolent men looking to create the Good Society. The rhetoric of Scripture and the ancient Greeks comes from a false understanding of humanity. A traditionalist definition of the Good Society is too dependent on intangibles. Scottish Enlightenment philosopher David Hume (1711–1776) claimed that it was more akin to habit. Habits are seen as actions the individual no longer consciously observes while performing—in other words, mindless. This is another distinction between the ancient and modern, because the ancients revered a person who acquired the skill of habit. The traditional institutions of society perpetuated the thoughtless habitual acts of custom without the challenge of reform so that the institutions would reflect the current mindset. The problem with this particular desire is revealed in the differences that exist from one age to another—belief in the habits and customs of one's ancestors are barbarous and inhumane as they are not one's own.

The customs of the city aid in structuring the education and growth of the individual. The modern sentiment moves away from the community as an agent of social change and order because it is seen as enslaved to its own conventions—other options, for example the State, should be considered. The focus of the modern society is one of "happiness and fulfillment" of the individual as long as it does not harm another citizen and his or her attempts. Custom and convention are characterized as not just barbaric, but also as the vestige of an elite class or leisure class—one not equal before the law. Amid progressive ideologies (i.e., Fabians and Positivists vs. pragmatists and psychologists) a consensus could not be reached on how to achieve the modern vision of Western society. According to Marc Stears:

> The Fabians and Positivists, though, argued that social progress would best come from the purposeful direction of an informed elite: "we believe in a government of the people, and for the people, but not by the people", as David Croly declared. Finally, the pragmatists and psychologists urged the development of an ever more participatory democracy, so distanced from the Fabian ideal of rigid instruction from the centre that its citizens "would not understand what a state is if the word were used in the present sense".[67]

It is clear that modern ideologies were not malicious, but traditionalists worried that they did not reflect the characteristics of human nature.

Before the modern industrial age, the leisure class served a purpose as it was a stage in the evolution of Western culture, but now that age passed and it no longer expressed the values of the influential in society. In *The Theory of the Leisure Class* (1899), Veblen indicted the pre-modern leisure class for its lack utility, saying: "The leisure class as a whole comprises the noble and priestly classes, together with much of their retinue. The occupations of the class are correspondingly diversified; but they have the common economic characteristic of being non-industrial."[68] The modern industrial age is completely different as it generally holds the belief that the individual is a product of the environment, rather than a transcendent Being who created with purpose. The self is then a construct or sum total of experiences. For the moderns an archaic mind-set hinders progress and humanity is in a constant state of progress. According to Veblen, the modern mind-set provides the clearest explanation: "Not only have the habits of men changed with the changing exigencies of the situation, but these changing exigencies have also brought about a correlative change in human nature. The human material of society itself varies with the changing conditions of life."[69] The changes in culture are indicative of the lack of an objective or universal definition of the Good. Self-knowledge cannot be attached to a higher form of the Good, but rather reflects the evolution of stylistic expression: "The changing styles are the expression of a restless search for something which shall commend itself to our aesthetic sense; but as each innovation is subject to the selective action of the norm of conspicuous waste, the range within which innovation can take place is somewhat restricted."[70] Systems of meaning and knowledge are subject to such trends as well and therefore need to reflect the values and desires of the age, rather than the so-called abuses of the leisure class.

In the modern sense, self-knowledge cannot reflect the Good Society if it does not possess a distinct utility. This cannot be achieved if the definition of the Good Society comes from a detached and elite ruling class. The industrial age had created a greater demand on the time and efficient use of resources from its participants. Even those with means could not devote their lives to the study of knowledge for its own sake. Veblen believes that knowledge for its own sake is vacuous and serves no purpose beyond the individual knower, thus profiting nothing for the society of which the knower is a member. Thus, John Dewey's pragmatic pedagogy appeals to the society effected by these realities. As Stears puts it: "What was required, Dewey concluded, was a continual programme of 'instruction' that prepares individuals to flourish in their 'social dependencies and interdependencies.'"[71] For adults and children alike, education necessitated a focus on public responsibility rather than the individual.[72] Dewey's influence was still felt at all levels of education thirty years later (and even in the late twentieth century) as evidenced by Mortimer Adler and Robert Hutchins' devotion of the first volume of *The Great Books* to the definition of a liberal education—one largely in opposition to Dewey.[73] The value of wisdom and study seen in the pre-moderns does not translate to the paradigms of utility in the modern industrial age. It is bound up in the ideas of the soul, whereas the moderns are more apt to define such things through the systematic (scientific) discipline of psychology, or in the words of William James: "The theory of the Soul is the theory of popular philosophy and of scholasticism, which is only popular philosophy made systematic. It declares that the principle of individuality within us must be substantial, for psychic phenomena are activities, and there can be no activity without concrete agent."[74]

The insights of William James spoke of a measurable knowledge of the Self based on collected data. For James, the metaphysical component is not valid because it is fragmentary, irresponsible, and half-awake especially during its interaction with a natural science.[75] The Self becomes something more easily explained despite its complexity (consciousness, memory, facts, reality, etc.). James could not get on board with the pre-moderns who valued the immortality of the Soul, as this is distinctly metaphysical. He viewed immortality as nothing more than a desire, stating, "The demand for immortality nowadays is essentially teleological. We believe ourselves immortal because we believe ourselves fit for immortality."[76] James falls in line with Veblen's broader implications of what defines society as he believed that self-knowledge did not lead to the individual's recognition of the community over the Self. Any attempt at this does not create the Good Society, but is a symptom of something James called "social self-seeking": "Our social self-seeking, in turn, is carried on directly through our amativeness and friendliness, our desire to please and attract notice and admiration, our emulation and jealousy, our love of glory, influence, and power, and indirectly through whichever of the material self-seeking impulses prove serviceable as a means to social ends."[77]

Veblen uses different language to define the same sentiment: "To this class the modern culture owes much in the way of the conservation of traditions, usages, and habits of thought which belong on a more archaic cultural plane, so far as regards their widest acceptance and their most effective development."[78] Moderns did not see the Good Society as a product of virtuous or divine intent. Therefore, the newly formed customs of the age augment the definition to better reflect present values, instead of allowing the past a significant influence.

Veblen believes that the institutions of the pre-modern world are alive and well and have not faded out because habits of thought persist indefinitely.[79] The modern industrial age faced the responsibility of removing the influence of the non-industrialists due to circumstances that enforce a new cultural stage. An emulation of leisure class ideals does not incorporate one into the leisure class, and for Veblen, it is merely the reflection of a "selective and coercive process,"[80] which is not a tenet of a good society.

In the eyes of traditionalists, classical learning is diverse in that the humanities reflect a natural relationship. Classical learning is diverse, but is centered in the humanities. As a proponent of the modern attitude, Veblen believed that science and society interacted more naturally to better reflect the trajectory of Western society: "a scholastic discipline is sanctioned by the common sense of the community incorporated into the accredited scheme of life."[81] James and Freud would agree with Veblen as their specific contributions are kindled in the glow of modern knowledge. Science reflects the utility of everyday life. Veblen saw this reflected in the education system, specifically higher learning, but the leisure class greatly influenced higher learning with its concerns through the humanities[82] and the "unknowable" which only serves the "sacerdotal purpose" (i.e., religious and supernatural).[83] At the time, a liberal arts education, in the modern industrial age, did not reflect the majority of the community who were invested in the "industrial" endeavors of society because it was deeply situated within a leisure class of "non-industrial" people. It was only the leisure class who benefits, without sacrifice, from knowledge for its own sake (classical): "Knowledge for its own sake, the exercise of faculty of comprehensive without ulterior purpose, should, it might be expected, be sought by men whom no urgent material interest diverts from such a quest."[84]

Once modern society was characterized by the industrial process, the liberal arts could no longer serve the individual for the sake of the community—the self-knowledge of the pre-moderns did not act as a foundational pillar for the Modern Age. The sciences better prepared the individual for the realities of a mechanical and material society: "It is only the exigencies of modern industrial life have enforced the recognition of causal sequence in the practical contacts of mankind with their environment, that men have come to systematise the phenomena of this environment, and the facts of their own contacts with it, in terms of causal sequence."[85] Veblen's call for change reflects similar desires of James and Freud within a scientific age; therefore, the sciences must guide and define the Good Society—a society focused on knowledge of the physical world. Veblen's critique did, however, leave more room for dialogue where James and Freud eliminated the value of the pre-moderns altogether. The leisure class has much to learn from its critics and vice versa, one can only hope that self-knowledge is good for something, even if it does not reflect the current focus of modern society.

For many moderns, the institutions of tradition have upheld a standard of living that only benefits the few. Therefore, the past is guilty of vulgar atrocities and must be cast aside or at the very least, significantly altered to reflect the new age of Western civilization. During the process of casting off tradition for the sake of a broader sense of equality and the like, Western society's definition of human nature took a significant turn away from the pages of dialogue housed within Western tradition.

Modern society recognizes an illness, but does not see a cure in either custom or religion, so it must forge ahead. Human nature, according to the modern secular paradigm, is not fallen or depraved; it is material that can be repaired or altered toward a greater efficiency. Like a machine it needs systems upgrades and repairs. The reduction of humanity into a mechanized state is the basis for Donald N. Michael's critique on *The Problems of Cybernation* (1962). Michael claims that society will become adaptable members of the workforce whose purpose does not extend beyond efficiency of production. If an individual happens to fall into a state of unproductiveness, he or she will be redirected toward something better suited to one's ability to contribute.[86] English author Samuel Butler (1835–1902) provides an excellent example in his planned society of the Erewhonians. Their ill health is a direct result of their ill behavior. The diagnosis reflects the idea that the functions of the machine directly affect its well-being.[87] Ironically, for the Erewhonians, the fight for individual rights and freedom could only be achieved through a structure of collectivism or the development of a public mind.[88] Convention can be viewed as arbitrary or cruel, therefore, is problematic when associated or even originated in religious tradition.

The alternative to reliance on the system is self-reliance. Echoed throughout the works of Ralph Waldo Emerson (1803–1882) and Thomas Paine

(1737–1809) is the sacredness and freedom of one's own mind as the only path to truth and understanding. The tradition within the *Great Books* recognizes the discrepancies of free-thought. For instance, St. Augustine recognizes the necessity of one's own reason to comprehend human nature. However, he is not completely sold on the ability of reason unaided to divine human nature. In this sense, Emerson's concept of freedom exists in custom and convention, not mentality.[89] The accumulated knowledge of humanity, both physical and metaphysical, needs to be compiled into a canon and shared with all walks of society. In his *Age of Reason* (1794), Paine believes, "My own mind is my own church,"[90] and given the access to knowledge is able to determine truth on its own accord. German philosopher Arthur Schopenhauer's (1788–1860) *On Education* (1819) points out that much like the encyclopedists of the French Enlightenment, progressives wish to edit and redefine the traditions of the West because they are criticized as discriminatory, full of bigotry, and elitist.[91] The consciousness of the past is not easily reconciled with the desires of the modern. The modern challenges each individual to stop leaning on the crutch of custom and look to the ability and discernment of the self.[92]

Traditionalists make a compelling argument for the possibility of upholding the traditions of the past alongside the benefits of free thought and other modern principles. The exercise and creation of good habits of mind can keep the individual from being kept at bay by unhealthy customs in order to elevate his or herself to a standard of virtue. In Michael Faraday's (1791–1867) *Observations on Mental Education* (1854), one must avoid blind dependence on dogma. The conception of tradition is that it is blindly bound to dogmatism. There are instances of this, but they are more often than not remedied when detrimental to society. Faraday also points out that a good habit of mind cannot be achieved without a body of knowledge to study.[93] Western thought has been dominated by certain perspectives and institutions, but the liberal arts have provided a sanctuary from totalitarian thinking. Tradition is devoted to certain principles—what traditionalists refer to as "permanent things." Based on this assessment, one could make the argument that Western thought is not blindly devoted to dogma, but rather, possesses a consciousness of ideas that exist in all ages. From the early Greeks to the modern scientific age, Western heritage challenges the individual person to form good habits of mind and clear and precise ideas for the sake of virtue, faith, community, and empirical truth.[94]

A good habit of mind can produce good behavior and sound morals, despite the lack of universal holding to this idea. One of the first modern advocates of the *Great Books* tradition, Columbia University professor of English John Erskine (1879–1951) wrote an essay on the link between intelligence and morality titled, *The Moral Obligation to be Intelligent* (1915). Erskine argued that morality is something more than a derivative of what is best for the current society. He believed that universal morals can be practiced and discovered when education and intelligence are a societal priority, one which is passed down through custom—intelligent beings create intelligent societies.[95] Rudyard Kipling (1865–1936), in his *Mowgli's Brothers* (1894), is in opposition to this theory. He states that custom is nothing more than the tool of a hierarchy that wishes to govern behavior in society. In the story, Mowgli is orphaned and raised by a pack of wolves. Kipling uses the story to exemplify the dynamic of Mowgli's learned traits as a wolf, and his innate traits as a man. The two mutually exclusive identities present a difficult disposition for Mowgli as he attempts to be both what he is by birth and what he has become in the jungle. Therefore, custom is not a natural occurrence within societies devoted to tradition, but is something forced upon society.[96] Nonetheless, the tradition of the West has been one that values education despite what it may bring. The problem for twentieth-century progressives was the tendency of tradition to include the perspective of Christianity. Erskine saw this as a distinct difference between the two: "At this moment they are readily divided into those who wish to be men—whatever that means—and those who wish to be intelligent men, and those who, unconscious of blasphemy or humor, prefer not to be intelligent, but to do the will of God."[97]

Regardless of the perspective, pre-modern or modern, Western society consciously debates the debt it owes to the ideas and institutions associated with tradition. Traditionalists recognize custom and convention may be misguided at times, even barbaric, but in its consistency, it weathered the tides of change. Modernity cannot claim perfection either, but it is given preference because of its commitment to relativity. Traditionalists recognize the difficulty of living by custom and convention, but it does not deter them from an attempt to live by a higher creed. Acting on one's own desires is clear, but traditionalists' definition of humanity looks at life as something more than just "happiness" and individual fulfillment. It asks the individual to seek a virtuous life in pursuit of truth, beauty, and goodness in a tradition passed down through the humanities. In light of such pursuits, there has been a small and occasionally successful resistance to the newer ideas of progressivism.

NOTES

1. T. S. Eliot, "Tradition and the Individual Talent," *The Sacred Wood: Essays on Poetry and Criticism* (London: Methuen, 1960), p. 33.
2. Eliot, "Tradition and the Individual Talent," pp. 30–31.
3. *Ibid.*, p. 30.
4. Russell Kirk, *The Essential Kirk: Selected Essays*, ed. George A. Panichas (Wilmington: ISI Books, 2007), p. 275.
5. Russell Kirk, *The Conservative Mind: From Burke to Eliot* (Washington, D.C.: Regnery Publishing, Inc., 2001), p. 47.

6. Pieper, *Tradition*, p. 3.
7. Kirk, *Essential Kirk*, p. 208.
8. Pieper, *Tradition*, pp. 9–11.
9. Isaiah Berlin, *The Proper Study of Mankind: An Anthology of Essays*, eds. Henry Hardy and Roger Hausheer (New York: Farrar, Straus & Giroux, 1997), p. 344.
10. "Conservatism," *American Conservatism: An Encyclopedia*, eds. Bruce Frohnen, Jeremy Beer, and Jeffrey O. Nelson (Wilmington: ISI Books, 2006).
11. British Idealist F. H. Bradley (1846–1924) championed the philosophical ideas of Immanuel Kant and G. W. Hegel. Bradley and other notable Idealists (Bernard Bosanquet, Edward Caird, T. H. Green, Harold Joachim, and J. M. E. McTaggart) held "that our everyday conceptions of the world (as well as those more refined ones common among his philosophical predecessors) contain hidden contradictions which appear, fatally, when we try to think out their consequences. In particular, Bradley rejected on these grounds the view that reality can be understood as consisting of many objects existing independently of each other (pluralism) and of our experience of them (realism)." "Francis Herbert Bradley," *Stanford Encyclopedia of Philosophy*, last updated Feb. 19, 2013, http://plato.stanford.edu/entries/bradley/.
12. Allan Bloom, *The Closing of the American Mind* (New York: Simon and Schuster, 1987), p. 107.
13. *Ibid.*, p.108.
14. Terence Ball, *Reappraising Political Theory: Revisionist Studies in the History of Political Thought* (Oxford: Clarendon Press, 1995), pp. 4–5. Scott Jaschik, "Disappearing Liberal Arts Colleges," *Inside Higher Ed* (October 11, 2012).
15. Mortimer Adler identified 103 Great Ideas contemplated, debated, and defined by the Western canon of thought. For example, "beauty," "state," "temperance," "poetry," "progress," among others.
16. C. S. Lewis, *God in the Dock* (Grand Rapids: Eerdmans, 1970), p. 202.
17. Alfred North Whitehead, *Science and the Modern World* (Cambridge: Cambridge University, 1953), p. 255.
18. Mortimer J. Adler, "Chapter 14 Custom and Convention," *The Great Ideas: A Syntopicon of Great Books of the Western World*, 2 vols. (Chicago: William Benton, 1952), p. 268.
19. Nussbaum, *Not for Profit*, p. 18.
20. J. S. Mill, *On Liberty* (Indianapolis: Hackett Publishing, 1978), p. 35.
21. *Ibid.*, pp. 41, 56, and 67.
22. Russell Kirk, *Prospects for Conservatives* (Washington, D.C.: Regnery Gateway, 1989), pp. 228–9.
23. H. G. Wells, *Mr. Belloc Objects to* The Outline of History (New York: George H. Doran Co., 1926), p. 80.
24. *Ibid.*, p. 30.
25. Joseph Pearce, *Literary Converts: Spiritual Inspiration in an Age of Unbelief* (San Francisco: Ignatius Press, 1999), p. 7
26. *Ibid.*, p. 93.
27. A. J. Ayer, *The Concept of a Person and Other Essays* (New York: St. Martin's Press, 1964), p. 97.
28. Ted V. McAllister, *Revolt Against Modernity: Leo Strauss, Eric Voegelin, and the Search for a Postliberal Order* (Tulsa: University of Kansas Press. 1996), p. 273.
29. Garry Wills, "Catholics and Population," *National Review* (July 27, 1965), p. 644.
30. Allitt, p. 250.
31. Colin Duriez, *Tolkien and C.S. Lewis*, p. 59.
32. Bertrand Russell, *Why I am Not a Christian and Other Essays on Religion and Related Subjects* (New York: Simon & Schuster, 1957), p. 8.
33. *Ibid.*, pp. 158–9.
34. Guy Ortolano, "F.R. Leavis, Science, and the Abiding Crisis of Modern Civilization," *History of Science* 43, no. 2 (June 2005), p. 161.
35. C. P. Snow, *The Two Cultures: A Second Look* (Cambridge: Cambridge University Press, 1965), p. 11.

36. Francis Bacon, *The Advancement of Learning*, "Book I, Ch. V, #1, ed. Mortimer Adler, *Great Books of the Western World, Vol. 30* (Chicago: Encyclopedia Britannica, 1990), p. 15.
37. Mortimer J. Adler, "Custom and Convention", pp. 269–71.
38. *Ibid.*, p. 272.
39. Mill, p. 54.
40. Michel de Montaigne, "Of Custom" in *The Complete Works*, trans. Donald M. Frame (New York: Alfred A. Knopf. 2003), p. 104.
41. See Charles Taylor, *A Secular Age* (Boston: The Belknap Press of Harvard University Press, 2007).
42. John Tavener, *The Music of Silence: A Composer's Testament*, ed. Brian Keeble (London: Faber & Faber, 1999), p. 98.
43. McAllister, *Revolt Against Modernity*, p. 278.
44. Ernst Cassirer, *An Essay on Man: An Introduction to the Philosophy of Human Culture* (New Haven: Yale University Press, 1956), p. 42.
45. Pieper, *Tradition*, p. 20.
46. Nicolas Berdyaev, *The Fate of Man in the Modern World* in *Sources* in *Western Civilization: The Twentieth Century, 1914–1964*, ed. Arthur P. Mendel (New York: The Free Press. 1965), p. 90.
47. *Ibid.*, p. 93.
48. *Ibid.*
49. Allitt, p. 44. For Lukacs' full article see: "Intellectuals, Catholics, and the Intellectual Life," *Modern Age* 2, no. 1 (Winter 1957–58), pp. 40–53.
50. John Tracy Ellis, "American Catholics and the Intellectual Life," *Thought* 30 (Autumn 1955): 351–88.
51. Allitt, p. 45.
52. Leo Strauss, *Political Philosophy: Six Essays by Leo Strauss*, ed. Hilail Gildin (Indianapolis: Pegasus, 1975), p. 81.
53. Allitt, p. 52.
54. According to Brian Domitrovic, More's restlessness eventually led him to Christianity, although not an orthodox version. "Paul Elmer More: America's Reactionary," *Modern Age* 45, no. 4 (Fall 2003): 343–49.
55. Lewis, "De Descriptione Temporum," p. 5.
56. McAllister, *Revolt Against Modernity*, p. 69.
57. Kronman, *Education's End*, p. 69.
58. McAllister, *Revolt Against Modernity*, p. 75.
59. *Ibid.*, p. 79.
60. *Ibid.*, p. 80.
61. Kevin Reilly, Charles Steger, James Barker, and James Bernhard Machve, "Do Humans Still Need to Study the Humanities?" *The New Republic*, last modified March 17, 2015. http://www.newrepublic.com/article/121308/what-purpose-do-humanities-serve.
62. The understanding throughout is one where all circumstances are in reference to the West as this type of freedom does not characterize the entire world.
63. Plato, *The Republic* in *Six Great Dialogues*, trans. Benjamin Jowett (Mineola: Dover Publications Inc., 2007), pp. 222–23.
64. *Ibid.*, p. 314.
65. *Ibid.*, p. 299.
66. Stratford Caldecott, *Beauty for Truth's Sake: On the Re-enchantment of Education* (Grand Rapids: Brazos Press, 2009), p. 123.
67. Stears, *Progressives*, p. 49.
68. Thorstein Veblen, *The Theory of the Leisure Class* (Oxford: Oxford University Press, 2007), p. 7.
69. *Ibid.*, p. 141.
70. *Ibid.*, p. 115.
71. Stears, *Progressives*, p. 213.

72. See John Dewey, *Reconstruction in Philosophy* (London: University of London Press, 1921); Dewey, *Democracy and Education* (New York: Macmillan, 1922); Dewey, "Vocational Education," *New Republic*, 11 March 1916.

73. See Robert M. Hutchins, *The Great Conversation: The Substance of a Liberal Education* (Chicago: University of Chicago, 1952); Alexander W. Astin, "Liberal Education and Democracy: The Case for Pragmatism" in *Education and Democracy: Re-imagining Liberal Learning in America*, ed. Robert Orvill (New York: College Entrance Exam Board, 1997).

74. William James, *The Principles of Psychology, Vol. 1* (Digireads.com Publishing, 2010), p. 225.

75. *Ibid.*, p. 5.
76. *Ibid.*, p. 228.
77. *Ibid.*, p. 203.
78. Veblen, *Theory of the Leisure Class*, p. 47.
79. *Ibid.*, p. 127.
80. *Ibid.*, p. 126.
81. *Ibid.*, p. 236.
82. *Ibid.*, p. 247.
83. *Ibid.*, p. 237.
84. *Ibid.*, p. 249.
85. *Ibid.*, p. 251.

86. Donald N. Michael, *The Problems of Cybernation* in *Sources in Western Civilization: The Twentieth Century, 1914–1964*, ed. Arthur P. Mendel (New York: The Free Press, 1965), p. 144.

87. Samuel Butler, "Customs and Opinions of the Erewhonians," eds. Robert M. Hutchins and Mortimer J. Adler, *The Gateway to the Great Books, Vol. 2* (Chicago: Encyclopedia Britannica, Inc., 1990), p. 483.

88. *Ibid.*, p. 499.

89. Ralph Waldo Emerson, *Self-Reliance*, eds. Robert M. Hutchins and Mortimer J. Adler, *The Gateway to the Great Books, Vol. 2* (Chicago: Encyclopedia Britannica, Inc., 1990), p. 537.

90. Thomas Paine, *The Age of Reason: Parts I & II*, ed. Moncure Daniel Conway (New York: Merchant Books, 2010), p. 22.

91. Arthur Schopenhauer, *On Education*, eds. Robert M. Hutchins and Mortimer J. Adler, *The Gateway to the Great Books, Vol. 2* (Chicago: Encyclopedia Britannica, Inc., 1990), pp. 197–98.

92. *Ibid.*, p. 198.

93. Michael Faraday, *Observations on Mental Education*, eds. Robert M. Hutchins and Mortimer J. Adler, *The Gateway to the Great Books, Vol. 2* (Chicago: Encyclopedia Britannica, Inc., 1990), pp. 216–17.

94. *Ibid.*, p. 220.

95. John Erskine, *The Moral Obligation to be Intelligent*, eds. Robert M. Hutchins and Mortimer J. Adler, *The Gateway to the Great Books, Vol. 2* (Chicago: Encyclopedia Britannica, Inc., 1990), pp. 9–10.

96. Rudyard Kipling, *Mowgli's Brothers*, eds. Robert M. Hutchins and Mortimer J. Adler, *The Gateway to the Great Books, Vol. 2* (Chicago: Encyclopedia Britannica, Inc., 1990), p. 130.

97. Erskine, *Moral Obligation*, p. 11.

Chapter Three

G. K. Chesterton

Mouthpiece of Tradition

Modernity's reactionary attitude toward past traditions it deemed as malignant defined a significant portion of twentieth-century progressivism and the conscious attempt to act in the name of reform—even if the definition was vague.[1] The concepts of modernity sought to reinvent commonly held ideas in order to usher in a new understanding of human nature and the universe for the sake of progress and improvement of public interest and the common good. The progressive understanding of the "common good" was not necessarily synonymous with the traditionalist idea of the "common mind." The preservation of tradition was not a highly esteemed practice at this point; rather it was seen as an archaic method that upheld contemporary power structures for the benefit of the privileged. The plausibility of the pre-modern world was called into question by the emergence of the modern era and its new knowledge. A vanguard from Oxford's the Inklings, to the New Humanists, to other traditionally minded intellectuals shared in the desire to preserve what they found to be critically important ideas within the tradition of Western thought. These groups and individuals were indebted to one particular traditionalist, G. K. Chesterton.

Traditionalists were well aware of the distinction between the traditional and progressive schools of thought. For the authors involved, the dialogue was an appropriate mirror of scrutiny to hold up to modernity as it struggled to reflect a deep history and tradition versus an ideology increasingly suspicious of its "primitive ancestors." As Sanford Schwartz puts it: "In a manner akin to Rousseau's critique of European ethnocentrism, Chesterton demonstrates that the same 'primitive' arts and artifacts that modern scientists associate with subrational humanity might well have been produced by creatures with minds as rational as our own."² By linking other traditionalists to Chesterton, one must evaluate the idea that they possessed a self-awareness or common sense of the importance of their life's work.

Modern thought of the twentieth century provided myriad methodologies and paradigms for philosophers. The explanations were exercises that took Westerners toward a type of transcendence or kept them firmly established in a more empirical intellectual enterprise. In either case, modernity criticized contemporary tradition and upon recognizing the good, the bad, and the ugly attempted to abandon the metaphysical notion of the past in favor of a new learning, namely humanism. There were those, however, who boisterously defended their disciplines against the changing sentiments—even the changes they feared did come to pass.

British historian and essayist G. K. Chesterton upheld an anti-modern sentiment and argued for the preservation of conservatism and tradition—a common sense. André Gushurst-Moore defines Chesterton's "common sense" in saying:

> Conscience, then, is a vital part of the *sensus communis*, and it is easy to see how the Christian civilization of the Middle Ages leads to the authority of human reason and democracy in succeeding ones. Common sense is in opposition to *gnosis*, that knowledge that is only revealed to a few, and is hidden from the multitude, and insofar as heresy is a form of *gnosis*, a special revelation of truth, common sense, is orthodoxy.³

At this time, the common sentiment regarding conservatism and tradition was one of either apathy or distaste. In *What's Wrong with the World* (1910) he concluded that modern philosophers and historians did not feel a strong pull on their heart strings to preserve historical principles, but instead they saw them as a total sum of Western faults which should be cast aside for a revised interpretation and methodology: "The modern man no longer presents the memoirs of his great grandfather; but is engaged in writing a detailed and authoritative biography of his great-grandson."⁴ The aspects necessary for this context engaged Chesterton's conservative traditionalism, his affinity for Anglo-Catholic traditions, and his success or failure in defining the path of anti-modern sentiment for those who wished to follow.

An understanding of the context of Chesterton's traditional conservative perspective sheds light on the process behind his anti-modern views. First, a definition of classical conservatism and modern liberalism needs to be reiterated because of the variety of ways these terms are utilized. Classical conservatism reflects a definition in keeping with the structures and institutions as they exist pre–French Revolution and Napoleonic Era. In Chesterton's mind, "the essential of the Darwinian argument had been already urged against the French Revolution. Man, said [Edmund] Burke in effect, must adapt himself to everything, like an animal; he must not try to alter everything, like an angel."[5] It is an ideology of the pragmatic practice of power. Conservatives tend to defend the traditional established institutions of the Church and monarchy. The intentions of an enlightened monarchy are geared toward the preservation and focus of three main characteristics: authority, unity, and stability.

For theorists and leaders, like Edmund Burke and Klemens von Metternich, an updated version of the *ancien régime* would be an ideal structure to uphold. They believed, as did Chesterton, that the ability to uphold the law could only come from a legitimate authority and this authority came from God and tradition: "whether we can preserve the tradition of a central thing which is even more human than democracy and even more practical than politics; whether, in a word, it is possible to re-establish the family, freed from the filthy cynicism and cruelty of the commercial epoch."[6] These three characteristics can be seen throughout Chesterton's works and even in those who claim him as an influence on their own ideas. In order to understand what it is to be anti-modern, one must also understand the tenets of modernity as they were expressed through the movement of modern liberalism's creation of ideologies or as Russell Kirk defined them, utopian systems full of false promises: "Ideology, in short, is a political formula that promises mankind an earthly paradise; but in cruel fact what ideology has created is a series of terrestrial hells."[7]

With the advent of the Enlightenment in the mid-eighteenth century, a host of new ideologies sprouted from the soil of intellectual growth which was fed by secularization and the light of reason. It affected all aspects of European society from the theories of economics (Adam Smith), to politics (J. S. Mill), and even to the artistic (Romantics). At the core of this movement the idea of freedom stood above all else. New institutions would be established to regulate free enterprise, an open system of justice defined by a government made up of a representative assembly, while also allowing for the freedom of expression through religion, art, et cetera. Essentially, a new society, unlike that of the past, would be created to provide an environment with thinly defined barriers on the individual and one that did not necessarily describe the past accurately. In his *A Short History of England* (1917), Chesterton claims popular histories are "written against the people; and in them the populace is either ignored or elaborately proved to have been wrong."[8] These movements have proved beneficial in many cases (e.g., elevation of women and minorities in society); however, Chesterton saw the modern concept of freedom as not all that free. He saw it as selective and often elitist on a national level; "democracy has one real enemy, and that is civilization. Those utilitarian miracles which science has made are anti-democratic, not so much in their perversion, or even in their practical result, as in their primary shape and purpose."[9]

Chesterton was horrified by the utilitarian ideas that framed society as a mathematical equation that possessed a definitive solution. Within this equation, the Western individual was the standard by which all was measured to achieve an efficient social system. For Chesterton, the new modern society: "[Had] endeavored to substitute for the moral or social ideals which have hitherto been the motive of politics a general coherency or completeness in the social system which has gained the nickname of 'efficiency'.... But, as far as I can make out, 'efficiency' means that we ought to discover everything about a machine except what it is for."[10] Modern liberalism purposefully made strides to sacrifice the medieval epoch of doctrine and the unity of creed through oaths. The Modern Age sought an egalitarian redefinition of the concept of societal contracts when it ushered in rotating ideologies, specifically socialism, romanticism, nationalism, utilitarianism.[11] Chesterton, although a contemporary of modern society, saw more value in the mode of thinking and virtue of the Middle Ages because of its adherence to doctrine and creed—for him an authority of common sense for all Westerners. In the minds of traditionalists, doctrine and creed, although definitive, promotes unity and stability. Meredith Veldman recognizes Chesterton's affinity for the past, saying: "To Chesterton, the medieval era offered the present an example of a vital community life, a cohesive society held together by a common religion and thus a shared sense of purpose."[12] Rather than focus on intolerance and boundaries, believers had cause to rally around common core values. These ideas were not subject to modern fashions of understanding that inferred relativity while it attempted to form an all-inclusive definition under the banner of fact. Chesterton found that doctrine and creed were best evidenced through his Anglo-Catholicism.

The story of Chesterton's conversion to Catholicism and the reasoning behind it amounts to another essay in itself. The important aspect here is the fact that he saw something, perhaps many things, wrong with the Church of England.[13] The features of Catholicism informed and shaped his anti-modern sentiment. Chesterton defended the features of Catholicism's authority, unity, and stability in the face of modern criticism. Chesterton incorporated the ideas of "collective identity," "dogma," "Truth," and "creed" in his definition of the common and at once found himself in opposition to a segment of society which saw such ideas as archaic and oppressive. He freely admitted that his conservative ideas were both politically and socially unpopular, but someone had to keep the candle of truth lit even in periods of human darkness.[14]

Another aspect of distinction for Chesterton was his belief that the preservation of tradition as it existed in the Catholic Church upheld the idea of transcendence. Chesterton was clear that progress in and of itself is not inherently evil. He echoes Christopher Dawson's four stages of spiritual development (Shaman, static archaic, rise of world religions, and scientific development) saying: "a complete human being ought to have all these things stratified in him, so long as they are in the right order of importance, and that man should be a prince looking from the pinnacle of a tower built by his fathers, and not a contemptuous cad, perpetually kicking down the ladders by which he climbed."[15] His concern was focused on the tenets of twentieth-century progressivism and its hostility to the past. It is interesting to note that Chesterton and Christopher Dawson both converted from the Church of England to Catholicism, while others like C. S. Lewis and Charles Williams did not convert despite their agreement with the Catholic Church and the intellectual company they kept, for example J. R. R. Tolkien and Hans Urs von Balthasar. One can view this as simple coincidence or as a message about where these individuals stood when it came to the possibilities of sectarian Christianity. One thing they all agreed on was Christianity's ability to transcend culture and possess an absolute truth. It must transcend the earthly realm if it is to represent the centrality of *jus divinum*. Chesterton quotes Edmund Burke as saying, "humanity was everywhere molded by or fitted to its environment and institutions."[16] The focus and necessity of unity and stability was so integral to Chesterton's view of divine justice in history and religion that he was willing to respect (not accept) other forms of this devotion, "we are all, one hopes, imaginative enough to recognize the dignity and distinctness of another religion, like Islam."[17] It is this level of commitment to unity and the devotion to one law that led to his nod to Islam and his refusal to convert back to the Church of England. Calvinism received the brunt of most of his distaste for Protestant Christianity. He focused his attack on "will worship," Bernard Shaw, and superstition tied to determinism as "they stick to their central doctrine, that he is judged before he is born."[18] Society, before the modern era, had its problems, but for traditionalists those problems were accelerated by a sickness of selfish endeavor enhanced by the tenets of modern identity. For Chesterton, a steady dose of conservative tradition aided in the repairs to a society that was not dead, but stricken by aspects of modernity. Joseph McCleary supports the idea that tradition is not easily replaced, noting that Chesterton saw no reason to abandon it: "Chesterton noticed that the unconsciously held traditions of a society may extend their influence for many years during which the conscious principles are opposed to these traditions; or there may be a mixing of logically incompatible customs the inconsistency of which remains invisible to their practitioners."[19] Chesterton took it upon himself to promote the idea of healing (reconciliation) that defined the path of anti-modernity, "you mend a thing because you like it; you end a thing because you don't."[20]

Where does the Chestertonian path lead? There were subsequent followers of the path carved out by the presence and conviction of such a large personality like Chesterton. They kept to the path of the preservation of conservative traditional views as they interacted with a modernized secular

West. These followers were few in number, yet known in their respective fields. According to Carpenter, although the list is larger than C. S. Lewis and J. R. R. Tolkien, they best embodied the general principles of Chesterton, "in this attitude [Lewis] was in agreement with two ultra-orthodox defenders of the faith, G.K. Chesterton, whose apologetic writings had been an influence on him during his conversion, and Tolkien."[21] The Inklings, in their works and worldviews, saw the beauty in the blueprint. They enjoyed and reveled in the fusion of their mythic writings with their Anglican and Catholic theologies. Their propensity to align themselves with tradition allowed for them to investigate and grow their appreciation for important medieval themes, such as friendship, myth, unity, and authority. If one subjects the self to an authority outside of oneself then he or she typically favors dogma. The characteristics mentioned above are seen prominently throughout medieval literature, which Chesterton and the Inklings picked up on: "I claim a right to propose as a solution the old patriarchal system of a Highland clan, if that should seem to eliminate the largest number of evils; for instance, the unnatural sense of obeying cold and harsh strangers, or bureaucrats and policemen."[22] The simple fact that the Inklings verbally and literally give credit to the likes of Chesterton is enough to deduce that Chesterton did indeed pave a path to the preservation of conservative traditional ideas.

The ideas of being like a child in innocence, faith, and the voluntary subjection to authority united the Inklings around the core of ideas promised by Chesterton to those who agreed that it was a good fight. As the Inklings grew deeper in their faith, their camaraderie provided an opening to the continuation of the valued principles of the medieval world to remain untouched by the world of modernity. The creation of a platform from which to profess both scholarly and imaginative sentiments defined the Inklings as the successful offspring of the traditional movement's resistance to what Chesterton declared as "the huge modern heresy of altering the human soul to fit its conditions, instead of altering human conditions to fit the human soul."[23]

Through literature and a devotion to traditional, often medieval concepts, the traditional historical scope of literature as well as the medieval and romantic sentiment was salvaged. At first glance these ideas presented themselves as esoteric to a time forgotten by modernity. They were a set of ideas that had the potential to pass away if not actively kept alive, but that was not a deterrent for students of Chesterton and fellow believers. For traditionalists, a balance between faith, the mystical, and the rational was linked to the divine. For example, Lewis, in *The Pilgrim's Regress* (1933), critiques modernity's failure to create connections between these concepts. Instead, modernity's goal is one of toleration and comfort as evidenced through the character of Mr. Sensible and his dreams of a nuanced way of life: "It leaves us free to establish a really tolerable and even comfortable civilization."[24]

According to traditionalists, a complete understanding of humanity is nonexistent without the transcendent. Without the transcendent, the knowledge of humanity is then limited to material and pragmatic definitions that do not leave room for immaterial realities. For some, the imagination aided moral and ethical dilemmas while providing another level of reflection with regard to the use and abuse of human knowledge and capability.[25] A number of traditionalists believed that imagination was cast off because of its disconnection with an empirical reality. The modern world began to reduce the mystical and imaginative to certain forms of the occult. Charles Williams saw this type of relationship in objects like the Holy Grail, which he claimed led to the idea that the pre-modern individual was in tune with "ancient desire; he longed to be married to the whole universe for a bride."[26] The affinity for the mystical and the importance of myth can be derived from the Inklings' fields of study. Imaginative literature allowed for the platform of explanation of the fantastic and the potential for insight into the apparently incomprehensible.

G. K. Chesterton was on a quest to rediscover the permanent foundations of Western culture and reconcile them to the shifts of modernity. Although Chesterton did touch on education and politics, his focus relied more on the tools of philosophy and theism. Through this lifelong endeavor he managed to criticize contemporary modernity, while initiating a dialogue to rediscover the past's definition of humanity's telos. Chesterton's body of work is extensive. This section will look at two of his books—*Heretics* (1905) and *Orthodoxy* (1908)—to ascertain his perspective. Chesterton used similar wording in discussing these topics, but it is important to keep in mind that, for him, orthodoxy referenced the origins of humanity and therefore, in the modern context, had become the new heresy. A line of connection can be drawn between the ideas of pre-moderns to Chesterton, the Inklings, and beyond. Chesterton's twofold approach produced a rooted and fruitful discussion of tradition, conservatism, and Christian humanism. Ultimately, his Christian humanism superseded all other aspects of his traditional ideas and beliefs in order to pin down a definitive common mind. For Chesterton, the final goal was the comprehension of humanity and reconciliation with its Creator. There are many threads to follow, as Chesterton wove into his text many one-lined, often paradoxical, quips, but essentially his message is focused on a few key ideas. Like others cut from the same cloth, Chesterton was concerned with the perceived crisis of Western civilization, specifically the waning interest in Christianity, and unearthing a rational plan to preserve those core beliefs concerned with the relationship of humanity to a Creator.[27]

It is important to understand what Chesterton attempted to achieve and the methodology he implemented in order to address the crisis provoked by the rise of modern Western culture. Like many other traditionally minded conservatives, Chesterton pointed out specific problems he had with modernity, but was clear that he did not wish to destroy his contemporary culture. In "The Seclusion of the Old Lady" found in his collection of short stories, *The Club of Queer Trades* (1905), the character of Mr. Grant states, "I never said a word against eminent men of science. What I complain of is a vague popular philosophy which supposes itself to be scientific when it is really nothing but a sort of new religion and an uncommonly nasty one."[28] According to James Lothian in *The Making and Unmaking of the English Catholic Intellectual Community*, Chesterton's first principle "was that the world was a magical place in which life was both 'precious and puzzling.' Scientific laws failed to account completely for this belief, or intuition rather, of Chesterton, so he reasoned that 'this world does not explain itself' but rather must have a cause or explanation outside of itself."[29] He would rather point out its breakdown in morality and "letting loose of vices"[30] in order to reform culture so that it could be geared more toward the transcendent and divine instead of the finite world. In order to do so, Chesterton asserted that these shortcomings lie in modernity's insistence that it is concerned with the progress of human civilization. In Chesterton's view, modernity is more concerned with the appearance and rhetoric of truth.[31] The rhetoric of modern culture he speaks of is one that professes the goal of truth as the acceptance of all perspectives. For Chesterton, standards could not be developed (specifically dogmatic tradition) by avoiding what it meant to be human in the traditional sense. Crafted and planned societies based on science alone have the tendency to confine the religious component of culture, and thus reduce the scope of a comprehensive picture of the human being:

> He is making himself inhuman in order to understand humanity. An ignorance of the other world is boasted by many men of science; but in this matter their defect arises, not from ignorance of the other world, but from ignorance of this world ... all attempts, therefore, at a science of any human things, a science of history, a science of folklore, a science of sociology, are by their nature not merely hopeless, but crazy.[32]

The recognition of modern science's understanding of the human animal prompts an explanation of what a human is, and thus the road is paved toward a reconciled apologetic that involves Christian humanism.

Chesterton, often calling it a crisis, reacted to the secularization of Western culture more than the use of science and philosophy as systems of understanding. His fear was not the systematic tools used to understand, more completely, God and the self, but if used to perpetuate the components of spiritual truth they could serve as engines of self-serving regimes, ideologues, and opponents of religion. In *G.K. Chesterton, Theologian*, Aidan Nichols explains how Chesterton's *Orthodoxy* addressed the depth of his disdain for secularism, using words like "mad," "lunacy," and "heresy."[33] Chesterton responded by offering orthodoxy as a solution that guards the liberty, creativity, and innovation of the individual because it is explicitly concerned with preserving one's true nature. Orthodoxy's concern is the divine and its relation to the temporal—a discussion continued through Christian humanism. Chesterton writes, "The secularists have not wrecked divine things; but the secularists have wrecked secular things, if that is any comfort to them. The Titans did not scale heaven, but they laid waste the world."[34] Cosmic truths may appear meaningless to modernity because they are not completely quantifiable. If the ability to assess and diagram objectives as opposed to outcomes is not achieved, then any such knowledge is void of pragmatic value. Thus, for Chesterton, the application of such knowledge is not to be denied as it is largely formulaic and empirical, even if its principles contain flaws. He saw it as a concerted effort to replace the human components of Western society with the "terrible quality of a machine."[35]

If humans become mechanized in a variety of capacities, they become sterile and emotionless beings—Nussbaum's "obstuseness"—with one determined repetitive purpose. Christian humanism describes a possible reconciliation of creation to its Creator; hence the Incarnation is the key component to the God–person relationship. A machine is not endowed with faith or the exercise of will. Modernity interjects that it actually fulfills the definition of free will because it allows for the individual to explore fully all the world has to offer. Chesterton is quick to point out that this is exactly what orthodoxy is not. Although Chesterton's paradoxes bring about confusing imagery, nonetheless, orthodoxy seemed corralled by the Modern Age into a definition that intended to make belief in the transcendent a heresy, which made dogma a heresy rather than a necessity. The nineteenth and twentieth centuries were characterized by a crisis of meaning—one that found the ancient and modern world at odds or seeking reconciliation. The modern definition of progress continues to regard dogma and tradition as a form of "heresy" through the rhetoric of freedom, equality, and in some cases the public good. For moderns, to embrace seriously "progress" and "liberty," one must prioritize the questions of permanence with the concern toward the direction and sensation of moving forward.[36] Most likely, Chesterton reacted to the relativistic ideas from what B. O. Flower called, nineteenth-century prophets of progress, namely Mazzini, Carlyle, and Marx.[37] In light of modernity's acceptance of relativism, how could a common direction take shape? It is in this argument that Chesterton explains that orthodoxy is humanity's adherence to creeds and dogma, for example the Apostles' Creed. Creed and dogma, for Chesterton, are historic constants that provide evidence for traditionalists to respond to the reliance on only the self and mankind: "It would be much truer to say that a man will certainly fail because he believes in himself. Complete self-confidence is not merely a sin; complete self-confidence is a weakness. Believing utterly in one's self is a hysterical and superstitious belief."[38]

Popular forms of modernity rely on the ideas of fixed scientific laws based in empirical facts that exclude the fantastic, imaginative, and miraculous. Such characteristics have no place in a modern scientific society and are filed under magic and superstition. As a voice for imaginative conservatives, Chesterton diagnosed flaws regarding this exclusion. By excluding these possible characteristics, the intellectual borders on anti-intellectual because of his or her inability to attach law, order, and so forth, to something beyond the self or the human systems of knowledge.[39] The belief in the transcendent extends beyond the tendency to associate one thing to another in order to achieve a sense of certainty in the explanation. The quantity of associations within the natural world attempts to give the modern person a feeling of connectedness similar to the connection achieved through the common sense or common mind found in Christian humanism's treatment of the Western canon.[40]

The willingness to accept magical or imaginative ideas anchors orthodox-minded conservatives in the Incarnation as they investigate the paradoxes inherent in the world. Christian humanism investigates the uniqueness of the paradox of the Incarnation in Western history. Modernity has abandoned what it has deemed primitive and superstitious. Orthodoxy maintains its commitment to dogma as appropriately humane in its understanding of the link between the divine and the temporal.[41] If Chesterton defines Christianity as human, then secularized thought, logically, is inhuman. Without dogma, existentialism turns out to be one of the few remaining options for Western society. Still, Chesterton possessed a level of compassion, almost pity, for existentialism, as in Bernard Shaw's character of the sad Caesar: "He who has never hoped can never despair."[42] Christian humanism seeks meaning and purpose for human existence despite a limited access to comprehensive knowledge. For Chesterton, orthodoxy leads to the recognition that humanity is an active participant in the recovery and reconciliation of humanity to God. Modern-scientific society either cannot or will not define human existence as anything more than the accumulation of knowledge for the sake of progress carried out through science and technology, which is precisely why the twentieth century was largely a new spin on Gnostic philosophy.[43] Chesterton felt orthodoxy, on the other hand, allowed for conversation with the imaginative.

Acceptance of the imaginative and mystical also allows for the acceptance of paradoxes as truths that define the foundational characteristics of orthodoxy. First and foremost, the Incarnation is a paradox owing to the fact that Christ was both transcendent and completely a participant. One possible paradox is that one cannot remain an objective observer if one wishes to participate.[44] In the eyes of Chesterton, paradoxes abound, but the paradox of Christianity is key to understanding his devotion to orthodox thought: "The primary paradox of Christianity is that the ordinary condition of man is not his sane or sensible condition; that the normal itself is an abnormality."[45]

Modernity's philosophical response to the Absolutes held up by orthodoxy builds on pragmatism. Again, Chesterton pointed out that even the careful and simplistic philosophy of merely tending to human needs is affected by paradox. Pragmatism teaches its followers to focus on the needs of individual and community, but Chesterton points out that, for centuries, the needs of people involved the transcendent, and therefore they naturally required what was beyond the temporal needs.[46] If paradox affects philosophy and science at every obvious juncture, then it is indeed an ally of Truth.

Although Chesterton has much to say about the modern person, it was not the scientific individual with whom Chesterton is at war; Chesterton takes issue with the modern systems of understanding which also plague the scientific community. Both *Heretics* and *Orthodoxy* address the ways in which these systems hijack tradition and the meaning of humanity. Modernity teaches Western culture that "liberty" and "progress" are humane virtues brought forth by certain tenets of secular knowledge. Chesterton, who was eventually echoed by Dawson and Kirk, saw implications for orthodoxy's effects on education and politics, but his main concern was mankind and the purpose of human existence—Christian humanism centered on philosophy. His concerns and explanations tie the ideas of tradition (reflected in orthodoxy, conservatism as a system of morality tied to tradition, and Christian humanism) to an essential definition of paradox; "that pagan virtues are the reasonable virtues, and that the Christian virtues of faith, hope, and charity are in their essence as unreasonable as they can be."[47] For a secularized society the greatest offenses are the obstruction of justice, the hindering of liberty, and the breaking of laws. Chesterton does not take issue with modern ideals of order (or propriety), but rather calls into question the hierarchy of their importance, in that he identifies the most egregious fault of society as the process of dehumanization. For Chesterton, the definition of humanity is more concerned with the power of hope and reconciliation than with the power of empirical laws.[48] Christian humanism parallels this sentiment, but it also discerns numerous points of view as they are all part of human insight. Chesterton's distinct perspectives had a lasting effect on a number of traditionalists. The next few chapters will divide these groups up in order to examine their influences, methods of reaction, the strength of their connection to one another, as well as their reaction to the new marketplace of the Modern Age. While they may not have shared his polemic delivery, they often agreed with many of his conclusions. The dilemma for traditionalists is that they were no longer the only fulfilling commodity on the market.

NOTES

1. Nugent, *Progressivism*, p. 3.

2. Sanford Schwartz, *C.S. Lewis on the Final Frontier: Science and the Supernatural in The Space Trilogy* (Oxford: Oxford University Press, 2009), p. 52.

3. Gushurst-Moore, *The Common Mind*, pp. 168–69.

4. G. K. Chesterton, *What's Wrong with the World* (Hollywood: Simon and Brown, 2012), p. 24, Kindle.

5. *Ibid.*, pp. 257–58.

6. *Ibid.*, pp. 179–80.

7. Kirk, *The Essential Russell Kirk*, p. 367. Kirk goes on to list three vices of ideology: (1) Ideology is inverted religion, denying the Christian doctrine of salvation through grace in death, and substituting collective salvation here on earth through violent revolution. Ideology inherits the fanaticism that sometimes has afflicted religious faith, and applies that intolerant belief to concerns secular. (2) Ideology makes political compromise impossible: the ideologue will accept no deviation from the Absolute Truth of his secular revelation. This narrow vision brings about civil war, extirpation of "reactionaries," and the destruction of beneficial functioning social institutions. (3) Ideologues vie one with another in fancied fidelity to their Absolute Truth; and they are quick to denounce deviationists or defectors from their party orthodoxy. Thus, fierce factions are raised up among the ideologues themselves, and they war mercilessly and endlessly upon one another, as did Trotskyites and Stalinists.

8. G. K. Chesterton, *A Short History of England: The Collected Works of G.K. Chesterton Vol. 20* (San Francisco: Ignatius Press, 2001), p. 423.

9. Chesterton, *What's Wrong with the World*, p. 99.

10. *Ibid.*, pp. 9–10.

11. Joseph R. McCleary, *The Historical Imagination of G.K. Chesterton: Locality, Patriotism, and Nationalism* (New York: Routledge, 2009), p. 69.

12. Veldman, *Fantasy, the Bomb, and the Greening of Britain*, p. 33.

13. Suggested further reading on this subject: "Why I Am a Catholic" from *Twelve Modern Apostles and Their Creeds* (1926); reprinted in *The Collected Works of G.K. Chesterton, Vol. 3* (San Francisco: Ignatius Press, 1990).

14. Chesterton, *What's Wrong with the World*, p. 115.

15. Chesterton, "On Man: Heir of All Ages," in *In Defense of Sanity: The Best Essays of G.K. Chesterton*, selected by Dale Ahquist, Joseph Pearce, and Aidan Mackey (San Francisco: Ignatius Press, 2011), p. 245.

16. Chesterton, *What's Wrong with the World*, p. 257.

17. *Ibid.*, pp. 16–18.

18. *Ibid.*, pp. 184–85.

19. McCleary, pp. 75–76.

20. Chesterton, *What's Wrong with the World*, p. 265.

21. Carpenter, p. 51.

22. Chesterton, *What's Wrong with the World*, p. 34.

23. *Ibid.*, p. 109.

24. C. S. Lewis, *The Pilgrim's Regress: An Allegorical Apology for Christianity Reason and Romanticism* (Grand Rapids: Eerdmans, 2014), p. 106.

25. Gareth Knight, *The Magical World of the Inklings: J.R.R. Tolkien, C.S. Lewis, Owen Barfield, Charles Williams* (Cheltenham: Skylight Press, 2010), p. 186.

26. Charles Williams, *War in Heaven* (Grand Rapids: Wm. B. Eerdmans Pub. Co, 1947), Loc. 758, Kindle.

27. For further reading on the awareness of the twentieth-century-assault on Christianity see Maurice Cowling, "The Assault on Christianity in the Twentieth Century," *Religion and Public Doctrine in England*, Vol. II: Assaults (Cambridge: Cambridge University Press, 1985): 185–286.

28. G. K. Chesterton, "The Seclusion of the Old Lady," in *The Club of Queer Trades* (London: Harper & Bros. Publishers, 1905), p. 241.

29. Lothian, *The Making and Unmaking*, p. 114.

30. G. K. Chesterton, *Orthodoxy* (Amazon Digital Services, Seattle, 2012), p. 22.

31. G. K. Chesterton, *Heretics*, edited by Jim Manis (Hazleton: Pennsylvania State University Press, 2014), p. 5.

32. *Ibid.*, pp. 71–72.
33. Aidan Nichols, *G.K. Chesterton, Theologian* (Manchester: Sophia Institute Press, 2009), p. 58.
34. Chesterton, *Orthodoxy*, p. 133.
35. Chesterton, *Heretics*, p. 27.
36. *Ibid.*, p. 16.
37. B. O. Flower, "A Nineteenth-Century Prophet of Twentieth-Century Civilization," *Twentieth Century Magazine* IV, (April–October): 167–68.
38. Chesterton, *Orthodoxy*, p. 6.
39. *Ibid.*, p. 44.
40. A number of articles typically point to a "modern spirituality" found through meditation. Here is one such example, Kay Goldstein, "Mind/Body/Spirit: The Meditation Connection," *The Huffington Post*, updated Nov. 17, 2011. http://www.huffingtonpost.com/kay-goldstein/mindbodyspirit-the-medita_b_109041.html. This shows the desire to recognize a spiritual component, but one that is anchored in the temporal and certainly more plausible.
41. Chesterton, *Heretics*, p. 145.
42. *Ibid.*, p. 43.
43. Jens Zimmerman, *Incarnational Humanism: A Philosophy of Culture for the Church in the World* (Downers Grove: InterVarsity Press, 2012), p. 194.
44. *Ibid.*, p. 157.
45. Chesterton, *Orthodoxy*, p. 151.
46. *Ibid.*, p. 28.
47. Chesterton, *Heretics*, p. 79.
48. *Ibid.*

Chapter Four

Raising the Temple of Science

A New Marketplace

Insofar as the modern scientific age was characterized by the advancements and revelations brought on by science and technology, such that religion was all but replaced in certain venues, the wealth of knowledge gained by humanity created an increased attitude of self-reliance. Suddenly, Western civilization had faith in itself to achieve knowledge of all things via ever-increasing discovery and advancement. The radical shift that was the West's adoption of progressivism did not occur overnight. Donald Kelley points out the presence of early twentieth-century debates between "revolutionaries and traditionalists," saying: "On the one hand was a positivist doctrine tied to the progressive and cumulative advance in science, highlighted by stories of heroic men like Galileo. . . . One the other hand was a story of gradual enlightenment begun by 'percursors' and continued by 'postcursors' within a tradition that preserved connections with religion."[1] It did, however, occur quickly enough that when active traditionalists found themselves pleading their case in the Western academy, their arguments largely fell on deaf ears. That is, many Moderns moved on from the debate before it ever started and overlooked ancient and medieval input. Modernity and the accompanying modes of interacting with reality were centuries old by the time any of the twentieth-century traditionalists were born. The sense that modernity already won out over tradition was one of the many things that united the Inklings and other traditionally minded intellectuals, and it in turn informed how they approached their various scholarly endeavors, many of which were dogged attempts to reassert traditions of the ancient and medieval world as valuable critiques of the temple of science—something slowly erected over the past three and a half centuries.

Despite the fact the ethos was at a disadvantage, traditionalists recognized the complexity of the twentieth-century intellectual climate and remained committed. In Chesterton's historical treatise, *The Everlasting Man*, he challenges the conclusions of social scientists and nihilists. Religion had undergone distinct stages of development. A new wave of late nineteenth and early twentieth-century intellectuals concluded that religion, specifically Christianity, was in its final stages with science waiting in the wings to provide salvation. Chesterton however, reached a different conclusion, one that characterized the attitude of traditionalists. He proposed Christianity's resistance to dissolution, saying:

> Christendom has had a series of revolutions and in each one of them Christianity has died. Christianity has died many times and risen again; for it had a God who knew the way out of the grave. But the first extraordinary fact which marks this history is this: that Europe has been turned upside down over and over again; and that at the end of each of these revolutions the same religion has again been found on top. The Faith is always converting the age, not as an old religion but as a new religion.[2]

Those who identify with Chesterton would agree with the sentiment of tradition's rebirth through the ages. Perhaps they felt responsible for the preservation of the permanent things in order to ensure their continuity in the face of much sexier options.

When supporters spoke up on behalf of tradition their arguments were scrutinized by contemporaries. A reduction in the prominence of traditional Western ideas began and continues to this day. Why was there a noticeable waning? The answer is twofold. From a sociological perspective Rodney Stark (1934–) assesses that people seek rewards and avoid costs. An age of anxiety and pessimism would not stand, thus, civilization shifted catalysts of progress into a new stage of beliefs. Modernity marketed itself better, and tradition lost out. The second reason came out of a radical shift in the Western marketplace of ideas. Where Christianity had replaced the temples of Poseidon and other gods, modernity replaced the Cathedral of Christ with the Temple of Science. The Western Agora was radically altered, having been recast in the shadow of scientism as the modern temple rose, stone by stone, on the horizon. Lewis saw evidence of this in relation to the perspective of miracles. Although he did not outright lament the change, he did recognize the clear distinction in that the pre-modern era did not view miracles as interruption in the natural order. However, the progress of science is concerned with the definition of what is normal and the greater the level of revelation, the greater the shift in attitude and perspective. Lewis states, "The progress of science has in just this way (and greatly to our benefit) made all sorts of things incredible which our ancestors believed; man-eating ants and gryphons in Scythia, men with one single gigantic foot, magnetic islands that draw all ships towards them, mermaids and fire-breathing dragons."[3] This is where the nineteenth and twentieth centuries ignited the perceived direction of the West since the late sixteenth to early seventeenth century.

THE NEW MARKETPLACE

From at least the early seventeenth century, Western culture's intellectual and political elites placed an ever-increasing trust in the natural sciences and the technologies their application produced. In *Novum Organum* (1620), Francis Bacon (1561–1626) articulated the tenets of empiricism (the "scientific method") and insisted that it was the only reliable method for acquiring progressive knowledge about the material world. Only through inductive reasoning grounded in controlled observation of nature could philosophers eliminate errors in thinking brought about by various "idols," such as the misuse of language, that frequently plagued the human mind. Bacon also argued in *The New Atlantis* (1627) that scientific progress could improve both material and social conditions for a society's inhabitants. The influence of Bacon's ideas grew steadily through the seventeenth and eighteenth centuries. Leading thinkers of the Enlightenment found empiricism congenial to their own emphasis on unassisted human reason as the means of addressing longstanding social, economic, and political problems. Although Bacon himself was a Christian, his proposed method for investigation of the natural world became a major element in the program of others, such as Voltaire, A. R. J. Turgot, and the Marquis de Condorcet—whose vision of human progress included the secularization of society.

One challenge for empiricists, of course, was the impossibility of direct observation of many phenomena for which they desired an explanation, such as the origin of life or the choices made by the human mind. For Christians and others who were comfortable with the acknowledgment of sources beyond those provided by science, explaining unobservable reality was by no means an insurmountable challenge. However, philosophical materialists and agnostics continued to struggle well into the nineteenth century to find plausible natural explanations for many things they observed every day. Indeed, many of them still lacked confidence that material explanations would be forthcoming. Auguste Comte, who is acknowledged by many as the father of sociology, theorized in works such as *A General View of Positivism* (1848) that as society progresses toward its highest stage of development—the "positive" stage—Enlightenment ideas about abstract laws of nature would be abandoned, and replaced by a total reliance on empirical methods. A new "social science" would then uncover solutions to the problems of human society without reference to abstract notions such as "human rights," which ultimately relied on the existence of a creator deity. A new standard of information would create new standards of measure, thus a new value system.

A religious economy is a reality due to the rational nature in which people make both religious and secular decisions. American sociologist Rodney Stark relies on the idea of a cost-benefit paradigm in order to show that human beings rationally tend to seek rewards and avoid costs.[4] In any case, a marketplace best illustrates not necessarily the truth in transcendence, but the values attached to and directed by humanity in light of the relationship between religion and culture. Stark deciphers religious activity as an economic market, saying: "To shift the focus from demand to supply, the concept of a religious economy is useful: a *religious economy* consists of *all the religious activity going on in a society: a 'market' of current and potential adherents, a set of one or more organizations seeking to attract or maintain adherents, and the religious culture offered by the organization(s)*."[5]

Realistically, culture may not directly create religion, but it does create a marketplace for the evaluation of religion. The illustration of society as a marketplace of ideas, beliefs, and truths creates a dialogue where the preservation of tradition can be evaluated in relation to the values of different ages. Within a pre-modern Western marketplace, the Christian religion was the dominant commodity. Stephen Paul Foster notes that it "possessed a novel compelling invisible world model" during the decline of ancient paganism.[6] Modernity represented a conscious effort to reduce the legitimacy of the religious voice. Unfortunately for religion, the "incredible invisible God" began to wane with increasing momentum among the intelligentsia of the nineteenth and twentieth centuries.[7]

Taken as a whole, the ideas of these thinkers provided a comprehensive way to interpret human life and ethics without reference to religion or any non-material phenomena. In 1903 the philosopher Bertrand Russell summarized the universe that scientific secularism claimed to have revealed:

> That man is the product of causes which had no prevision of the end they were achieving; that his origin, his growth, his hopes and fears, his loves and his beliefs, are but the outcome of accidental collocations of atoms; that no fire, no heroism, no intensity of thought and feeling, can preserve an individual life beyond the grave; that all the labours of the ages, all the devotion, all the inspiration, all the noonday brightness of human genius, are destined to extinction in the vast death of the solar system, and that the whole temple of Man's achievement must inevitably be buried beneath the debris of a universe in ruins—all these things, if not quite beyond dispute, are yet so nearly certain, that no philosophy which rejects them can hope to stand. Only within the scaffolding of these truths, only on the firm foundation of unyielding despair, can the soul's habitation henceforth be safely built.[8]

Around the same time, sociologists Max Weber (1864–1920) and Emile Durkheim (1858–1917) proposed their theories of secularization, arguing that the modernizing of the world would inevitably lead to a decline in religiosity. Many followers of the great modernists confidently predicted that science would eventually explain the religious impulse itself. In lectures presented at King's College, London, in 1902, Greville Macdonald declared, "Like all other human attributes, the religious sense is an inheritance from mighty small beginnings, else man is a special creation: a theory we cannot study biology and hold."[9] He claimed to find the roots of religious behavior in sponges and flowers and went on to call for increased study of the evolutionary progression of the religious sense.[10]

Although sociology does not attempt to provide proof of God or the absolute truth of religion, it can aid in understanding the status of religion if culture is viewed as a marketplace. Sociology takes on the task of defining religion as it pertains to culture and the individual. It examines its subject through the use of empirical analysis involving the dynamic of how humans sought religion throughout the ages by their own inherent drive and strength of being. Weber explains, "Whoever possesses the requisite charisma for employing the proper means is stronger even than the god who he can compel to do his will."[11] Those in the traditionalist camp did not view religion and spirituality as something characteristic of a particular age. One must be aware of the possibility that sociology may attack transcendence or coerce a definition of religion while simultaneously acting as a form of investigation toward the relationship between religion and culture. Nonetheless for traditionalists, transcendence is an important voice in the evaluation of different stages of practice and belief.

Rodney Stark and Christopher Dawson produce analyses that best suit this particular discussion due to their interactions with religion's relationship to the cultural marketplace and their ability to distinguish the shift of religion's replacement with the more "market-friendly" ideologies of modernity. In turn, Peter Berger's (1929–2017) insights into modernity's effect on the relationship between religion and culture provide evidence of traditionalist concerns coming to fruition. Despite Max Weber's eminence in the field, some challenge that his conclusions do not reflect the reality of how traditionalists saw themselves and their era. According to David Pacini, Weber falls prey to the "problematic assumption that it is culture which defines the character of modern religious thought . . . [which] is lodged in a misconceived notion of dialectic that emphasizes the sociological pole at the expense of the ideological."[12] As much as humanity wants to clearly define all things and bring about certainty through knowledge, religion occupies too many unknowns and metaphysical characteristics to extend into the realm of categorized and empirical knowledge. A general theory would only serve in an attempt to categorize a theoretical characteristic, thus failing again to address the reality of transcendence as a valuable commodity in the marketplace. It is therefore necessary to recognize basic arguments to provide context for the field and discussion of the ongoing dynamics.

There are a number of dissenting views regarding the topics of religion and culture, but all can agree that the interaction between religion and culture is extremely complex. Stark sees the participation in religion as a cost-benefit analysis. In looking at all human interactions, including those with God, it is beholden to the individual to ask if these interactions are solely based on nothing more than an evaluation of the cost-benefit relationship for the individual. In short, what is the maximum reward for the minimum cost? Traditionalists who sought to preserve something that did not align with intellectual trends of modernity stood out as an anomaly. They may not have evaluated themselves in this manner, but there clearly seems to be little benefit for the cost they were willing to incur. True to his discipline, Stark does not include the characteristic of transcendence, but he does point out that these discrepancies and the rise and fall of popularity of religion is not birthed by culture, but by individuals. He states: "Obviously, there was a clash of ideas *and* there were significant social aspects of these religious changes. But it is vital to focus on the primary fact: these were *religious* revolutions initiated by individuals."[13] The tendency of moderns is to treat religion as a product in a marketplace where the consumers' wants and desires often begin to trump the consumers' needs. Progressivism became a more attractive and coveted option in place of rigid tradition—one that reflected the shift in public desire. The pluralistic phenomenon of modernity affected different eras and communities in the West in different capacities.

In a consumer economy, the market is determined by the perceived wants and demands of the consumers, rather than an outside force. The pluralism of the modern marketplace has proven Stark's notion of cost-benefit ratio, which Berger also sees as fitting: "If the secularization thesis holds, the stronger party, of course, is the modern world in which the supernatural has become irrelevant. The theologian who trades ideas with the modern world, therefore, is likely to come out with a poor bargain, that is, he will probably have to give far more than he will get."[14]

In *The Heretical Imperative* (1979), Berger demonstrates that in the 1970s, American orthodoxy and conservatism ceased to be the norm and were suddenly not elevated among the many choices of religious and political deviation—something traditionalists, earlier in the century, saw on the horizon. Berger's claims are an expansion of Durkheim's theory of a pluralistic society which leads its members to social pathologies through moral uncertainty.[15] Berger examines religion through a similar lens, stating: "Modernity has plunged religion into a very specific crisis, characterized by secularity, to be sure, but characterized more importantly by pluralism. In the pluralistic situation . . . the authority of all religious traditions tends to be undermined."[16] For Berger, pluralism forces religions to compete in a market situation because they are evaluated beyond a "taken-for-granted" mentality.

Pluralism and secularization define the modern marketplace, while simultaneously convincing people that if multiple options exist, how can only one contain absolute truth? As is evidenced above, the advertisement of variety and the shift in focus onto the individual rather than the common mind had its foundations in the sixteenth century and began to grow and effect change as time continued. A surge occurred during the Scientific Revolution of the seventeenth century and again with the eighteenth-century Enlightenment due to the constant turmoil of the changing Western world. Westerners began to realize as Pacini states, "the heart of the modern Western intellectual enterprise could scarcely have arisen in a stable social and moral order."[17] The inclusion of the incredibly brief span of forty-five years where the Western world trudged through World War I, the Great Depression, and World War II provides compelling motives to abandon the ways of the past. The changes in the marketplace began to reflect the changes in Western society. In *Religion and Society in Twentieth-Century Britain*, Callum Brown recognizes that statistical discrepancies exist as to the pace and characterization of decline in religiosity, especially the differences between the working class and intelligentsia.[18] After the great storms of the first half of the twentieth century, religion was cast off as a Jonah into the belly of obscurity, and people began to seek after new navigators. For instance, Pacini notes: "Humans fashion their civil world—their civilization and its institutions—not out of whole cloth or out of infinitely malleable material, but from the eruption of ideas, events, and forces that give voice to the experiences of the time."[19]

One example of disruption involves the wares being peddled by modernity versus those of Christianity. If people feel that they have no connection between their lives and their religion, they will seek out another option. The pluralism[20] of modernity allowed for the consumer to try new and ever-changing products. The onset of pluralism led to secularization, but it did not reach this end magically or immediately. It was a process that grew out of contemporary events that altered the marketplace. The more options available and the more impulsive the choices from society, new doors open with the promise of new, more scientific truths. According to David Bebbington, there are two notable periods of secularization in the university that provide the opportunity to challenge Christianity and its proponents with the ideas of Albert Camus, Friedrich Nietzsche, Jean-Paul Sartre, and Sigmund Freud, to name a few.[21] The plausibility of the dominant belief system begins to wane under the pressure of other options presumably offering alternative characteristics to tradition.

The culture, at the time, was not devoid of religion. Therefore, any fracturing of the Church then fractured culture as well. According to Dawson, modernity provides a number of life-preservers that rescue the individual from the effects of pluralism and secularization:

> Thus the social detachment which results from a spiritual alienation from the dominant culture and the religion that is associated with it does not necessarily produce social impotence or failure. For the detached elements acquire a greater degree of social fluidity which enables them to respond more easily to new needs and situations. On the other hand, they inevitably undermine the existing synthesis of religion and culture and tend, often unconsciously and unintentionally, toward the secularization of culture.[22]

The axioms of the Christian faith found naysayers in certain strands of humanist thought, which valorized the possibility that secular philosophy might become a comfort, and, once understood, an alternative that fostered certainty and tolerance. Dawson maligns the consistent lack of confidence in established institutions as fertilizer for modern thought to grow and strengthen to the point where it sprouts, competes, and then offers an abundance of options to a plurality of individuals. After the establishment of modernity in the marketplace, Christianity and all other religions cannot help but begin any given transaction in a state of bankruptcy.

It is individualism that Christopher Dawson points to as a key ingredient to secularization. For Dawson, the destruction of unity and the decline in value of Christianity is ushered forth by the reevaluation of definitive philosophies (e.g., natural theology)[23] in European civilization along with the growing focus on the importance of the individual, due to the events in the sixteenth century. To understand the rapid change from the pre-modern to the modern marketplace, one must understand the foundation of the new marketplace. Once the origins are laid out, then the changes in consumer attitudes from myth to modernity begin to make sense.

Modernity affected the marketplace on multiple levels and because of this, it opened the doors for almost any mode of thinking to explore a new understanding of humanity and the universe. It is because of this detachment from the pre-modern world that the following two things occurred: first, tradition was devalued and either abandoned or reformed; second, a new set of methodologies started up with progress as the fuel. Paul Brockelman makes the case that modernity gave life to these two occurrences and it continues tirelessly because it broke with tradition; it introduced meaninglessness and fanaticism; it made the pursuit of religious understanding impossible; it reduced the notion of interpretation to factual truth; it blinded humanity to the spiritual idolatry and danger of the time—pursuit of technological power and progress; and it nurtured a multiplicity of religious traditions and practices that are often in conflict with one another.[24] A blinded culture allowed for a strong secular and pluralistic temperament to flourish, thus causing a fractured disunity. For Dawson and others, disunity played a pivotal role in Western culture's abandonment of the myth and imagination of the Middle Ages toward its courtship with science and reason. Dawson clearly states that "medieval synthesis appeared to achieve complete cultural unity and to embrace every aspect of social and intellectual life."[25] This perception of the pre-modern world is exactly why it is important to recognize what individuals like G. K. Chesterton and groups like the Inklings were attempting to do in their respective works, namely provide a defense for traditional modes of thought during an era that usurped all else.

Both Dawson and C. S. Lewis each wondered if hope was strong enough to carry the West through a secular age, respectively: "A key ingredient of most (but not all) theodicies is hope. The specific content of such hope varies. In earlier periods of human history, when the concept of the individual and his unique worth was not as yet so sharply defined, this hope was commonly invested in the future of the group."[26] "Hope ... means a continual looking forward to the eternal world . . . one of the things a Christian is meant to do. . . . Aim at Heaven and you will get earth 'thrown in': aim at earth and you will get neither."[27] Traditionalists lamented the possibility of these future outcomes. However, the attractiveness of possibility and progress through science quickly outsold traditional allegiances. During the twentieth century, a mass exodus ensued which left the believers in faith and religion looking to survive the change in the marketplace. The modern mindset turned Western civilization into a marketplace, viewing religion as a commodity that competed with other forms of "truth." For those in opposition to this trend, the purpose behind the preservation of tradition was an act of the preservation of the permanent, pre-modern ideas as received truth in order to convince others of their inherent value. However, twentieth-century progressivism and modern ideologies were advertised as more effective catalysts of change. In his recognition of modernity's effects, J. B. Bury quotes Seneca in order to show a distinction exists between modern progressivism and pre-modern attitudes toward knowledge and its ends:

> Yet, at least, it may be said, Seneca believed in a progress of knowledge and recognized its value. Yes, but the value which he attributed to it did not lie in any advantages which it would bring to the general community of mankind. He did not expect from it any improvement of the world. The value of natural science, from his point of view, was this, that is opened to the philosopher a divine region, in which, "wandering among the stars," he could laugh at the earth and all its riches, and his mind "delivered as it were from prison could return to its original home."[28]

Secular empiricists made occasional progress in the nineteenth century's early decades. Charles Lyell's *Principles of Geology* (1830–1833) popularized the uniformitarian theory of geological change, thus convincing many that the Earth was older than the six thousand years suggested by a literal reading of the book of Genesis. Nevertheless, the biggest breakthroughs for the secular scientific interpretation of reality came between the mid-nineteenth and early twentieth centuries due to the work of Charles Darwin and the other scientists featured in this chapter, who collectively erected a theoretical edifice that allowed for a naturalistic and morally relativistic view of human life and society.

It is difficult to overestimate the impact of Charles Darwin's ideas on the modern world. He was not the first thinker to posit that the origin of human life came about through purely natural processes. Some classical thinkers such as Lucretius had written as much. However, his theory of natural selection, outlined in *The Origin of Species* (1859) and *The Descent of Man* (1871), provided the modern mind with a plausible alternative to the traditional Christian account of creation. His theory of biological evolution appears to remove the need for an appeal to a divine creator to explain the panoply of life observable in the modern world. It posits, instead, a process of "natural selection" in which accumulations of tiny variations in species over long periods of time eventually lead to the development of entirely new species.

In *Origin of Species* Darwin did not explicitly state his belief that humanity is also the result of this process, and some observers thought he had left room for special creation of the human species. However, in *The Descent of Man*, Darwin made very clear his conviction that similarities among the morphologies of humans and other mammals indicates human descent from a lower form of life. He went on to attack the conventional wisdom that human intelligence was of a different kind than those of other animals. Instead, he argued that a continuous spectrum of intelligence existed within the animal kingdom and that there was "no fundamental difference between man and the higher mammals in their mental faculties."[29] Many came to believe that this argument undermines the traditional claim that the rational nature of human beings is evidence of their being made in the image of God (*Imago Dei*). Some Christian thinkers attempted to harmonize Darwinian thought with Christian orthodoxy by suggesting that no necessary contradiction exists between the two if God guides the evolutionary process. However, Darwin himself resisted the notion of a deterministic force lying behind and guiding natural selection. He wrote that "if God ordained that variations should be along beneficial lines, natural selection would be redundant."[30] The measure of Darwin's effect on twentieth-century science is undeniable. Perhaps more than any factual advancements, his theory allows for a more substantial and varied grasp on the Baconian ideals of mastery over nature. For instance, there existed a small, but notable attempt to control the interaction between the scientific and supernatural worlds.

John West notes that the goals of scientists and magicians overlap in that both hope to achieve power over nature in pursuit of human ends; thus, in some respects they are "twins."[31] At certain historical junctures, such as the seventeenth century's Scientific Revolution, scientists frequently engaged in magical experiments and vice versa. According to Lewis, the relationship is complimentary due to his claim that lawless applied science is the son and heir of Magic.[32] Chesterton shares a similar view in that applied science and ancient magic are curiously similar. He states, "Magic (in the ancient sense) and Medicine (in the modern sense) are really in one way very like each other, because they are both very unlike the pure and abstract idea of Science as conceived by the Ancient Greeks."[33] The early twentieth century was another such era. According to Mark Morrisson, "during the period from the turn of the [twentieth] century to just before World War II, the trajectories of science and occultism briefly *merged*."[34] The increase in popularity of occult societies is evidence of a conscious spiritual grappling with the new scientific discoveries of the era, especially radioactivity; occultists "increasingly focused on alchemy as a material science validated by the new atomic chemistry and physics, even if it was a science with spiritual implications."[35] Peter Gay writes: "To find a congenial doctrine among the varieties of spiritualism was a welcome move for thousands, educated and uneducated alike, who could no longer accept the Christian legend of a divine Saviour . . . but found it repugnant to embrace what they thought the chilly, deadening materialism of natural science."[36]

Hermeticism, an esoteric school of thought attempting to blend the scientific and magical, had lain seemingly dormant since the seventeenth century, but it experienced a significant revival in the late nineteenth century with the formation of organizations such as the Hermetic Order of the Golden Dawn. The Theosophical Society, another such group, blended Western hermeticism with tenets of Hinduism and Buddhism; its co-founder, Helen Blavatsky (1831–1891), taught that adepts who learned to pierce the veil between man and astral bodies "would be capable of knowing all that had been known or could ever be known."[37] Its members hoped to bridge religion and material science, effectively seeking to re-enchant scientific experiment.[38] Anthroposophy, originally an offshoot of theosophy, attempted to encompass both natural science and Christianity within a spiritual vision that focused on the inner development of the individual. These organizations and others like them questioned the certitude of the scientific community in regard to the material world. In the process, they attracted a number of prominent philosophers, literary figures, and even some scientists. Mystical societies fought a constant battle to resist scientism's attempts to reduce all knowledge to the material, and they had to justify their spiritual perspectives in the face of an "ever-growing public faith in the authority of science."[39] At the same time they attempted to ride the coattails of science's prestige by incorporating as much of the scientific method as possible into their proceedings. Nonetheless, a faithfulness to empiricism maintained a dominant function within the twentieth-century scientific community.

The expectations of the scientific community hinged on the certainty of factual knowledge in order for Western society to progress toward some version of a realized utopian society. The tenets of positivism, scientism, and the like led Westerners into the next phase of progress and evolution. Modern European historian Paul Johnson describes the unique intellectual atmosphere of the 1920s: "At the beginning of the 1920s the belief began to circulate, for the first time at a popular level, that there were no longer any absolutes whether of time and space, of good and evil, of knowledge, above all of value."[40] Granted, scientists cannot anticipate what will be done with their discoveries, but they share in the hope of the scientific process maintaining a character of constant development. They too benefit from previous endeavors and succeed where others have failed.

The inability to anticipate what would be done with subsequent discoveries was enough to cause concern in the traditionally minded intellectuals of the period. Their voices were a boisterous minority amid the cacophony of academic lecture halls, journals, and popular media. Due to the level of scientific exposure, attitudes and ideas on the trajectory of science took on a more widespread and popular sentiment. Traditionally minded intellectuals sought to preserve tradition and the ideas associated with a more holistic knowledge of humanity. They did not want to succumb to a version of "popular science" that condemned the spiritual for lack of evidence, yet still maintained certain theories of its own without sufficient evidence (e.g., prehistoric Caveman). Inspired by Lewis's essay "Is Progress Possible?", Yannick Imbert claims: "Scientific progress deified [scientism] through human hubris could never become the instrument through which humanity's hopes and desires could be achieved."[41] Secular humanists, as well, are concerned with the effects of scientism. Kronman warns: "Our scientific knowledge of the world is today greater than ever before. But earlier ages knew more about humanity than we do. . . . And the very science which has advanced our knowledge of the physical world and produced technological wonders beyond number, has at the same time diminished our understanding of the human condition itself."[42] An unknown, otherworldly element of the universe was often separated from scientific age of the twentieth century, due to an inability to be empirically verified as well as the impracticality to the everyday world.

Resistance to scientific secularism did not come exclusively from adherents of the occult or traditionalists. Even as theological modernists attempted to negotiate a partial surrender to the *zeitgeist* by revising several venerable doctrines in a more "rational" direction, other forces within Western Christianity renewed an emphasis on theological orthodoxy. In the English-speaking world, these forces were active on both sides of the Atlantic, but in

Britain their most visible manifestation before World War II came from the so-called Oxford Group, which emphasized prayer and other devotional activity and had the support of many Anglican clergy as well as high-profile figures in the media and sports.[43] The controversy over proposed revisions to the Book of Common Prayer in 1927–1928 showed that theological matters could still command the attention of Parliament and broad segments of the public.[44] Christian orthodoxy resurfaced in other areas as well. For example, literary historians Harry Blamires and Amardeep Singh agree on the existence of a "minor" or "small" Christian literary renaissance that stretched throughout the 1930s and 1940s, including works by not only members of the Inklings, but also T. S. Eliot, Helen Waddell, James Bridie, Christopher Fry, Dorothy Sayers, David Jones, Graham Greene, Evelyn Waugh, Rose Macauley, Edwin Muir, Andrew Young, and Francis Berry.[45]

Among the opponents of progressivism, one of the more evident worries was that of reductionism—the reduction of all things to basic material components. According to West, fear arose that scientific reductionism removes the identity of man as a rational moral agent and opens man to scientific manipulation.[46] Imbert claims certain Inklings (specifically Lewis and Williams) saw the culmination of such ideas leading toward a form of scientific reductionism that creates "deified science," yet also perpetuates "scientific naïveté and the threat it poses to the integrity and freedom of humanity, but also to the integrity of science itself."[47] Imbert sees (as did many of the traditionalists) the eventual result being, "an absolute separation of the spiritual and the natural—in many ways synonymous with the absolute separation of myth and history."[48] The rapid development of the modern scientific era allowed for advancements to seemingly come one right after another, thus anchoring its popularity and usefulness in the eyes of the public. James Herrick is in agreement that the potential for scientism did not grow in secret societies or government labs, but it was constructed in stages in the open air of the marketplace: "By contrast the new science, or scientism, developed out of an impulse to see through nature by deconstructing its processes until everything in it—including the human being—was explained as a matter of mere physical causality. Scientism's ultimate goal is placing all of nature under human control."[49]

RAISING THE TEMPLE

The nineteenth and twentieth centuries showed a vigorous and abundant advancement in the prestige, trust, and efficiency of the sciences, namely, psychology, sociology, chemistry, physics, and genetics (eugenics). Under the influence of scientism, eugenics gained large numbers of adherents in the early twentieth century. This social philosophy aimed to encourage reproduction among members of society with "desirable" characteristics (e.g., good health, intelligence, ambition) and discourage reproduction among those with "undesirable" characteristics. In the eyes of twentieth-century historian George Mosse, Britain's two most influential eugenicists, Sir Francis Galton (1822–1911) and Karl Pearson (1857–1936), took Darwin's theories on environmental influence, extracted the "good and reliable facts," and applied them to their studies in heredity.[50]

C. P. Blacker suggests, as early as 1869, Galton's *Hereditary Genius* attempts to determine the civic worth of an individual by "genetic" characteristics, specifically "physique, ability, and character."[51] Galton's work focuses on heredity without empirical knowledge or proof of his genetic theories—something that would give pause to both the non-scientific and scientific communities. Scientific development can only move forward with facts, not with hypothetical theories. This is not to say that those who never achieved empirical conclusions were failures, rather their theories acted as stepping stones for those who would go on to discover scientific truths.[52] Galton was certain "that a man's natural abilities are derived by inheritance, under exactly the same limitations as are the form and physical features of the whole organic world."[53] Eminent individuals who surpass environmental hindrances provide examples for the exegesis of Darwin's natural selection. These individuals rose to eminence regardless of circumstance and therefore must possess a genetic superiority to those in similar situations. If this were true then the development of a society imbued with favorable characteristics could be realized. Galton hypothesizes the propagation of superior qualities most likely come from this first-class group of specimens, explaining:

> If a man is gifted with vast intellectual ability, eagerness to work, and power of working, I cannot comprehend how such a man should be repressed. The world is always tormented with difficulties waiting to be solved—struggling with ideas and feeling, to which it can give no adequate expression. If, then, there exists a man capable of solving those difficulties, or of giving a voice to those pent-up feelings, he is sure to be welcomed with universal acclamation. We may almost say that he has only to put his pen to paper, and the thing is done. I am here speaking of the very first-class men—prodigies—one in a million, or one in ten millions, of whom numbers will be found described in this volume, as specimens of hereditary genius.[54]

A protégé of Galton's, Karl Pearson, also argues for the predominance of hereditary influence in *The Relative Strength of Nature and Nurture* (1915). For decades he held an endowed chair in eugenics funded by Galton's estate at the University of London. Other British eugenicists such as Julian Huxley (the grandson of T. H. Huxley) believe that eugenics is necessary to prevent the genetic destruction of humanity.[55] These ideas were not isolated to the United Kingdom, but spread to the continent and across the Atlantic through academic journals (e.g., *Journal for Racial and Social Biology*, 1904) and societies (e.g., Galton's *Eugenics Education Society*, 1907; *National Academy of Sciences*, 1863).[56] Historians of the British Empire commonly agree that much of the British population saw their scientific breakthroughs as a formal expression of Britain's rung on the ladder of creation—even visual displays (such as the Crystal Palace unveiled at the World's Fair, 1851) were seen as gifts to the world.[57]

The most prominent socialists in Britain saw eugenics as a viable path toward the betterment of society. Literary elites—many of them socialists—also found much to admire in eugenics.[58] H. G. Wells, George Bernard Shaw (1856–1950), D. H. Lawrence (1885–1930), and W. B. Yeats (1865–1939) were part of a sizeable contingent of authors who favored eugenics in the Western world. John Carey argues that even the literary elite saw eugenics as a new humane ethics with the hopes to create a civilization worthy of Western civilization's potential.[59] In works such as H. G. Wells' *Anticipations of the Reaction of Mechanical and Scientific Progress upon Human Life and Thought* (1901) and W. B. Yeats's *On the Boiler* (1938), one finds arguments for a scientifically driven "purification" of society via management of the masses' reproduction. In the 1950s, the popular science fiction of W. E. Johns, Percy F. Westermen, and George E. Rochester incorporated themes of progressivism, social Darwinism, xenophobia, and scientific racial beliefs into a not-so-distant future.[60]

The impact of eugenics on the West in the early twentieth century is familiar to many. Britain and other Western nations openly considered legislation that would enforce the principles of the eugenics movement (e.g., the compulsory sterilization of the mentally and physically disabled). Progressive British and American citizens, Christian or secular, saw themselves as "social scientists" studying organisms in search of, "empirical evidence, evaluated and sifted by experts in sociology, political economy, and allied sciences, who would then devise programs and policies that governments would effectuate for the benefit of the social organism."[61] These discussions found their way into newspapers, journals, academic societies, and even royal commissions. According to Victoria Brignell's research:

> A Royal Commission on the Blind, Deaf and Dumb concluded in 1889 that intermarriage between these groups was to be strongly discouraged. Its report was based upon advice from Alexander Graham Bell, the inventor of the telephone, who had warned in his 1883 work Memoir upon the Formation of a Deaf Variety of the Human Race that the "passions of the deaf and dumb are undoubtedly strong." In 1896 a pressure group entitled the National Association for the Care and Control of the Feeble Minded was set up in Britain to bring about the lifetime segregation of disabled people.[62]

Although Parliament never passed legislation mandating compulsory practices, eugenics remained an eminently respectable field until its association with Nazism forced it out of vogue in the middle of the century. A number of traditionalists did not find issue with the biological theory of evolution, but could not accept a theory that designated others to subhuman status. Sanford Schwartz, in *C.S. Lewis on the Final Frontier*, writes:

> For the most part Lewis is less concerned with the prospect of subhuman ancestry than with a conceptual apparatus that consigns other human beings to subhuman status. . . . These issues were increasingly acute in the early twentieth century, when projects for the "transformation of humanity" turned from speculative fictions into real-life legislative agendas for the improvement of the species, and at their most extreme, into lethal crusades to secure the future of the evolutionary process itself.[63]

The problems of social reorganization presented a greater difficulty that the Church and the State were unable to bear. The scientific community offered insight, certainty, and possibility in achieving the goals set by humanity's endeavors.

It is not surprising that British intellectual elites ushered in the secular orientation of the twentieth century. Historian Peter Gay writes that even before 1900, "Western civilization seemed to be entering a post-Christian era."[64] Most likely, the scientific community of the early twentieth century was aware of this sentiment and characterized by it. The development of scientific thought was on the brink of a number of major discoveries, predictions, and changes. The alarm from traditionalists did not necessarily originate from the competing scientific theories, but with the justification of those theories by politicians and government. The Fabian Society (British socialist organization) believed central government possessed three criteria of an external agency to enact social evolution—power, knowledge, and impartiality—in order to complete "the task of enabling individuals to pursue their social perfection."[65]

The work of four individuals who popularized science during the twentieth century, H. G. Wells (1866–1946), J. B. S. Haldane (1892–1964), James Watson (1928–), and C. H. Waddington (1905–1975), mark important milestones of the development of the sciences and the promotion of the scientific agenda for the betterment of civilization. At this point it may be helpful to examine the major ideas of these contributors in order to create a body of evidence that explains the discoveries and hopes of progressivism made real through the development of scientific knowledge. There was an abundance of discoveries during this century, so only a few will be highlighted for the sake of brevity. Scientism may or may not serve as the end goal, but it did not develop overnight and much of its early failures came due to the lack of discovery and advancements in the hard sciences. The following sections focus on the scientists who either predicted the course of scientific development or had a hand in bringing it to light.

H. G. WELLS

British author H. G. Wells sought to invigorate the current spirit of Britain and provide it with the "nourishment" it craved. This is recognized by a number of historians, including Christopher Dawson who wrote in reference to Wells' own belief that he provided sustenance in a wilderness of books: "And so Wells felt himself inspired to bring food to the hungry multitude in the wilderness. And he was right. He knew what they wanted and they accepted what he gave them, and *The Outline of History* sold by the millions."[66] Dawson also notes that Wells downplays the common moral education given by the religions of Islam and Christianity toward a common idea of human purpose and destiny.[67] Despite Wells' underestimation of religion, and perhaps even because of it, he was wildly popular. Joy Davidman, future wife of C. S. Lewis, recalls becoming an atheist at the age of eight after reading his *Outline of History*.[68] As a popular science fiction novelist, Wells had the audience of educated individuals eager to get a handle on the postwar world.[69]

Wells set out to write a comprehensive history (one that became a best seller) of human beings from a progressive, evolutionary perspective. It admittedly expressed and even celebrated the developmentalism and emergent evolution of the human species through its success and failure in discovery. With Wells' recognition of the seventeenth-century Scientific Revolution as a peak era, he emphasizes the importance of this era through key figures such as Roger Bacon and Francis Bacon. Wells found no use for tradition as scientific thought was not concerned with a conversation with the past, but eagerly sought to propel humanity into the future.[70] Wells claims that history should focus solely on scientific incendiaries like Roger Bacon as they serve as benchmarks of progress: "There are but some of the brightest stars amidst that increasing multitude of men who have from the fifteenth century to our own time, with more and more collective energy and vigour, lit up our vision of the universe, and increased our power over the conditions of our lives ... Roger Bacon is of more significance to mankind than any monarch of his time."[71] This was a jab at the powerful institution of the monarchy and the dogma of tradition. Wells argues that the Christian cosmogony is unsound and at some point this was bound to happen because of the nature of discovery and the advances in science and technology.[72] But Wells may have faltered when he insisted it was an indication of the falsehood of religion—something even Einstein would not have agreed with: "You may call me an agnostic, but I do not share the crusading spirit of the professional atheist ...

I prefer an attitude of humility corresponding to the weakness of our intellectual understanding of nature and of our own being."[73] Einstein may not have agreed with the crusading spirit, but his discipline provided a welcomed substitute for the uncertainty of religion and faith.

Dawson points out the benefits of substituting the ideal of progress for the governing spirit of Christianity due to the fact that it is a working religion. A working religion empirically quantifies and maps humanity and the universe in order to better understand it.[74] New knowledge was resisted by some Christians and traditionalists, but it was a minority opposition. Wells argues that the effects of Darwinian ideas on the Western world lead to a noticeable loss of faith.[75] His pronouncement of the death of faith, along with his popularity, made him, according to Dawson, "an evangelist for science."[76] Wells, like Haldane, places his faith in the technological and mechanized approach of science as a savior for humanity.

J. B. S. HALDANE

J. B. S. Haldane was more than a scientist. He popularized scientific theory and its dominance as well as planted seeds for future applications of the important groundbreaking work being done in the twentieth century. Haldane, like many of his contemporaries, bought in wholeheartedly to the promises of science and the agenda of scientism. He would come to see all things determined under the dogmatism of empirical knowledge. Although Haldane wrote extensively, two of his books are best suited for the context of this discussion, specifically *The Causes of Evolution* (1932) and *Daedalus* (1924). These works reveal the stages of development in the scientific endeavor to reconstitute the definition of what it means to be human from traditional paradigms in order to explain humanity in terms of matter that abides by and is confined to the natural laws of the universe. His view is often seen as extreme in comparison to other evolutionists, setting himself apart: "The hypothesis that mind has played very little part in evolution horrifies some people. Shaw's preface to 'Back to Methusaleh' is a good example of a strong emotional reaction. He admits that Darwinism cannot be disproved, but goes on to state that no decent-minded person can believe in it. This is the attitude of mind of the persecutor rather than the discoverer."[77] As he stood on the shoulders of Darwin and others, Haldane created a popular following for the new conventional definition of the human animal—a definition of beings devoid of metaphysical implications and who live at the mercy of an empirically crafted society.

Haldane's *The Causes of Evolution* examines the reality of the twentieth-century person and his or her position in the progressive evolutionary chain of being. Haldane establishes a distinct perspective, many of whom (e.g., C. S. Lewis, C. Lloyd Morgan) categorize it as developmentalism or emergent evolution. His perspective holds to the idea that all things are in a constant state of progression toward the most adaptable specimen: "Characters appear to go on developing past their point of maximum utility."[78] Thus, humanity, naturally, should weed out flaws and weaknesses through evolutionary progress. For Haldane this does not reflect a transcendent teleology or intelligent design:

> Nor are the facts any more consonant with the view that evolution represents the working out of a purpose, and is intelligently directed. On numerous occasions related species have gone through very similar changes as a prelude to extinction. We should have to suppose the directing mind intelligent enough to design new types of organism (perhaps only a biochemist can form an adequate idea of the difficulties of doing this), but not intelligent enough to learn from its own mistakes.[79]

The vision of Haldane and others is one where humanity looks nothing of the past and certainly not like the twentieth-century individual. Desire rested more in focused areas of industrial, electronic, and automated society.[80]

Haldane does not agree with Darwin's idea that evolution and the phenomenon of natural selection is intended to unfold over a long period of time: "But if we come to the conclusion that natural selection is probably the main cause of change in a population, we certainly need not go back completely to Darwin's point of view. In the first place, we have every reason to believe that new species may arise quite suddenly, sometimes by hybridisation, sometimes perhaps by other means."[81] It is by these "other means" that Haldane believes change can occur in a shorter period of time. Unfortunately for Haldane, his theory of short-term evolution has yet to be proven, thus acquiring the moniker of "Haldane's Dilemma."[82] Humanity can become a product of its own paradigm created to ensure compulsory ideals toward the survival of the species.

The faith he possesses in science is best expressed through a paper addressed to the "heretics"[83] at Cambridge University titled *Daedalus*. The paper explains the implications of his social Darwinism and belief that science held the cure for the problems of modern society, stating, "scientific knowledge is going to revolutionize human life."[84] Science reacts to the degree necessary in order to fix humanity or at the very least provide it with a means of what Haldane calls "our gradual conquest of space and time."[85] If human beings are a product of their environment and not a transcendental or metaphysical source, then science is the best option. Science as a means to improve humanity and society was not the concern of traditionalists, but rather the reductionist view of humanity in conjunction with a narrow faith in scientism. The religious and metaphysical lost representation as the values and needs of humanity nor did they promise finality[86] in the modern scientific age and therefore hindered progress if valued above the empirical nature of scientific thought. Productivity and utility are the marks of necessity for Haldane's future society: "Developments in this direction are tending to bring mankind more and more together, to render life more and more complex, artificial, and rich in possibilities—to increase indefinitely man's powers for good and evil."[87] Haldane goes to great lengths to propose that lingering religious tendencies may be satisfied as well by scientific knowledge because of its material origins: "We already know however that many of our spiritual faculties can only be manifested if certain glands, notably the thyroid and sex glands, are functioning properly, and that very minute changes in such glands affect the character greatly."[88]

Science has the platform to become a secular substitute for religion as people had already begun to trust their doctor over their priest (an alien characteristic prior to the scientific revolution): "Apart from the important social consequences which have flowed from the partial substitution of the doctor for the priest, its net result has been that whereas four hundred years ago most people died in childhood, they now live on an average (apart from the late war), until forty-five."[89] There are many scientists who have bought into the idea that science (specifically, genetics) can explain all things characteristic of humanity and its way of life. Due to the efforts of individuals like Wells, Haldane, Watson, and Waddington, the popularity of such claims increased among the public. To date, there are studies claiming genetic links to disease, spirituality, and even a distaste for meat and the dislike of school. Moderns claimed that a secular religion of science (in many cases scientism) provided opportunities to feed the "religious" tendencies (as they are a product of evolution not yet phased out). Take for instance what Haldane said about surgery: "The biological invention then tends to begin as a perversion and end as a ritual supported by unquestioned beliefs and prejudices. Even now surgical cleanliness is developing its rites and its dogmas, which, it may be remarked, are accepted most religiously by women."[90]

The similarities between religious theology and scientific theory reached a pivotal phase during the nineteenth and twentieth century, where one took on the ability to satisfy the other. Haldane and his ilk thrived in an era that saw modern problems in terms of theory versus practice. In *Physics and Philosophy* (1958), eminent theoretical physicist Werner Heisenberg (1901–1976) addressed the difficult relationship, concluding that at some point the classical theories needed to be tested and, if not proved, removed from scientific thought.[91] Haldane, like many scientists, held out hope for the development of theories and ideas in the future. Many of these ideas would come to fruition within the next seventy-five years.

Haldane also discussed ideas of alternative energies, the abolition of disease, and even the synthesis of food.[92] They were not bereft of consequences, but the benefits far outweighed the damages due to the simple fact that a mechanized society was thought to be the only hope for modern society. One of Haldane's visions, ectogenesis, lends credibility to the process of scientific discovery for the individuals discussed in this chapter. The reality of reproducing human beings in a controlled and artificial womb-like environment would make the theory of eugenic practices a reality. It would provide a non-invasive environment to practice gene therapy leading to the production of the right kind of specimens.[93] It also claims to alleviate the inconvenience and pains of childbirth. In a modern industrial society, production cannot be halted by pregnancy. Thus, ectogenesis solves the problem. Without the commitment to development, these theories cannot be put into practice. Development and progress are championed by traditionalists as well, but to an extent that recognizes a consistent narrative of morality and relationship with an immaterial knowledge of human beings. A traditionalist's problem is with the progress of science at the expense of the metaphysical. The reality remains that with each new success, scientific progress gains new followers and believers.

JAMES WATSON

The one, really two, who were most affected by the growing field of genetics were James Watson (1928–) and Francis Crick (1916–2004). The eugenics movement stalled in the late nineteenth century due to the lack of discovery regarding the genetic composition of man, but the field remained full of wild possibilities until its public demise at the hands of the Nazis. The universe is full of mystery and wonder and it presents humanity with all manner of knowledge both elementary and advanced. Human beings do not wish to carry on merely in awe of the world around them, but labor at the process of discovery and comprehension. It is this innate desire that drives curiosity toward the "how" and the "what" of scientific reasoning. Watson and Crick possess this curiosity and desire to know; it led them to one of the more important discoveries in the history of science, namely the double helix. Watson published the accounts of their journey to success in *The Double Helix* (1969). He claims scientific thinking often desires knowledge regarding the most basic and rudimentary components of the natural world in order to develop a deeper more complex understanding: "genes were the key components to living cells and that, to understand what life is, we must know how genes act."[94] The implications of scientism are diverse, with genetics serving as one of the more ethically challenging fields of study. The building blocks of the human body demand awe and wonder, something experienced by scientific and non-scientific communities, but traditionalists do not wish to pursue manipulation and mastery.

The scientific process benefits humanity when it reflects the pragmatism in discovery. The reality of scientific knowledge is that it is not birthed out of thin air, but rather from a constant state of growth and development. Specifically, for Watson and Crick, their research is a development of the information found through X-ray crystallography and biochemistry, neither of which satisfied Watson's lingering curiosity about DNA:

> For why should I get excited learning boring chemical facts as long as the chemists never provided anything incisive about the nucleic acids? . . . Though this work had been going on for over fifteen years, most if not all of the facts were soft. Ideas put forward with conviction were likely to be the products of wild crystallographers who delighted in being in a field where their ideas could not be easily proved.[95]

The reality of the field provided the lacuna that Watson and Crick eventually would fill.

Regardless of its new theories and hypotheses, the scientific community had always relied on the demands of evidence beyond intuition. Watson and Crick were correct in their assumptions because it was through this understanding of the natural interaction between hydrogen molecules with the base pairs of DNA (guanine, cytosine, adenine, thymine) that the structure of the double helix began to take shape: "Furthermore, the hydrogen-bonding requirement meant that adenine would always pair with thymine, while guanine could pair only with cytosine."[96] It was this type of empirical progress that gave traction to the popularity and reliance in scientific knowledge, but also brought forth possibilities in service to the agenda of scientism. Mastery of the basic elements of nature leads to the ability to determine actions and outcomes of those elements. Measurable success and reliable knowledge provide the information necessary to produce consistent and replicable results. Data is necessary to give credibility to planned theories associated with the betterment of society. In the case of genetics and the redefinition of the human person, there are plenty of examples of proposed applications. One of the more egregious of these applications, eugenics, may not be a surprise.

Watson's account of the process of discovering the double helix shed light on the breakthroughs that transformed scientific thought into demonstrable evidence. Great discoveries are not a dime a dozen and often come out of years of development, trial and error, and frustration. The scientific process has every element of material interaction, but it also reveals a very human component as well. Scientific endeavor is without a doubt an innate characteristic shared in human nature. It is not always problematic. Some ages of history reflect a desire to advance more than others. The endeavors of Watson and Crick altered the field of genetics from one of complacency to one of activity: "All that most of them wanted out of life was to set their students onto uninterpretable details of chromosome behavior or to give elegantly phrased, fuzzy-minded speculations over the wireless on topics like the role of the geneticist in this transitional age of changing values."[97] Much like their predecessors, they acted as dwarves standing on the shoulders of giants. They developed commonly held ideas into a fuller and more accurate knowledge of DNA. The natural process of scientific endeavor builds on existing facts and plants seeds for further growth. Watson and Crick joined the ranks of Moseley, Mendeleev, Einstein, and Curie in their ability to proceed with their theoretical assumptions until their hypothesis could be demonstrated empirically. They showcased the ability to endure the difficulties and process of great discovery. The scientific process is one that does not often occur overnight, but over a long and arduous road that few have the strength to endure. Despite the marvel of these breakthroughs, traditionalists still asked the question as to whether or not humanity was capable of the responsible use of these discoveries and a deeper knowledge of the physical world?

C. H. WADDINGTON

According to a number of twentieth-century authors, Western society was poised to achieve a deeper knowledge of the physical world as well as respond ethically to the challenges and implications of discovery. Embryologist C. H. Waddington's *The Ethical Animal* (1960) examined the contemporary progress of human evolution. Waddington's insights are deeply influenced by the research of Darwin, T. H. Huxley, and Julian Huxley—amounting to the basic thread that "the evolutionary picture could be reduced to natural law."[98] For these scientists, humans are a product of evolution and therefore all aspects of humanity are subject to its effects. Progressive evolutionists maintain that every step of evolution in a species is a movement toward its betterment as evidenced by adaptability, increased levels of survival, and superiority amid similar specimens.

The changes in human beings caused drastic shifts in political, cultural, and religious perspectives lending to different spirits of an age. The reactions to these shifts may or may not reflect the best course of action, but they occurred nonetheless. Since the increase of scientific knowledge, modern intellectuals believed themselves to be the most prepared version to deal with the realities of modern issues. The numerous developments and stages in scientific thought promoted a popular acceptance of these ideas. Waddington echoes Julian Huxley's axioms on the relation of an animal to its environment: "He lays particular stress on two factors of the animal's relation to its environment: firstly, the attainment of increasing independence of the environment, for instance, by the evolution of systems maintaining a constant body temperature and so on; and secondly, the ability to control the environment."[99]

The reductionist view of materialism gained momentum during this era. The place for metaphysics dwindled at an alarming rate. In the face of scientism, all aspects of humanity had a scientific explanation; those that did not, simply had no place in a species committed to knowledge and understanding. For Waddington, even ethics was subject to evolution as it too is a material function.[100] The extension of scientific theory into the realm of ideas, largely kept by the humanities, was an important development of the age. The importance of man's survival and progress rested in the realization of an underlying theme of the mastery of nature. The Modern Age had its own unique stresses and environmental realities and therefore it needed new and unique solutions. For traditionally minded individuals, this did not mean complete abandonment of the past, but this is a difficult attitude to pass on to the Waddington's committed to the ideas of the modern scientific age: "As soon as one begins to think about the development of the individuals in an evolving population, one realizes that each organism during its lifetime will respond in some manner to the environmental stresses to which it is submitted, and in a population there is almost certain to be some genetic variation in the intensity and character of these responses."[101]

Waddington is a product of the developments of Darwin, Watson, and Haldane. He may even be the next logical step in applicable knowledge that involved evolution. A systematic comprehension of these human processes is possible because of the work of those before Waddington. The development of causal systems led to their application in aspects of society and the individual from planned economies to ethical morality: "The processes of evolution have produced the phenomenon that the human race entertains ethical beliefs. Man can then, not so much through experiment but rather by taking account of its results, use evolution to guide the way in which those beliefs will develop in the future."[102]

Of the group, Waddington appears to be the most cognizant of the impact science may have on humanity. He quotes Heisenberg to express the dilemma of modern civilization: "If, starting from the conditions of modern science, we try to find out where the bases have started to shift we get the impression that it would not be too crude an oversimplification to say that for the first time in the course of history, modern man on this earth now confronts himself alone, and that he no longer has partners or opponents."[103] Nonetheless, he did not abandon the scientific theory for something else—something that kept him at odds with the likes of traditionally minded contemporaries. Authors like C. S. Lewis maintain that ethics and morality have their origins in transcendence. Waddington and a host of other scientists rely on the subjective patterns they themselves develop in order to process the knowledge of the universe. Waddington recognizes modernity's ability to remove the human being as a unique variable, instead of incorporating the individual into a series of immaterial and material structures. Quoting Austrian physicist Erwin Schroedinger (1887–1961): "This is the reason why the scientific world view contains of itself no ethical values, no aesthetic values, not a word about our own ultimate scope or destination, and no God, if you please."[104] The modern scientific age succeeded in creating a believable factual analysis of humanity. However, was it completely objective? Without subjectivity there can be no ethical component. As Waddington believes the human creature to be a "biological entity," there may not be a need for such things as they often cause problems in progress.[105]

Using this logic, ethical problems cannot be defined in personal relationships; they are often a choice for the sake of progress.[106] The most widely used example of this era is the invention of the atomic bomb. The actions of Western society are viewed as material products that interact with the environment. Regardless, Waddington sees the course of humanity as one of progress and healthy growth due to its proven ability to accept empirically transmitted facts and transmit this ability genetically.[107] He believes in the progressive ability of modern society and not the characteristics of pre-modern society. The implications of scientific thought are vast, but scientism is confident in its ability to instruct society toward a promising future. Modernity began to convince the majority of the public that science possessed the necessary tools to solve the ills of civilization. Waddington maintains that hope in the metaphysical is not the evolved reality of the Modern Age, instead natural laws hold the keys to the kingdom of Earth: "The hope, more especially, that we may someday find "the laws of motion of society," just as Newton found the laws of motion of physical bodies, is nothing but the result of these misunderstandings. Since there is no motion of society in any sense similar or analogous to the motion of physical bodies, there can be no such laws."[108] Even though the Modern Age adopted a more secular view, the recognition by Waddington of its limitations did give some weight to the arguments that humans could not be reduced to material at the expense of the immaterial.

The reduction of the human being to nothing more than matter (materialism) allowed for the application of nineteenth and twentieth-century scientific discoveries. In the face of modern problems, science promised solutions. If humans are nothing more than matter, then the solution will come undoubtedly in the form of a system that can plan the outcome of their behavior, genetic makeup, et cetera. Once humanity becomes a determined and examinable material, the veil of mystery disintegrates. Einstein points out that the mysteries of the book of nature are countless and because of this reality, humans will continue to seek out knowledge unsatisfied by "arbitrary interpretations of observable evidence."[109] Human beings desire answers to the unsolved mysteries of the physical universe. Einstein believes that scientific development was a natural occurrence: "Human thought creates an ever-changing picture of the universe."[110] Einstein may express a distinct definition of science, but the force of scientism creates a rhetoric of authority over all disciplines of knowledge.[111]

Scientism's momentum continued to accelerate through the first half of the twentieth century with the development of schools of thought such as logical positivism. Thinkers associated with this movement insisted that only statements that could be verified through logic or empirical methods could be considered "cognitively meaningful." All other statements were relegated to the status of "pseudostatements," cognitively meaningless musings not fit for serious consideration by philosophers. Logical positivists thus attempted to banish discussion not only of metaphysics and the claims of religion, but also notions such as causality, on which even scientists often relied. Science is undoubtedly an important component to the human species. Some humanists argue, because it is not the only component, it may not be the most important. Intellectuals aside, the British people reveled in their contributions to the Industrial Revolution, as well as their contribution to the Scientific Revolution (Humphrey Davy, Arthur Eddington, Michael Faraday, James Clark Maxwell). The progress of the modern scientific age began to convert possibility into reality. The Haldanian dreams of feeding and healing humanity increase science's credibility while the fancies of the humanities do not produce the same type of measured improvement in the lives of its participants. The collective reaction of traditionalists attempted to preserve the value of the humanities in an increasingly hostile world.

NOTES

1. Kelley, *The Descent of Ideas*, p. 209.
2. G. K. Chesterton, *The Everlasting Man* (Lexington: EMP Books, 2013), p. 213.
3. Lewis, *Miracles*, p. 75.
4. Rodney Stark, *Discovering God: The Origins of the Great Religions and the Evolution of Belief* (New York: HarperCollins, 2007), p. 116.
5. Stark, p. 116.
6. Stephen Paul Foster, *Melancholy Duty: The Hume-Gibbon Attack on Christianity* (Boston: Kluwer Academic Publishers, 1997), p. 292.
7. Hans Knippenberg, *The Changing Religious Landscape of Europe* (Amsterdam: Het Spinhuis, 2005), pp. 7–9.
8. Bertrand Russell, "A Free Man's Worship," 1903. www.philosophicalsociety.com.
9. Greville Macdonald, *The Religious Sense in its Scientific Aspect* (London: Hodder and Stoughton, 1904), p. ix.
10. *Ibid.*, p. xvi.
11. Max Weber, *The Sociology of Religion* (Boston: Beacon Press, 1993), p. 25.
12. David S. Pacini, *The Cunning of Modern Religious Thought* (Philadelphia: Fortress Press, 1987), p. 17.
13. Stark, p. 384.
14. Peter Berger, *A Rumor of Angels: Modern Society and the Rediscovery of the Supernatural* (Garden City: Anchor Books, 1970), p. 22.

15. See Emile Durkheim, *Suicide: A Study in Sociology* (New York: The Free Press, 1979).

16. Peter Berger, *The Heretical Imperative: Contemporary Possibilities of Religious Affirmation* (Garden City: Doubleday, 1979), p. xi.

17. Pacini, p. 23.

18. Callum Brown, *Religion and Society in Twentieth-Century Britain* (New York: Routledge, 2006), pp. 10–12, 47–50.

19. Pacini, p. 97.

20. Pluralism is being used here as an expression of modernity's offering of numerous "plausible" options regarding truth, belief, et cetera.

21. He argues that there were two major periods of secularization, 1850–1920 and 1920–1990. The former was an attempt to resolve the antagonisms of rival Christians and the latter explained a wider representation of society. See David Bebbington, "The Secularization of British Universities Since the Mid-19th Century" in *The Secularisation of the Academy*, eds. G. Marsden and B. J. Longfield (New York: Oxford University Press, 1992): 259–77.

22. Christopher Dawson, "Religion and Cultural Change," in *Religion and Culture* (University of Virginia: Sheed & Ward, 1948), p. 204.

23. "This, I take it, is the classical experience of the humanist Natural Theology. . . . a rudimentary theology or as Bacon put it, 'that knowledge or rudiment of knowledge concerning God which may be obtained by the light of nature and the contemplation of his creatures.'" Christopher Dawson, "Natural Theology and the Scientific Study of Religion," in *Religion and Culture*, p. 6. Essentially, the idea of natural theology had a definition steeped in the assumptions of faith.

24. Paul Brockelman, *The Inside Story: A Narrative Approach to Religious Understanding and Truth* (Albany: SUNY Press, 1992), pp. 38–48.

25. Dawson, "Religion and Cultural Change," p. 201.

26. *Ibid.*, p. 61.

27. Lewis, *Mere Christianity*, p. 119.

28. Bury, p. 14.

29. Charles Darwin, *The Descent of Man*, ed. Mortimer Adler, *Great Books of the Western World, Vol. 49* (Chicago: Encyclopedia Britannica, 1990), p. 287.

30. *Stanford Encyclopedia of Philosophy*, "Darwinism: Selection, Adaptation, Teleology," 19 January 2010.

31. John G. West, "The Magician's Twin," in *The Magician's Twin: C.S. Lewis on Science, Scientism, and Society*, ed. John G. West (Seattle: Discovery Institute Press, 2012), pp. 29, 23.

32. Lewis, *Miracles*, p. 245.

33. Chesterton, "About Beliefs," *In Defense of Sanity*, p. 318.

34. Morrisson, p. 10.

35. *Ibid.*, p. 12.

36. Peter Gay, *Modernism: The Lure of Heresy* (New York: Random House, 2007), p. 28.

37. As quoted in George L. Mosse, *Toward the Final Solution: A History of European Racism* (New York: Howard Fertig, 1985), p. 95.

38. Morrisson, p. 95.

39. *Ibid.*, p. 53.

40. Johnson, p. 4.

41. Yannick Imbert, "From Myth to History and Back Again: Inklings Arthuriana in Historical Context" in *The Inklings & King Arthur: J.R.R. Tolkien, Charles Williams, C.S. Lewis, and Owen Barfield on the Matter of Britain*, ed. Sorina Higgins (Berkeley: Apocryphile Press, 2017), p. 188.

42. Kronman, *Education's End*, p. 240.

43. Robert Graves and Alan Hodge, *The Long Week-End: A Social History of Great Britain 1918–1939* (New York: W.W. Norton & Co., 1941, reissued 1994), pp. 193–95.

44. *Ibid.*, p. 196.

45. Harry Blamires, "Against the Stream: C.S. Lewis and the Literary Scene," *Journal of the Irish Christian Study Centre 1 Christian Study Centre 1* (1983), p. 15. Amardeep Singh, *Literary Secularism: Religion and Modernity in Twentieth-Century Fiction* (Newcastle: Cambridge Scholars Press, 2006).

46. West, p. 31.
47. Imbert, "From Myth to History and Back Again," p. 187. Imbert also references the agreement of Richard Olson's *Science Deified, Science Defied* and Edward J. Larson's "C.S. Lewis on Science as a Threat to Freedom" in *Magician's Twin*.
48. *Ibid.*
49. James Herrick., "C.S. Lewis and the Advent of the Posthuman," in *The Magician's Twin: C.S. Lewis on Science, Scientism, and Society*, ed. John G. West (Seattle: Discovery Institute Press, 2012), p. 242.
50. Mosse, p. 72.
51. C. P. Blacker, *Eugenics, Galton, and After* (London: Duckworth Overlook, 1952), p. 108.
52. Certain characteristics of Mendeleev's "Period Table of Elements" did not have empirical proof at the time of conception, but eventually his theories were proved by future scientists.
53. Sir Francis Galton, *Hereditary Genius*, eds. Robert M. Hutchins and Mortimer J. Adler. *The Gateway to the Great Books Vol. 8* (Chicago: Encyclopedia Britannica, Inc., 1990), p. 227.
54. *Ibid.*, p. 254.
55. West, p. 27.
56. Mosse, p. 75; West, p. 27.
57. See Joseph Loconte's "The Promise of the Crystal Palace" in *A Hobbit, A Wardrobe, and a Great War* (Nashville: Nelson Books, 2015), pp. 5–10; Richard Drayton, "Science, Medicine, and the British Empire," *The Oxford History of the British Empire Vol. V: Historiography*, ed. Robert Winks (Oxford: Oxford University Press, 1999), pp. 264–76; Donald Mackenzie, "Eugenics in Britain," *Social Studies of Science, Special Issue: Aspects of the Sociology of Science: Papers from a Conference, University of York, UK 16-18 September 1975* 6, no. 3/4 (September 1976): 499–532.
58. West, p. 27.
59. John Carey, *The Intellectuals and the Masses: Pride and Prejudice among the Literary Intelligentsia, 1880–1939* (London: Faber & Faber, 1992), pp. 63, 124–25.
60. John M. Mackenzie, "The Popular Culture of Empire in Britain," *The Oxford History of the British Empire Vol. IV: The Twentieth Century*, eds. Judith M. Brown and W. M. Roger Louis (Oxford: Oxford University Press, 1999), pp. 212–31.
61. Nugent, *Progressivism*, p. 58–59.
62. Victoria Brignell, "The Eugenics Movement Britain Wants to Forget." *The New Statesman,* 9 December, 2010.
63. Schwartz, *C.S. Lewis on the Final Frontier*, p. 6.
64. Gay, *Modernism*, p. 28.
65. Stears, *Progressives, Pluralists, and the Problems of the State*, p. 42.
66. Dawson, *Dynamics*, pp. 366–67.
67. *Ibid.*, pp. 370.
68. Carpenter, p. 234.
69. H. G. Wells, *The Outline of History: Being a Plain History of Life and Mankind*, rev. ed. Roger Postgate (New York: Garden City Books, 1961), p. 9.
70. *Ibid.*, pp.604–6.
71. *Ibid.*, pp. 607.
72. *Ibid.*, p. 776.
73. "Letters from Einstein about God (and Toys) Sell for $420, 625," NBC.com, last modified June 11, 2015. http://www.nbcnews.com/science/science-news/letters-einstein-about-god-toys-sell-420-625-n373991.
74. Dawson, *Dynamics*, p. 34.
75. Wells, *Outline*, p. 777.
76. Dawson, *Dynamics*, p. 368.
77. As quoted in Imbert, "From Myth to History," p. 188. J. B. S. Haldane, *The Causes of Evolution* (Ithaca: Cornell University Press, 1932), p. 163–64.
78. J. B. S. Haldane, *Causes of Evolution* (New York: Longman's, Green & Co., 1932), p. 23.
79. *Ibid.*, p. 28.

80. Snow, p. 30.
81. *Ibid.*, pp. 138–39.
82. Essentially, any beneficial variable within a species that would ensure its survival and adaptability would need a significant length of time to become a normal trait through evolution. This dilemma challenges the idea of the conventional timetable stating that man evolved from apes.
83. Heretics is a reference to the Heretics Society which was an intellectual club who challenged tradition and religious dogma.
84. J. B. S. Haldane, *Daedalus* (New York: E.P. Dutton & Co., 1924), p. 80.
85. *Ibid.*, p. 27.
86. *Ibid.*, p. 16.
87. *Ibid.*, p. 20.
88. *Ibid.*, p. 70.
89. *Ibid.*, p. 54.
90. *Ibid.*, pp. 49–50.
91. Werner Heisenberg, *Physics and Philosophy* (London: Penguin Books, 1958), pp. 12–16.
92. Haldane, *Daedalus*, pp. 23–25, 72–73, and 37–40, respectively.
93. *Ibid.*, p. 66–67; Haldane, *Causes of Evolution*, pp. 128–29.
94. James Watson, *The Double Helix: A Personal Account of the Discovery of the Structure of DNA* (New York: Atheneum, 1969), p. 13.
95. *Ibid.*, p. 31.
96. *Ibid.*, p. 196.
97. *Ibid.*, p. 74.
98. C. H. Waddington, *The Ethical Animal* (Chicago: University of Chicago Press, 1960), p. 98.
99. *Ibid.*, p. 136.
100. *Ibid.*, p. 137.
101. *Ibid.*, p. 89.
102. *Ibid.*, p. 81.
103. *Ibid.*, p. 77.
104. *Ibid.*
105. *Ibid.*, pp. 72–80.
106. *Ibid.*, p. 16.
107. *Ibid.*, p. 5.
108. *Ibid.*, p. 68.
109. Albert Einstein, *The Evolution of Physics*, eds. Robert M. Hutchins and Mortimer J. Adler. *The Gateway to the Great Books, Vol. 8* (Chicago: Encyclopedia Britannica, Inc., 1990), p. 490, 493.
110. *Ibid.*
111. See D. R. Stoddart "Darwin's Impact on Geography," *Annals of the Association of American Geographers* 56, no. 4 (December 1966): 683–98; Paul White, "Darwin's Emotions: The Scientific Self and the Sentiment of Objectivity." *Isis* 100, no. 4 (December 2009): 811–26; Sarah Winter, "Darwin's Saussure: Biosemiotics and Race in *Expression*," *Representations* 107, no. 1 (Summer 2009): 128–61; Ernst Mayr," Darwin's Impact on Modern Thought," Proceedings of the *American Philosophical Society* 139, no. 4 (December 1995): 317–25; Jonathan Smith, "Domestic Hybrids: Ruskin, Victorian Fiction, and Darwin's Botany," *Studies in English Literature, 1500–1900* 48, no. 4, *The Nineteenth Century* (Autumn 2008): 861–70.

Chapter Five

Fellowship of Tradition

Laughter and stinging (yet well-intended) criticism, shared over drinks and tobacco, characterized the fellowship of the Inklings. Indeed, an influence on *The Fellowship of the Ring*, the Inklings' weekly meanings came to parallel a quest of sorts that meant friendship, camaraderie, and companionship. They were not an amorphous group, but one compiled of different personalities and eccentricities that ultimately valued many of the same things. This chapter is an expository discussion of the group's significant core concepts, and how these ideas are appropriated in an effort to understand the foundation of the Inklings' ideas as well as the value they placed on certain pre-modern concepts. Most prominent of these are the use of fantasy in imaginative literature, the meaning of myth, and, of course, the task of keeping these ideas alive amid the strong influence of certain perspectives of the scientific age.

A REACTION TO SCIENTISM

The Inklings themselves offered a variety of responses to the climate of scientific secularism. At times they offered simple rebuttals to what they considered false claims of secularists. At other times they argued from evidence that scientism (not science in general) necessarily presents an incomplete view of reality, one that tradition still incorporated. Occasionally they fired salvos at scientism's foundational tenets in an effort to call into question its entire project. Several of these arguments resonated in academic and popular culture and continue to enjoy serious consideration among philosophers and Christian apologists.

Of the four main Inklings, C. S. Lewis dealt, in the course of his popular work in Christian apologetics, most frequently with popular misconceptions about tradition, religion, or its adherents occasioned by vulgar scientism in British and American culture. Meredith Veldman suggests that Lewis "call[ed] on Britain to reevaluate, question, and retreat from contemporary values and to reclaim a rapidly retreating cultural tradition."[1] One example of addressing contemporary misconception is that ancient and medieval people "believed in a flat earth with the stars only a mile or two away," and that this made the teachings of Christianity plausible to them, whereas modern science, revealed the true vastness of the universe, rendered it ridiculous to think that an omnipotent God "could be interested in us tiny little creatures crawling about on an unimportant planet."[2] J. B. S. Haldane deploys this very argument in his hostile review of Lewis's *Space Trilogy*, claiming that "five hundred years ago . . . it was not clear that celestial distances were so much greater than terrestrial."[3]

Lewis replies to this particular argument by pointing out that Ptolemy's *Almagest*, the most influential text in ancient and medieval astronomy, displays a perfect awareness of the sizeable distance between the earth and the stars, although modern encyclopedias and histories of science fail to mention this fact:

> The enormous size of the universe and the insignificance of the earth were known for centuries, and no one ever dreamed that they had any bearing on the religious question. Then, less than a hundred years ago, they are suddenly trotted out as an argument against Christianity. And the people who trot them out carefully hush up the fact that they were known long ago. Don't you think that all you atheists are strangely unsuspicious people?[4]

The increase of human power, partly through the continued acquisition of knowledge about the material world and partly through the devaluing of traditional, religious restraints on human behavior, may be the most enticing benefit of the scientific age. A culturally pervasive notion was the belief in inevitable, science-led human progress that managed to survive in many quarters following the devastations of two world wars. Scientists and secularists create a narrative difficult to unseat due to their focus on the betterment of humanity. They often point out tradition's resistance to change and dub traditionalists as enemies of progress and the pronouncement that an understanding of the laws of nature could very well lead to a mastery of nature and a sort of secular salvation.[5] According to its adherents, scientism should lead the human race to correct all that is wrong in nature, self, and society. As James Herrick writes, "Technology now advances at a rate more rapid than even the most dedicated observer is capable of tracking. Our contemporary moral guides offer us the astonishing speed of progress as assurance of the unquestionable correctness of progress; *rate* of change now equals *rightness* of change."[6]

Members of the Inklings saw this progress trending toward "anti-nature," or "modern industrialism, scientism, totalitarian politics"; evidence of this can be seen in both their personal letters and the subjects of their fiction.[7] J. R. R. Tolkien's well-known technophobia led him to see despair, not hope, in the fast-paced age of technology:

> There is the tragedy and despair of all machinery laid bare. Unlike art which is content to create a new secondary world in the mind, it attempts to actualize desire, and so to create power in this World; and that cannot really be done with any real satisfaction. . . . And in addition to this fundamental disability of a creature, is added the Fall, which makes our devices not only fail of their desire but turn to a new and horrible evil.[8]

Tolkien did not see the effects of technology as harmless and material trifles, but thought that they would lead to paths of moral compromise. Towards the end of World War II, he expresses his concerns, in a letter to his son Christopher, after hearing news of "Atomic bombs": "The utter folly of these lunatic physicists to consent to do such work for war purposes: calmly plotting the destruction of the world! Such explosives in men's hands, while their moral and intellectual status is declining."[9] The intuition of Tolkien was validated by World War II, but clearly began during the First World War. Historian Joseph Loconte examines this phenomenon in a chapter titled "Funeral of a Great Myth." The confidence in human progress led the early twentieth-century West "to believe that, with the help of modern technologies, wars could be fought and won with minimal cost in life and treasure. . . . The belief in progress led others to argue that the West would soon dispense with war altogether as the remnant of a primitive, unenlightened epoch."[10] Loconte goes on to contextualize this unique movement as one that fosters human improvement, mastery of nature, and new gospels under the Myth of Progress. He states: "The Myth of Progress proves to be irresistible, especially to those repelled by traditional Christianity and its unpleasant doctrines of guilt, judgement, and repentance. . . . Science, not religion, was driving human achievement. Its new dominance left many believers struggling for resources with which to shore up the credibility of their faith."[11]

Lewis himself once held a view opposed to tradition; as a young adult he "still had all the chronological snobbery of [his] period and used the names of earlier periods as terms of abuse."[12] After his conversion, though, he vigorously attacked this popular view, in part by questioning the goals toward which scientism's progress tended. In this he remained a steadfast defender of tradition. For example, in *Mere Christianity* he writes, "We all want progress. But progress means getting nearer to the place where you want to be. And if you have taken a wrong turning, then to go forward does not get you any nearer. If you are on the wrong road, progress means doing an about-turn and walking back to the right road; and in that case the man who turns back soonest is the most progressive man."[13]

For Lewis, a corrupt and excessive use of technology develops a culture that erodes the nature of humanity, a culture in which science, rather than explaining things, increasingly explains them away.[14] For example, in a short poem titled "On the Atomic Bomb," Lewis challenges, in language similar to Tolkien's, the claim that all scientific advancement improves the quality of life: "This marks no huge advance in/ the dance of Death."[15] The poem points out death was a reality long before modern ills that science claims it can cure—humanity is never out of death's pincer-like grasp and history will go on despite the impact of each generation.

Lewis provides his most thorough critique of the progress scientism promises in *The Abolition of Man* (1943). Although many of his contemporaries looked eagerly toward an age of limitless increase in scientific knowledge and power promised since the Enlightenment, Lewis warns that such a panacea is a logical impossibility:

> Each generation exercises power over its successors: and each, in so far as it modifies the environment bequeathed to it and rebels against tradition, resists and limits the power of its predecessors. This modifies the picture which is sometimes painted of a progressive emancipation from tradition and a progressive control of natural processes resulting in a continual increase of human power.[16]

Ultimately a generation would arise that had enough power to control the succeeding generation to the extent that the latter would have less power than the former, and from that point human power would continue to decrease.

Lewis's critique of the view of limitless progress thus meshes with the fear of political tyranny manifest in his writing since the mid-1920s, before his conversion to Christianity. His pre-conversion political views were nuanced after his conversion, but he still found opportunities to reconcile tradition with the unique predicament of the age. His views on marriage are, again, helpful here as Lewis did not believe that all of England should be held to a Christian standard, especially those who were not Christians (a growing majority at the time). He explains his views on British divorce laws in *Mere Christianity*. Lewis held the position that two types of marriage should exist—those governed by the Church and those governed by the State. To make laws out of one's own views was an abuse of power for Lewis—something he feared would open new doors for scientism's link to politics. It was the tyranny of power, André Gushurst-Moore tells us, that brought even the most disparate of intellectuals together:

> For all George Orwell's antipathy for C.S. Lewis, and his Christianity, their visions of a scientific, totalitarian future, composed at the time of the Second

World War, were not very different. Orwell's violent vision of the future, "a boot stamping on a human face—forever," the Nietzschean will to power crushing the human values of pity, compassion, sympathy, and so on, is remarkably close to Lewis's *The Abolition of Man*, and in *That Hideous Strength*.[17]

Lewis saw that those who desire power over others can manipulate the promises of scientism to gain control over their fellows and future generations.[18] He examines scientism unchained in his fictional work *That Hideous Strength* (1945). The powerful group, ironically called the N.I.C.E. (National Institute of Coordinated Experiments), exercises a ruthless disregard for humanity. The reduction of humanity to material is not only a fear of Lewis's, but the possible realization in the hands of the State who emphatically sought to convince people of a better world through the tenets of scientific materialism.[19] Traditionalists maintain the flaw of scientism comes from those who use it to redefine humanity's place in Nature. The fear of Lewis and fellow traditionalists dealt with scientism's desire to strip humanity of any and all traditional characteristics of being. The character of Professor Filostrato clearly explains the intentions of the N.I.C.E. and by extension scientism: "It is for the conquest of death: or for the conquest of organic life if you prefer. They are the same thing. It is to bring out of that cocoon of organic life, which sheltered the babyhood of mind, the New Man, the man who will not die, the artificial man, free from Nature. Nature is the ladder we have climbed up by, now we kick her away."[20]

After reading *That Hideous Strength*, J. B. S. Haldane accused Lewis of believing that "the application of science to human affairs can only lead to hell."[21] Lewis denied the charge; rather, he expected that "any effective invitation to Hell will certainly appear in the guise of scientific planning" because every tyrant "must begin by claiming to have what his victims respect and to give what they want."[22] Scientific planning fits the bill for most modern Westerners; Lewis had envisioned such a dystopian world as early as 1926, when "twenty separate Boards of Education/Closed round" the titular character of *Dymer*: "He was passed through every test,/ Was vaccinated, numbered, washed and dressed,/ Proctored, inspected, whipt, examined weekly.[23]

Several of the Inklings advanced the proposition that scientism communicated a narrow view of reality. Without denying the value of empirical knowledge of the natural world, they attempted to point out blind spots from which scientism's adherents suffered. For example, in *Poetic Diction* (1928), Barfield shows the insufficiency of the modernist attempt to explain the poetic nature of ancient language; he labels as pure fantasy the influential view of Max Müller that at some point in the distant past an age of poets infused names for brute objects with metaphor.[24] Likewise, the ubiquity of myth in the ancient world exploded the "root" concept of language because it implies a parallel age of mighty philosophers that infused names with abstractions.[25] In reality, ancient language participated in what Barfield called "true metaphor," in which a given word could communicate several logically disconnected, but poetically connected ideas—a core concept to how he and others defined tradition. In a key passage, Barfield criticizes moderns for failing to discern meaning originating from outside their disciplines: "The naturalist is right when he connects the myth [of Demeter] with the phenomena of nature, but wrong if he deduces it solely from these. The psychoanalyst is right when he connects the myth with 'inner' experiences, but wrong if he deduces it solely from these."[26]

J. R. R. Tolkien in *The Lord of the Rings* (1954–1955) presents what can be interpreted as a subtle critique of scientism's claim that inductive reasoning is the only way to gain reliable knowledge. As Peter Kreeft points out, Tolkien often places characters, especially Frodo, in situations where reliance on pure reason or experience is more likely to lead them astray than when they follow their intuition. When the hobbits must decide whether to trust Strider upon meeting him for the first time, Frodo goes against the advice of both the innkeeper and Sam and confides in him, stating, "You have frightened me several times tonight, but never in the way servants of the Enemy would, or so I imagine. I think one of his spies would—well, seem fairer and feel fouler, if you understand."[27] Both Bilbo and Frodo take pity on Gollum when a reliance on calculating reason probably would have resulted in their killing him; Gollum, of course, later plays a critical role in the destruction of the One Ring.[28] Kreeft notes that a crucial element in the success of Frodo's frequent reliance on his intuition is his moral goodness; intuition "is only trustworthy in the virtuous." Tolkien can thus be interpreted to say that "epistemology depends on ethics; knowledge (of the highest and most important things) depends on goodness."[29] This view appears consistent with that of J. S. Ryan, who writes: "It is a commonplace of Tolkien criticism that it should be observed of the hobbits that they possess 'a Parzival-like innocence.'"[30] Ryan argues that Frodo, like Parzival, seeks "only to serve, from which acts come all true strength."[31] Traditionalists could hardly imagine a view further from that of scientism.

Two of the Inklings devoted considerable energy to their involvement with the esoteric or occult societies mentioned above as a means of overcoming the limitations of scientism. For decades, Charles Williams participated in the activities of an offshoot of the Hermetic Order of the Golden Dawn called the Fellowship of the Rosy Cross, organized by the poet A. E. Waite in 1915.[32] Members of the Fellowship attempted to revive an alleged centuries-old secret tradition whose practices led to an empirical union between the supernatural and natural.[33] According to Mark Morrisson, in Williams's novels the Holy Grail becomes "essentially a radioactive atom, a 'storehouse of power' 'encompassed' by 'radiations,' a 'material centre' that could be 'dissipated.'"[34] Likewise, Gavin Ashenden writes that Williams' treatment of the Grail echoes the Order's belief in the possibility of unity rather than dichotomy between the two realms. A belief that was a Neo-Gnostic synthesis of medieval images and symbols with the advent of a scientific, all-enlightening gnosis. For example, the nature of Christ exemplifies the idea that the body does not bow to the whim of the soul: "the body is unique and divine."[35] In the face of contemporary prejudices (e.g., a devaluing of the non-scientific), Williams promoted the use of myth to "supercede the limitations of a metaphysic truncated by a materialistic culture."[36]

Owen Barfield had similar concerns about scientism's attempt to discard the spiritual component to the existence of man. He was a lifelong devotee of Rudolf Steiner (1861-1917), the founder of anthroposophy, who in *Philosophy of Freedom* (1894) attempted to articulate a philosophical understanding of the relationship between humanity and nature. Where Williams was drawn to the mystical union of the material and immaterial, Barfield was drawn to Steiner's belief that the gaps between modern science and humanity's religious strivings could be bridged through a refocusing of scientific study on the evolution of the human soul: "We are sometimes asked to say 'in a few words' what Anthroposophy is. It is of course impossible. But let us in this context say that the kernel of Anthroposophy is *the concept of man's self-consciousness as a process in time*."[37] According to Steiner, modern science increasingly defines nature separately from humanity and focuses all its energy on observing the former. In the modern era, numerous theories, philosophies, and perceptions segregated or eliminated the spiritual component.[38] Steiner made the argument that these modern systems were evidence of a spreading scientism that would eventually redefine the relationship between humans and nature. Barfield clarifies the new perspective when he says: "It wasn't a new idea about the relation between man and nature; it was an idea of the new relation between them."[39] The response of philosophic anthroposophy was one that links the present with the consciousness of the past and its belief in classical "spiritual hierarchies."[40] Without Steiner's system, Barfield believed that the scientific outlook would move into a floundering existentialism. Anthroposophy could provide an objective method of inquiry that enables a recovery of the spiritual. If humans are more than matter, then they have a "divine relation to the Cosmos."[41]

Another way the Inklings suggested that scientism offered a narrow view of reality came through the contrast between the modern outlook and that of the Middle Ages. This is not to argue that the achievements of medieval science were greater than those of modern science. Traditionalists hoped to demonstrate that scientism's adherents had lost sight of some important truths. Before the modern scientific age, thinkers accepted another component to tradition; the adherence to an adequate knowledge of the world required engagement of both the material and the immaterial. In his fiction, Charles Williams sought to convey the distinction that the modern world reduced the mystical and imaginative to certain forms of the occult, whereas the pre-modern world was in tune with it. Principles relating to the immaterial were usually held a priori, but scientism's insistence on empiricism results in a modern acceptance of the material alone. Thinkers such as the logical positivists, whom C. S. Lewis dubbed "plaguey Philosophers,"[42] threatened to drain of meaning and render absurd humanity's free will and purpose.[43] The Inklings feared that the radical epistemological move to deny the immaterial would result in modern society's dehumanization.

The modern mind prizes utility to a much greater extent than did the medieval mind. Taking a cue from the Enlightenment, it also viewed knowledge as something attained rather than something received, another departure from the classical and medieval mind-set. Lewis argues that if this new knowledge is merely empirical, it will create a society of people who have an anthropological knowledge of themselves: "They are not men at all, they are artefacts."[44] In the eyes of those who value the metaphysical, the individual's understanding *sans* the transcendent reduces he or she to a material object. Unlike the pre-moderns, the scientific age will re-categorize the human spirit and replace it with empirical data. Adherents of solely empirical knowledge define human beings as objects functioning within the laws of nature. The posterity of humanity is not be a concern because the end of the story is known and there is nothing else to look forward to, or transcendentally received meaning and purpose to fulfill. Any duty to posterity will be filed under superstition.[45]

For the Inklings, the reinvention of humanity would lead to inevitable difficulties due to the denial of any possibility of metaphysical reality. Scientism's attempts to claim an omni-competence on the part of the natural sciences caused the Inklings to argue that science oversteps its bounds when it begins to address the question of "why," due to the reality that it is largely unconcerned with and unequipped to handle such questions—not necessarily seen as a negative characteristic. Many medieval thinkers were committed to scientific knowledge and discovery as well. The difference between the two eras is that the medieval mind was comfortable with conscious limitations regarding the answers it might discover. Medieval scientists were not necessarily concerned with more than the empirical, but they recognized the possibility of the metaphysical in their paradigm:

> The fundamental concept of modern science is, or was till very recently, that of natural "laws", and every event was described as happening in "obedience" to them. In medieval science the fundamental concept was that of certain sympathies, antipathies, and strivings inherent in matter itself. Everything has

its right place, its home, the region that suits it, and, if not forcibly restrained, moves thither by a sort of homing instinct.[46]

In *Saving the Appearances*, Barfield drew attention to a possible problem with the nature of scientific inquiry. He takes issue with the claims that scientific inquiry produces a more accurate and objective knowledge of all subjects, pointing to the problem of reconciliation between differing sets of scientific conclusions. The process of empirical research assumes that a consistent approach to any subject should result in replicable conclusions. When scientists reach divergent conclusions, especially in instances where for Barfield the sciences do not provide the appropriate methodology, one must resort to unscientific criteria for favoring one set of conclusions over another.[47]

The Inklings called for scientism's adherents to recognize that science can respect, even if it cannot explain, the mythic or metaphysical. They sought to recover a view more representative of the medieval mind-set toward humanity and nature. The Modern Age created a popular science—what Lewis called "a caricature of the true sciences"—that did not recognize the need for self-reflective exercises.[48] The Inklings hoped for a recovery of that self-reflection in the natural sciences and an admission that its scope was limited, that it could explain the order, but not what or who does the ordering.

The final way in which the Inklings responded to the expansive claims of scientism came by way of challenged first principles. Owen Barfield's *Worlds Apart* (1963) is perhaps the most elaborate example in their collective works. The work was arranged as a fictional dialogue among eight intellectuals in various fields: law, historical theology, rocketry, physics, biology, linguistics, psychiatry, and Waldorf-Steiner's anthroposophical education. The participants' attempts to penetrate the "watertight compartments" of their respective disciplines lead them to reexamine their underlying assumptions. Barfield refrained from presenting any one perspective as definitively correct, but as the dialogue proceeds, the emphasis shifts from the three physical scientists, who begin the process by confidently proclaiming the perspective of scientism, to the other characters, who point out the insufficiency of its foundational assumptions that are usually asserted but not argued:

> There are many different kinds of knowledge, and one kind is the kind which we require to enable us to control our material environment and make it serve our purposes.... But there is also another kind of knowledge—knowledge about *man* and about the values which make him man and the best way of preserving them; knowledge about his relation to God and God's creatures. The mistake you make—the mistake nearly everyone makes—is to assume that the first kind necessarily includes the second.[49]

Barfield's characters fail to reach a consensus on the various problems they discuss, but the direction of the dialogue indicates which perspective(s) Barfield favors. Not surprisingly, the anthroposophist speaks more than any other character in the final section.

One of C. S. Lewis's most discussed attacks on scientism is his challenge to the validity of reason given scientism's own assumptions. This argument appears in its fullest form in the third chapter of *Miracles*: "The Cardinal Difficulty of Naturalism." In abbreviated form, the argument begins by noting that the possibility of human knowledge depends on the validity of reasoning. Theism has grounds for asserting this validity because it holds that reason, specifically divine reason, precedes Nature, causes Nature's orderliness, and illuminates the human mind in its act of knowing.

For traditionalists, naturalism's grounds for making the same assertion are much more doubtful. It holds that reason is itself the product of nature; that it evolved through the Darwinian process of natural selection out of organisms' non-rational responses to their environment. The problem, as Lewis stated, is that "it is not conceivable that any improvement of responses could ever turn them into acts of insight, or even remotely tend to do so. The relation between response and stimulus is utterly different from that between knowledge and the truth known."[50] Likewise, experience can produce the mental behavior of expectation but not of reason, which infers connections between conjoined things or events and then attempts to discover those connections. To infer that a useful reason must develop from the sub-rational by appeal to the tendency of natural selection to favor the useful, begs the question of the validity of inference: "Reason is our starting point. There can be no question of attacking or defending it. If by treating it as a mere phenomenon you put yourself outside it, there is then no way, except by begging the question, of getting inside again."[51]

This argument against naturalism, now commonly known as the "argument from reason," occasioned debate when Lewis first proposed it, and it continues to do so in the twenty-first century, having influenced a number of other thinkers.[52] Lewis himself revised the argument after Oxford philosopher Elizabeth Anscombe criticized it at length in a 1948 paper. In recent years the debate continues to create opposing views. Peter van Inwagen judges the argument from reason a failure because it does not prove that naturalism is inconsistent with the thesis that beliefs are grounded in reasoning,[53] whereas Marcel Sarot maintains the argument's validity: "All Lewis needs in order to show that naturalism undermines rationalism is the claim that if a thought is caused, it is *not likely* to be grounded. As soon as we accept this claim, naturalism through its claim that *all* our thoughts are caused will lead to a distrust of our own thoughts."[54]

The dialogue between the pre-modern or medieval mind-set versus that of moderns or progressives characterizes the scholarly work and personal lives of the Inklings. Modernity saw itself as a new progression toward better economies, societies, governments, and specimens. Perhaps the Inklings saw a greater need to promote continuity between the Middle Ages and the Renaissance and a divisive progression in order to preserve the permanent things—largely because the modernity they reacted to is argued to have firm roots in the Renaissance. Without continuity, Jacob Burkhardt's idea that the Renaissance was "first-born among the sons of modern Europe" becomes damning of the medieval. It embodies a distinct break through the revival of antiquity and the early modern genius of the Italian people. For the Inklings, the eras were more closely aligned in that the Renaissance rediscovered the core ideas of medieval society—a common mind largely through Christian and secular humanism. Lewis examines the complexities of the eras in an essay titled, "The English Prose *Morte*."[55] His contention is that humanity possesses the ability to return to pre-modern principles, as the medievals recognized ideas of antiquity, thus, creating a possibility for the preservation of tradition in the modern scientific age.

FANTASY IN IMAGINATIVE LITERATURE

The pre-modern world, around which the Inklings congregated—as drifters congregate around a fire in a city of heated buildings—was laden with the manifold esoterica of elves, dwarves, and fairies. Nonetheless, the Inklings believed that they were rallying around sacred tales, which told universally applicable stories about human nature. Their eyes at times glistened with a child-like innocence and perspective of the world untarnished by cynicism, industrial endeavor, and philosophical debate that often permeates the worlds of fantasy within imaginative literature. Lewis, specifically, separates the language of the imaginative from that of the scientific, claiming the former is more suited to the conversation of religion.[56] The allure of this genre of literature betrays a desire to preserve traditional ideas. It is a hope in the possibility of the fantastic. It speaks to a sleeping truth deep within the soul that time forgets with increasing knowledge via other avenues. In any case, fantasy has held a place in the hearts and minds of Western society from as early as Homer's *Odyssey* to as recently as J. K. Rowling's *Harry Potter* series. Such stories are sought for the magic contained on every page, and the use of supernatural worlds and characters.

Fantasy literature remains distinct from science fiction due its lack of logical or scientific explanations for the often impossible events that occur throughout its lines of prose. Fantasy, for the Inklings, although differentiated from myth by definition, could serve as a bridge that reconnected the modern scientific age to the pre-modern mythical age.[57] Although twenty-first century comparative literature scholar Milton Scarborough seeks to reconcile myth to the realities of modernity, he does recognize modernity's perspective on myth, claiming: "On the other hand, consistent with modern presuppositions, they view myth as associated with what is primitive, past, subjective, and untrue—namely, all the things that modernity hopes to out distance."[58] Despite the differences in definition, myth and fantasy serve the same purpose as both can lead to the infusion of a religious or spiritual significance within the works of specific writers. One can easily argue for the presence of such themes in the more popular works of *The Lord of the Rings*, *The Chronicles of Narnia*, *The Hobbit*, or *The Space Trilogy*. A look into the elusive and characteristically pre-modern world of fantasy may aid in finding the reasons behind its being so emphatically cherished and embraced by the likes of George MacDonald (*Phantastes*, 1858) and J. R. R. Tolkien (*Tree and Leaf*, 1964). One can even argue that Charles Williams' *Outlines of Romantic Theology* (1924) embodies the use of similar methods of explanation and expression. Brief investigations surrounding a preoccupation with fairies, the ability to fantasize, and the niche of fantasy literature provide clarity when drawing some conclusions about the elite group of the Inklings and their place in the greater scope of anti-modern thought.

George MacDonald had a recognizable effect on certain elements within the works of the Inklings, Tolkien's use of fairy stories especially. Although this is but one component and theme of writing it speaks of a larger endeavor to preserve certain pre-modern ideas in the face of a civilization bent on moving past such themes. Lewis and Tolkien recognized their debt to MacDonald in their understanding of what fairy stories represented.[59] This ability gave them literary strengths to defend similar ideas. By no means did Tolkien's investment in myth make him popular with his colleagues, nor Lewis for that matter. Even some confidants met his chosen road with stiff criticisms. Hugo Dyson, when once asked to hear a draft of Tolkien's Middle-earth literature, famously blurted out, "Not another fucking elf!" MacDonald hints at the idea that fairies are different from humans; possibly they are the keepers of a deeper knowledge: "Ah! That is always the way with you men; you believe nothing the first time; and it is foolish enough to let mere repetition convince you of what you consider in itself unbelievable."[60] Deep knowledge, reminiscent of tradition extending through the ages, is a theme throughout a number of works in the genre of imaginative literature. It speaks to a pre-modern mentality before the emergence of strictly empirical evidence and a mechanized age. Both Tolkien and MacDonald wrote about fairy stories in the context of fantasy, but Tolkien went as far as defending the reasoned and logical presence of fantasy outside of the realm of make-believe. In his poem "Mythopoeia" he suggests that humans once had a place in the fantastical world, but the course of Western history caused a divide in the relationship: "I will not walk with your progressive apes,/ erect and sapient. Before them gapes/ the dark abyss to which their progress tends—"[61]

The pre-moderns appeared to accept metaphysical explanations without much disturbance in their methods and systems. Likewise, the Inklings were a group who projected the same level of ease in relation to the supernatural. The description of elves and the ways in which they interact with humanity and nature bring about the assumption that there was a harmony between elves and nature that is nonexistent or perhaps forgotten by the Modern Age. Tolkien and MacDonald bring forth a reverence that borders on envy of the relationship and knowledge that elves had with the world. In these stories, humans represent a chosen and unique species that lost its way. For MacDonald, the human heart hardened over time and people can no longer find Fairy Land, nor do they believe in it anymore: "My heart, softened by the dreams through which it had passed, overflowed in a sad, tender love towards them. . . . Very true! You speak like a sensible man, sir. We have but few sensible folks round about us. Now, you would hardly credit it, but my wife believes every fairy-tale that ever was written. I cannot account for it. She is a most sensible woman in everything else."[62]

Throughout the pages of imaginative literature, fairy remains an eternal child. This is not to say that they are impish little fiends who are full of naïve innocence and lacking in wisdom. Tolkien's "Of Fairy-Stories" argues just the opposite as it distinguishes the regality of some fairies (most likely the influence on his Elves) as they are not corrupted or swayed by the world and thus able to remain untouched, and innocent as children. In the worlds created by MacDonald and Tolkien, fairies were important in the sense that they were caretakers of the world; they were involved with revelation for their human counterparts who come into contact with them, quite possibly to bring them out of exile. Specific to the twentieth century, the Inklings imagined worlds, not devoid of progress, but which consciously reacted to its effects. It was as if parts were never affected by the Fall and therefore readers are led to believe that they were not subject to human desires. The things of God were desired by Elves, for example Tolkien's Silmarils, but they did not desire the creations of the Modern Age and the products of industrialism.[63]

There is, however, a realistic aspect woven into these fantastic stories which should give pause, and more importantly lead to questions regarding the possible importance of elves and fairies. The Inklings and other traditionalists framed the human species as unique. It is different from the animal kingdom through its possession of an intellect. Most of the traditionalists within the context of this discussion believed when God came down from heaven, He came as a man in Christ. In myths and stories, the gods and God hold a special place for mortals. Fairies and beings of supernatural form recognize the difference and the effect mortals have on their environment. It is either a recognition of human uniqueness or it is the influence of humanity's arrogance in its ability to progress that writers create a sense of envy in the immortals. In MacDonald, the fairies have prophecies about becoming men and women, "For there is an old prophecy in our woods that one day we shall all be men and women like you."[64] For Tolkien, Niggle's imagination of one painting of a tree shapes the place he resides with Parish before his journey on to the mountains. This gives the reader the idea that the individual also has the ability to shape the physicality of his or her own afterlife.[65]

The different aspects discussed above support the understanding of two central ideas regarding fantasy, namely the ability to fantasize and the place of imaginative literature. The ability to fantasize is not a simple task for the modern individual. In the eyes of the fairy world, modern individuals are often restless and asleep: "My soul was not still enough for songs. . . . From dreams of bliss shall men awake One day, but not to weep: The dreams remain; they only break the mirror of sleep."[66] The ability to imagine or fantasize carried with it a definition that Tolkien felt misrepresented the spirit of imagination. He would rather it be categorized under sub-creation, "the power of giving to ideal creations the inner consistency of reality."[67] The modern human condition interferes with the ability to fantasize in this light. As Western civilization became more and more technologically advanced and preoccupied with industry, its interests changed and with that its ability to wonder in the pre-modern sense. This new preoccupation silenced the Ents and nymphs of the world. Thus, their cries could not be heard as they were hacked to pieces to fuel the fires of industry. This shift in desire continues to progress and is on the verge of ushering in a Robotic Age focused on the material advancement of society and the betterment of all things man-made, for example phones that talk to thermostats—something that is not inherently evil, but may give traditionalists a source of contemplation.

The march of science increases its tempo with each era and moves farther and farther away from the simple civilizations of the ancients. In that, possibly inevitable, march the modern era made conscious attempts to quiet tradition or at least categorize it as the musings of barbarous ancestors.[68] Utility supplanted spirituality and metaphysical oneness. As twentieth-century intellectual historian Richard Weaver (1910–1963) notes: "We hear smooth words to the effect that there is no real conflict between science and religion or between science and literature. There is no real conflict anywhere when one side gives up. The question still at issue is whether the facts and the logic dictate so complete a surrender as has been urged by one party."[69] This was certainly the case as even Tolkien felt the need to support fantasy through scholarly endeavor. He felt the fantastic and reality deserved a reasoned argument for one to attach reality and valid knowledge to the fantastic—at the very least so that it did not lose its voice. It is not the fault of Tolkien that adults do not ask the questions that children ask, but rather suffer from a "blunted belief."[70]

"Is it a fact?" The inevitable question the modern mind asks of all things from the empirical to the mystical. Modern society does not seem satisfied unless it incorporates this factor into its search for knowledge. Did the desire to answer this question negate any validity of imaginative literature in the twentieth century? Ultimately, the fear of the unknown and any reminder of the existence of uncertainty was not held in high esteem especially when coupled with fantasy. MacDonald saw this as a healthy and appropriate fear of the unknown, stating, "it added the force of imagination to the power of fear within me."[71] Fantasy and myth, although they hold to different definitions, tell the stories of culture and religion from even the earliest of civilizations.

During the modern era, Western civilization attempted to sever all ties with the fantastic and spiritual, instead looking for science and reason to provide what religion never could—proof. Maybe the answer is as simple as to whether or not imaginative literature holds value or has a place in real life. If God cannot be proven by all the science in the world, then the possibility exists that imaginative literature is a medium to understand or commune with the Maker. David Lyle Jeffrey explains the connection based on George Steiner's definitions of "critic" and "reader": "The critical act is a function of the ego in a condition of will," so that in the end the critic is '*judge* and *master* of the text'. . . . By contrast, the 'reader' exhibits an opposite desire. His stance is one of the yielding acceptance; he favors personal encounter with the 'living presence' projected by the text."[72] For one, the Bible is heavy with imaginative literature. Throughout both the Old and New Testaments the prophets use parables, metaphors, and similes to reveal and describe the Kingdom of God. Meaning is not always clear and immediately present. Christians turn to the suggestion in Matthew 13 that the human race will not come to an understanding of God and the absolute core truths of reality through scientific and logical explanations alone. Christ can even be seen as the epitome of the fairy story.[73] The Bible also refers to humanity as the children of God. The subjects in imaginative literature suggest that there is value in the childlike. For example in *Phantastes*: "Fairy Land; and one who travels there soon learns to forge the very idea of doing so, and takes everything as it comes; like a child, who, being in a chronic condition of wonder is surprised at nothing."[74] This childlike endeavor could bring about a clearer explanation to the value of fantasy's use in imaginative literature.

The Inklings cherished this type of literature as a way of linking the ancient world, through the Middle Ages into the modern era. It gave them a platform to voice their concerns regarding scientism and other borderline progressive measures, something that was discussed in chapter 4 as part of the new marketplace. They believed traditional ideals and beliefs still held value and a place in modern institutions, but needed a concerted effort for preservation and reconciliation. MacDonald, Lewis, and Tolkien incorporated fantasy into the explanation of their faith and the Church. These two factors greatly influenced their understanding of a traditional perspective, which led to their defense of Christianity, not through the modern routes of science, but through reason and the literary roots of imagination. The Inklings' use of modern romantic ideas drew similar parallels to the ways in which the Jews utilized Hellenistic ideas. Both groups used the ideals and methods only as they suited their existing perspective and only where it did not directly contradict or conflict with their religious beliefs.[75]

The Inklings recognized that, historically, Christianity was in a state of decline in the West. In the first millennium AD, Christianity was pervasive, but only after careful interaction with Greco-Roman paganism. Christian apologists like Justin Martyr and Irenaeus saw success precisely because they did not abandon the mode of discourse invented by pagans, but mastered and utilized it on behalf of their burgeoning faith.[76] That the aforementioned Church Fathers found the Socratic apology a fitting mode of dispersing theological ideas was a factor in why the worship of Christ began to win over that of the classical pantheon. Christianity was thus framed as the consummation and fuller revelation of what paganism had sought for centuries, and not the mere replacement of it with entirely new ideas and modes of discourse (Paul in Athens). In the eyes of the Inklings, however, modernity's ascent over religion—especially Christianity—amounted to a gag order. The major Western revolutions of the second millennium AD stimulated the West's desire for more certainty in knowledge of the universe and less margin for error on the part of the Church and the Crown. In some way, all of Catholic Europe was dragged to guillotines in 1789 with every victim of the Reign of Terror. Traditionalists lamented this course of action, for they believed tradition was betrayed with a Judas kiss.

The increased reliance on a more scientific explanation of such attitudes created friction between pastoral and psychological diagnoses.[77] The Inklings saw a number of these ideas present in the Church, specifically the Roman Catholic Church and Anglican Church traditions. Some of them fused their love of romanticism with their desire to defend Christianity. Thus, the ability of the Catholic Church to represent unity and the intended purpose and actions of humanity was expressed in the blending of theology with natural laws. The Inklings relied on one another to build up the legitimacy of both their fictional and scholarly works.

USE OF MYTH

Charles Williams best represented his perspective in *Outlines of Romantic Theology*. Williams did not wish to separate the naturalism of the romantics from the dogma of Christian doctrine, but instead to create a unity between the two. The concepts of love, intimacy, and marriage are intricately woven into the understanding that the pure forms of each of these concepts are a direct representation of the relationship between humans, God, the Church, and Christ.[78] Williams provides a logical explanation of the relationship between the Church and humanity. In all of the Inklings' endeavors, they strove to remain a united front against the pessimism and cynicism of certain popular modern philosophies in an attempt to know God on a higher level, even if through the use of something so childlike as fantasy: "The pure devotion of a philosopher or an explorer plays its part in the search for the most holy Graal."[79] Myth and its meaning serve as tools in the justification of fantasy and imagination to the modern arguments of science and reason. The Inklings dutifully carved out a niche for such things in their search for the survival of myth in the modern world.

Myth has a rich and full history with regard to its use by humanity to build knowledge and explain the universe. Myth has been an integral characteristic in the development of religion and culture. Given the role of myth in the development of religion and culture, and its presence in poetry and literature, it remains relevant. If myth was a central idea of the pre-modern world, then its relevance in the modern world is a necessary aspect of the conversation. The subject is best approached by looking at what myth is, how it is viewed from the modern and Christian perspectives, and its importance in developing a core value of its keepers.

The definition of the word "myth" comes from the Greek *mŷthos* meaning "story" or "word." The derivation of the current meaning finds its roots in the decade of 1820–1830. The era of modern thought was in full swing at this point in Europe and so it is important to note the different definitions of myth and the order of their importance. There are two working definitions that are commonly attached to the present meaning of the word myth:

> 1) A traditional or legendary story, usually concerning some being or *hero* or event, with or without a determinable basis of fact or a natural explanation, especially one that is concerned with deities or demigods and explains some practice, rite, or phenomenon of *nature*. 2) A story about superhuman beings of an earlier age taken by preliterate society to be a true account, usually of how natural phenomena, social customs, etc., came into existence.

Both definitions infer that the meaning of myth comes from tradition or a preliterate society. Both accounts refer to "natural explanation" or "phenomena" and their link to deities, rites, and social customs. The assumption follows that myth as a tool is no longer relevant to the modern world because science provides society with the light of empirical knowledge, therefore voiding the necessity of tradition, legend, and deities. The definitions all deal with characteristics of fiction, imagination, fantasy, and invention. As the above definitions imply, and as the Inklings bear witness, one who values imaginative literature, especially myth, as popular opinion deems such things to be outside of scientific reality, thus relegating them to the category of fiction.

If myth had a specific meaning for primitive and ancient cultures, then why did that definition change with time? Why did the meaning change or lose value? One possibility is the issue of language and the effects of metamorphosis. In *Poetic Diction*, Barfield treated this metamorphosis from a historical perspective:

> Meanwhile, the historian would note how the anti-poetic, or purely rational, had begun to take effect. He would find meanings splitting up in the manner previously described and language beginning to change its character, to lose its intrinsic life. He might note, also, that the increased action of this principle was accompanied by the birth of hitherto unknown antitheses, such as those between truth and myth, between prose and poetry, and again between an objective and a subjective world; so that now, for the first time, it becomes possible to distinguish the *content* of a word from its *reference*.[80]

As definitions and meanings were reordered by the *Encyclopédie* of the Enlightenment *philosophes*, they shaped the acceptance and utility of popular meaning for Western society. The social sciences accepted the more scientific approach to the relationship between myth and culture and sided with the empirical knowledge of science that portrayed myth as something from the ignorant, superstitious, and primitive past.

For twentieth-century moderns, myth represented a world characterized by symbolic acts and magical pretense. The ancient meanings and uses of these meanings remain entombed within their respective eras. The modern world saw itself acting in reality. In his seminal work *Sociology of Religion* (1920), Weber saw the ancients acting in magical symbolism that substituted original naturalism, thus making gods and other supernatural components accessible through myth and mysticism.[81] An affinity for and defense of myth appeared discarded, essentially, by the progress of Western society. No longer was it necessary to attribute aspects of the natural world directly to transcendent beings. Rather, one only need find the explanation within the context of scientific reality. By eliminating the long-standing meanings, the moderns had no place to turn except the early stages of scientific knowledge. The Modern Age was unwavering in its certainty of the scientific process while the importance of myth became relegated to imaginative literature and religious practice. As Barfield points out, there was a time when the two were not separate forms of knowledge, but instead existed as one revelation that brought forth a more intimate relationship between humanity and the universe:

> [T]his meaning has been traced back to its source in the theocratic, "myth-thinking" period, and it has been shown that the myths, which represent the

earliest meanings, were not the arbitrary creations of "poets", but the natural expression of man's being and consciousness at the time. These primary "meanings" were *given*, as it were, by Nature, but the very condition of their being given was that they could not at the same time be apprehended in full consciousness; they could not be *known*, but only experienced or lived.[82]

The Modern Age voluntarily sought the removal of intangible aspects of history and knowledge and replaced it with the tangible.

Scientific knowledge claims to offer a more accurate vision of reality despite the Inklings' objections that it too might be just as incomplete. The loss of the mystical, regardless of one's opinion on the virtues or vices of myth as both a tool and an art, had an effect on the cultural fabric of modern Europe. The departure of myth signaled drastic reevaluations of long-standing abstractions, such as love. Charles Williams recognized the inherent discord in modernity's treatment of the abstract and divine, uncovering the reality that its participants often served two masters: "It is scepticism and devotion. That these two cannot always work together must, alas! Be admitted. The entire *dévot*, the entire agnostic, each tend to be scornful of the other."[83] Traditionalists determined a need for the proper balance of such extremes, but modernity struggled to embrace the need for balance during its devotion to fact and progress. Williams uses the backdrop of romantic love to pursue his investigation of meaning and how the progress of the age moves away from the understanding and experience of such divine delights. Williams consistently ties the ability to love with the ability to maintain a devout relationship with God—for him, the two are not exclusive.[84] He believed the modern romantics exorcized such "narrow-minded" insights of intimately human characteristics. Thus, they created another example of new meaning devoid of any historical significance and its relevance to their present era. In its most extreme forms, the modern world remained in a constant state of flux that sought to draw new meanings as progress continued. Barfield contended that meaning became tied to metaphor as it moved through time; it was the only way to comprehend the shifts and movements of definitions and the different use of concepts: "To anyone attempting to construct metaphysics in strict accordance with the canons and categories of formal Logic, the fact that the meanings of words change, not only from age to age, but from context to context, is certainly interesting; but it is interesting solely because it is a nuisance."[85] The nuisance that Barfield speaks of did not come from actual changes in meaning, but rather the need of a "desperate faith in the ancient system of *definitions*."[86]

A premature postmodern theory seemingly rears its head in the prose of Barfield. The Inklings believed that the tradition of myth was an important factor to transport into the modern era; even if Barfield's dedication in *Poetic Diction* reads: "To C.S. Lewis, 'Opposition is true friendship.'" Despite the realization that Lewis and Barfield held different interpretations, Barfield did not see them as different truths: "His experience, his *meaning*, is quite different from mine, for it is the product of quite different concepts."[87] This is an example of how the Inklings, some of whom subscribe to modern "concepts" (to quote Barfield) and some who do not, see myth as advantageous. Therefore, the Inklings suggest a precedent wherein myth does not necessarily signal a hatred of science and progress as the above definitions, and the scientists of the era alleged. The larger implication is that modernity won before the Inklings were born because it simplified what did not fit its paradigm until it was completely soluble. It reduced myth to its most basic form until it was entirely digestible.

Instead of the outright denouncement of fantasy and myth, Inklings found another way to approach this subject through Christianity and those who persevered to uphold the doctrines of the Middle Ages. What if Barfield recognized that, although humanity, myth, and meaning had changed such that the modern person could never entirely recover the mind of ancient myth, myth nonetheless possesses virtue and offers a modicum of the hope of a return to and rediscovery of true and absolute realities? For the Inklings, myth seemed lost or misplaced in the scuffle of the Scientific, Intellectual, and Industrial Revolutions. All three of the aforementioned revolutions happened relatively close to one another and caused a disorienting avalanche of ideas. Tolkien and Chesterton mounted defenses of fantasy under similar terms, respectively: "Fantasy is a natural human activity. It certainly does not destroy or even insult Reason; and it neither blunts the appetite for nor obscures the perception of, scientific verity."[88] "At the four corners of a child's bed stand Perseus and Roland, Sigurd and St. George. If you withdraw the guard of heroes you are not making him rational; you are only leaving him to fight the devils alone."[89]

Williams recognized a similar misconception in the modern perception of love. His position reflects an anti-modern sentiment in that the modern world did not mirror the relationship of pre-modern principles and therefore did not know how to love to the fullest potential. He equates it to humanity's attempts to "figure out" the Mass instead of letting love dictate: "As a matter of practice, therefore, the lover will probably be wise to meditate upon the particular teachings of Romantic Theology 'outside church' or during the opening ceremonies of the Mass, but when the Canon has been begun to put away so far as possible all methods of interpretation, and to keep only the intention to let the work of Love be fully accomplished in him."[90]

Our Oxford dons easily could have followed suit and snubbed such things as fantasy, but instead they saw the parallels between the ability to fantasize and the ability, not necessarily to imagine God, but rather to bear the image of God. One of the most important facets of myth as it exists in imaginative literature is the concept of "otherness." Jeffrey asserts that Lewis is integral to understanding how pre-modern ideas were reconciled to the modern mind-set:

> [T]hose who oppose the Christian faith will quite often come out on top. It is entirely appropriate, he thought, for Christians to try with utmost diligence to be persuasive about the truth and reasonableness of Christianity but unnecessary for them always to "win" an argument. . . . It is thus the heart of the faithful reader, not to the skeptic or technophile, that some of the meaning in irreducible mysteries may most likely come.[91]

Lewis did not believe all moderns made such distinctions as their ethos only allowed them to see what came from the individual and the physical universe. Anything with derivation from a supernatural or transcendent source was seen as ancient superstition and did not provide insight or truth to the rational landscape of humanity.

Even given the possibility that after the success of political and intellectual revolutions, myth was relegated unjustly by modern culture to either personal matters of faith or the superstitions found within human societies, the Inklings' unyielding frame of myth as something true and attainable was and is strange in no small way. Tradition allows for the continuance of myth amid the metamorphosis of the intellectual landscape. It is this strangeness, however, that gives myth, fantasy, and imaginative literature their identities. Barfield recognized this quality: "'Strangeness' may produce an aesthetic effect . . . that the strangeness shall have an *interior* significance; it must be felt as arising from a different plane or mode of consciousness, and not merely as eccentricity of expression. It must be a strangeness of *meaning*."[92] If one is willing to follow the logic of Barfield then the importance of the Inklings' action of the preservation of pre-modern ideas through imaginative literature increases in importance. Josef Pieper provides a helpful insight to tradition and the relationship between speech and original revelation. He states: "The concept of 'original revelation' betokens that at the beginning of history an event took place of a divine speech directed especially to 'the' man, that is to *all* men, and that what was shared at that time has entered into the sacred tradition of all peoples—in their myths, that—and is preserved and present there, more or less recognizably."[93] The ideas had not changed, only the relative meanings changed to fit current understandings in culture. If the individual is to be a proper critic of such mysterious ideas, then he or she must possess certain qualities and characteristics to best extract the truth: "A controlled and fundamentally sane consciousness, a gentle sympathetic imaginative understanding, not only of 'human nature' in the ordinary sense, but of the nature of inspiration and its function in human evolution."[94] With these ideas in mind the Inklings were translators of tradition who consciously avoided the tendencies of modernity and the clutches of scientism.[95]

The Inklings allow their imaginations to work in tandem with their reason, thus giving them a perspective in which to evaluate and resist certain promises of the modern scientific age.[96] They valued the place of tradition and felt that the Modern Age had a number of redemptive qualities, but was too concerned with materialism and utility. A focus on the material understanding of life would affect numerous aspects from spirituality to education. An association could be made, that is quite possibly the clearest way to glimpse what Lewis referred to as "Joy," through the paths of one's imagination even if he or she travels the mythical roads of Narnia, Middle-earth, or Fairy-Land. It was through this path that they maintained hope for their fellow travelers. It was the argument of reason that led Lewis to Christianity and allowed him and the others to defend it against outside instigators. For many, Christianity and tradition are something more than practice, custom, or habit—it is the definition of being human. The romanticism of the premodern world provided a strong foil to progressive twentieth-century ideology. Boenig references Lewis's idea that the Middle Ages evidenced most a pure medium of Joy because it was an age replete with poetry to enjoy and explicate the voices of the mystics.[97] The Inklings embodied a conscious recognition of "an emotional wish to inhabit a medieval world in reality, not just in imagination."[98]

George MacDonald's use of myth and fantasy in the medium of imaginative literature coupled with the anti-modern traditionalist sentiments of G. K. Chesterton were building blocks to a greater awareness of the assessment of the Modern Age. Myth, imagination, and the like became useful in coming to terms with the sterile and mechanical world of the modern era. If the premodern world and tradition were relegated to the superstition and fiction sections of knowledge, then the only means which kept them alive were a wholehearted commitment to the spirit of these ideas. Myth and imagination once linked God to humanity and was seen as truth; modernity began to view them as childish stories. In the pages of *The Future of an Illusion* (1927), Freud characterized myth as ancient archaic hokum explained as mass delusions and illusions of projected reality. Once the individual was convinced of this, he or she was able to pick up the tools of reason and science, move into a new era of technology and progress, and forget romantic naturalism.

The Inklings focused their collective energies toward the themes of the Middle Ages through the likeness of the Roman Catholic—by extension the Anglo-Catholic—tradition. Medieval tradition gave aid to Lewis, in particular, in the course of articulating Christianity precisely because it was where the paganism of late antiquity matured into the Christian religion.[99] The affinity of such themes, realities, and so on naturally led to an apology. These robust and subtle references ultimately define the Inklings as preservers of tradition and a common mind; possibly some of the last amid the increased popularity of modern thought until the bridge they built could be tended by a new generation of preservationists. Individuals of the late-modern world owe it to question the ancient and modern mind-sets equally, along with their validity and purpose. It is one thing to admit the extensive knowledge of the modern case, but it is another to recognize that there could be something deeper that modernity overlooked or ignored due to its focus on progress.[100] The number of modernity's intellectual opponents were few, but formidable.

NOTES

1. Veldman, *Fantasy, the Bomb, and the Greening of Britain*, p. 54.
2. Lewis, "Religion and Science," *God in the Dock*, p. 74.
3. J. B. S. Haldane, "Auld Hornie, F.R.S.", *Modern Quarterly*, n.s., 1 (Autumn, 1946): pp. 32–40.
4. Lewis, "Religion and Science," *God in the Dock*, p. 75.
5. Peter Williams, *C.S. Lewis vs the New Atheists* (Milton Keynes: Paternoster, 2013), pp. 49–50.
6. Herrick, "C.S. Lewis and the Advent of the Posthuman", p. 260.
7. C.S. Lewis, *The Collected Letters of C.S. Lewis Vol. 3*, ed. Walter Hooper (New York: HarperOne, 2004–2007), p. 498.
8. Tolkien, "Letter to Christopher Tolkien, 28 July 1944", *Letters*, p. 88.
9. *Ibid.*, p. 116.
10. Loconte, *A Hobbit, A Wardrobe, and a Great War*, pp. 2–3.
11. *Ibid.*, p. 14.
12. C.S. Lewis, *Surprised by Joy: In The Inspirational Writings of C.S. Lewis* (New York: Inspirational Press, 1994), p. 114.
13. Lewis, *Mere Christianity*, pp. 25 and 36.
14. Bruce Reichenbach, "C.S. Lewis and the Desolation of Devalued Science," *Seven Vol 4.* (1983): pp. 17–19.
15. C.S. Lewis, *The Collected Poems*, "On the Atomic Bomb," lines 13–4, p. 78.
16. C.S. Lewis, *The Abolition of Man* (New York: HarperCollins, 2001), pp. 56–7.
17. Gushurst-Moore, *The Common Mind*, p. 209.
18. See Michael D. Aeschliman, *The Restitution of Man: C.S. Lewis and the Case against Scientism* (Grand Rapids: Eerdmans, 1983).
19. C.S. Lewis, *That Hideous Strength* (New York: Scribner Classics, 1996), p. 23.
20. *Ibid.*, p. 177.
21. Haldane, "Auld Hornie."
22. C.S. Lewis, *Of Other Worlds: Essays and Stories* (New York: Harcourt, 1994), pp. 80.
23. C.S. Lewis, *Dymer: A Poem* (London: J.M. Dent and Sons, 1950), p. 3.
24. Owen Barfield, *Poetic Diction: A Study in Meaning* (Middletown: Wesleyan University Press, 1973), pp. 84–5.
25. *Ibid.*, pp. 89–90.
26. *Ibid.*, pp. 91–2.
27. Tolkien, *The Lord of the Rings* (Boston: Houghton Mifflin, 1993), p. 187.
28. *Ibid.*, pp. 73 and 643.
29. Peter Kreeft, *The Philosophy of Tolkien* (San Francisco: Ignatius Press, 2005), p. 123.
30. J.S. Ryan, "Uncouth Innocence: Some links between Chretien de Troyes, Wolfram von Eschenbach and J.R.R. Tolkien," *Inklings Jahrbuch fuer Literatur und Aesthetik* 2, (1984), p. 25.
31. *Ibid.*, p. 37.
32. Grevel Lindop suggests that Williams possibly possessed a membership in a Golden Dawn group as well. See *Charles Williams: The Third Inkling* (Oxford: Oxford University Press, 2015), pp. 64–6.
33. A.E. Waite, *The Hidden Church of the Holy Graal* (London: Rebman Ltd., 1909), p. 523.
34. Morrisson, p. 28.

35. Gavin Ashenden, *Charles Williams: Alchemy and Integration* (Kent: Kent State University Press, 2007), p. 134.
36. *Ibid.*, p. 158.
37. Owen Barfield, *Romanticism Comes of Age* (Middletown: Wesleyan University Press, 1966) p. 189.
38. *Ibid.*, pp. 188–89.
39. Owen Barfield, *Speaker's Meaning* (London: Rudolf Steiner Press, 1967), p. 138.
40. Barfield, *Romanticism*, p, 189.
41. *Ibid.*, p. 201.
42. C.S. Lewis, *The Collected Letters of C.S. Lewis, Vol. 3: Narnia, Cambridge, & Joy, 1950–1963* (New York: HarperOne, 2007), p. 540.
43. P. Williams, *New Atheists*, p. 12.
44. Lewis, *Abolition*, p. 64.
45. *Ibid.*, p. 44.
46. C.S. Lewis, *The Discarded Image: An Introduction to Medieval and Renaissance Literature* (Cambridge: Cambridge University Press, 1964), p. 92.
47. Barfield, *Saving the Appearances*, p. 38.
48. Lewis, *Discarded Image*, p. 17.
49. Owen Barfield, *Worlds Apart: A Dialogue of the 1960's* (Middletown: Wesleyan University Press, 1963), pp. 20–1.
50. C.S. Lewis, *Miracles* (San Francisco: HarperOne, 2015), p. 28.
51. *Ibid.*, p. 33.
52. An interesting juxtaposition exists on "the argument of reason" between Daniel Dennett, *Darwin's Dangerous Idea* (New York: Touchstone Books, 1996) and Victor Reppert, *C.S. Lewis's Dangerous Idea: In Defense of the Argument from Reason* (Westmont: Intervarsity Press Academic, 2003).
53. See Peter van Inwagen, "C.S. Lewis' Argument Against Naturalism," *Journal of Inklings Studies* 1, no. 2 (October 2011): 25–40.
54. Marcel Sarot, "The Cardinal Difficulty for Naturalism: C.S. Lewis' Argument Reconsidered in Light of Peter van Inwagen's Critique," *Journal of Inklings Studies* 1, no. 2 (October 2011): p. 49.
55. C.S. Lewis, *Image and Imagination*, ed. Walter Hooper (Cambridge: Cambridge University Press, 2013), pp. 248–76. Originally published in *Essays on Malory* (Oxford: Clarendon Press, 1963), pp. 7–28.
56. Mineko Honda, *The Imaginative World of C.S. Lewis: A Way to Participate in Reality* (Lanham: University of America Press, 2000), p. 30.
57. John D. Davidson, "Tolkien, Lewis, and a World Shot Through with Meaning," *The Washington Free Beacon*. Last updated July 11, 2015. http://freebeacon.com/culture/tolkien-lewis-and-a-world-shot-through-with-meaning/.
58. Milton Scarborough, *Myth and Modernity: Postcritical Reflections* (Albany: SUNY Press, 1994), p. 30.
59. *J.R.R. Tolkien Encyclopedia: Scholarship and Critical Assessment*, ed. Michael D.C. Drout (New York: Routledge, 2007), pp. 399–400.
60. George MacDonald, *Phantastes* (East Peoria: Versa Press, 2011), p. 5.
61. J.R.R. Tolkien, *Tree and Leaf* (Boston: Houghton Mifflin, 2001), p. 89.
62. MacDonald, *Phantastes*, p. 162 and 163, respectively.
63. J.R.R. Tolkien, "Of the Sun and Moon and the Hiding of Valinor" and "Of Men," *The Silmarillion* (New York: Houghton Mifflin, 1999): 98–105.
64. *Ibid.*, p. 35.
65. Tolkien, *Tree and Leaf*, pp. 93–101.
66. MacDonald, *Phantastes*, p. 139 and 155, respectively.
67. Tolkien, *Tree and Leaf*, p. 47.
68. See Ryan Somma, "Humanism," *Enlightenment Living: Essays on Living a Virtuous Scientific Life* (Mountain View: Creative Commons, 2012): 167–74.
69. Richard M. Weaver, *Visions of Order: The Cultural Crisis of Our Time* (Wilmington: ISI Books, 1995), p. 143.

70. *Ibid.*, p. 38.
71. MacDonald, *Phantastes*, p. 32.
72. David Lyle Jeffrey, *Houses of the Interpreter: Reading Scripture, Reading Culture* (Waco: Baylor University Press, 2003), p. 181.
73. Tolkien, *Tree and Leaf*, p. 72.
74. MacDonald, *Phantastes*, p. 29.
75. George Holley Gilbert, "The Hellenization of the Jews Between 334 B. C. And 70 A. D." *The American Journal of Theology* 13, no. 4, University of Chicago Press, 1909: 520–40.
76. For examples of their respective discourse with paganism, see: Justin Martyr, trans. Thomas B. Falls, "Chapter 22" in *The First Apology, The Second Apology, Dialogue with Trypho, Exhortation to the Greeks, Discourse to the Greeks, The Monarchy of the Rule of God* (Washington, D.C.: The Catholic University of America Press, 2008), p. 399: "Plato had learned all this in Egypt and he was especially impressed with doctrine of one God. Yet, because he feared the Areopagus, he did not dare mention to the Athenians the name of Moses, because the latter had taught that there was only one God. But, in his carefully written work, the *Timaeus*, which he discussed God's nature, he wrote as his own the same opinion as Moses concerning God." Irenaeus, "Book II" in *Against Heresies* (Pickerington, OH: Beloved Publishing, LLC, 2015), p. 129: "This opinion, too, that they hold the Creator formed the world out of previously existing matter, both Anaxoragas, Empedocoles, and Plato expressed before them; as, forsooth, we learn that they also do under the inspiration of their Mother. Then again, as to the opinion that everything of necessity passes away to those things out of which they maintain it was also formed, and that God is the slave of this necessity."
77. See Joanna Bourke, "Divine Madness: The Dilemma of Religious Scruples in Twentieth-century America and Britain," *Journal of Social History* 42, no. 3, (Oxford: Oxford University Press, 2009): 581–603.
78. See Charles Williams, "The New Testament in Romantic Theology" and "The Mass in Romantic Theology in *Outlines of Romantic Theology* (Berkeley: Apocryphile Press, 2005).
79. *Ibid.*, p. 72.
80. Barfield, *Poetic Diction*, p.94.
81. Weber, p.7.
82. Barfield, *Poetic Diction*, p. 102.
83. Williams, *Outlines of Romantic Theology*, p. 50.
84. *Ibid.*, introduction by Alice M. Hadfield, viii.
85. Barfield, *Poetic Diction*, p. 61.
86. *Ibid.*, p. 62.
87. *Ibid.*, p. 49.
88. Tolkien, *Tree and Leaf*, p. 55.
89. G.K. Chesterton, *Tremendous Trifles* (Create Space Publishing, 2009), p. 51.
90. Williams, *Outlines of Romantic Theology*, p. 45.
91. Jeffrey, *Houses of the Interpreter*, p. 180.
92. Barfield, *Poetic Diction*, p. 171.
93. Pieper, *Tradition*, p. 51.
94. *Ibid.*, p. 170.
95. Scientism was not the only problem, but certainly one of the more egregious as it made grandiose claims for the future of mankind. As shown in other chapters, not all traditionalists focused their efforts on the bout with scientism, but took up other crusades against modern thought, modern education, modern politics, et cetera.
96. See Lewis's explanation of the "magician's bargain" in *The Abolition of Man*, pp. 72–81.
97. *Ibid.*, p. 78.
98. *Ibid.*, p 53.
99. Lewis, *Surprised By Joy*, p. 227.
100. *Ibid.*, p. 141.

Chapter Six

The Broader Conspiracy

The Inklings were not the only group that took notice of the possible implications of progressivism. There were other intellectuals, marginalized perhaps, who, though they did not all identify as Christians, still traced the lineage of their beliefs to tradition. The authors discussed in this chapter were not all categorized as New Humanists; nonetheless, each one of them reflects the title in that they share a distinct genealogy of thought along with similar goals for the preservation of the permanent things. Traditionalists were aware of the stigma of obligation by their generation toward tradition. Pieper's response characterizes a general sentiment toward such suspicions, saying: "The praise due the act of tradition only makes sense when what is preserved and will continue to be preserved through the generations is *what is truly worth preserving*."[1] They evaluated the Modern Age in a number of different facets and determined what needed to be preserved for the sake of humanity. The Modern Age brought about an interesting turn in the acceptance of knowledge and technological advancement. Traditionalists maintained that even with an abundance of empirical data, humanity may not know anything more about its meaning and purpose. R. William Franklin and Joseph Shaw explain the ethos of the spirit of the modern scientific age which claimed, "this age or this world is all that belongs to reality."[2] If humans are merely a chance occurrence of molecules and atoms that simply drift through space and time, then there does not seem to be a need for a unique and distinct relationship to a Creator bound by a relationship of participation.

Traditionalists reflected a more orthodox view of what governed humanity's participation on a spiritual and intellectual level. One such definition can be found in Jens Zimmerman's description of *theosis* as the individual's participation in reconciliation and deification.[3] It is not enough to participate in the activities of temporal existence, but one needs to contemplate the proximity to possible transcendent expectations. Christian humanism augments the connection between the Incarnation and the human condition and actively seeks an understanding of both God and the human soul. In the mind of traditionalists, the Modern Age traded perceived higher standards and the humanities for the sake of progress through humanitarianism and utility. The responsibility of the Christian humanist envisions both activity and contemplation. In most cases Christian humanists do not wish to create a theocracy nor do they want to wait for messages from heaven. They do, however, wish to participate in humane pursuits through political, economic, intellectual, and spiritual outlets. The participation of traditional conservative authors Christopher Dawson, Russell Kirk, Hilaire Belloc, Irving Babbitt (1865–1933), Paul Elmer More (1864–1937), and John Henry Newman (1801–1890) created an awareness of what they called "the crisis of Western civilization" with the hope of reform in the modern West through such things as education.

This chapter discusses how these authors promoted tradition and conservatism through the exercise of humanism, Christian where appropriate, and the awareness that education would necessitate any lasting success in the preservation of the permanent things. They did not all share the same religious or political views, but they did value the conservative tradition of the Western canon. Literary scholar and professor of English Benjamin Lockerd points out Dawson's agreement with Babbitt only extends so far: "Though Babbitt insists on the spiritual dimension and wishes to draw on the collective spiritual wisdom of the ages, he declines the dogmatic claims of any particular religion and therefore is not far enough from the position he is opposing."[4] These intellectuals are included here to show that their connections extended beyond their personal views. The differences did not seem to matter as they all saw a necessity in the preservation of the permanent things and shared similar ideas on what best reenchanted the ebb of tradition in the modern progressive West. The reality is that the tradition of Western civilization, although classical, was definitively affected by Christianity. Nonetheless, nonreligious humanists were aware of a sense of obligation to defend tradition against certain twentieth-century ideologies. While it is clear that Kirk claimed Dawson's influence on his ideas, Babbitt and Belloc, More and Newman are juxtaposed in this chapter to provide grounds for reconciliation, especially in matters of tradition and liberal learning and despite some of their distinct differences.[5] All six interact with the Modern Age in matters of permanence, a natural tradition of humanity, the place of humanism in Western education, and the formation of good habits to reveal a complex relationship between tradition, conservatism, and different forms of humanism.

DAWSON AND KIRK

Human beings, in general, feel the need to reinvent the wheel. The reinvention, or at the very least the upgrading, especially for modern society, serves as a measure of progress. Is progress defined only by the act of moving forward in the attempt to change and improve existing methodologies? Those who believe in the tenets of tradition and conservatism would argue that progress is defined as a rediscovery of the permanent tenets of humanity alongside new developments. They are tenets that remain consistent with the traditional Western definition of what it means to be a human—the common mind. The foundational ideas of the West are conveyed and cultivated through humane learning. According to Christopher Dawson's *The Crisis of Western Education* (1961) and Russell Kirk's *Prospects for Conservatives: A Compass for Rediscovering the Permanent Things* (1954), the West deviated from tradition and was in need of something to re-establish the virtuous construct that it once forged. Their evaluations of modernity were critiques that reveal how they evaluated humanity's progressive endeavors in light of whether or not the progress damaged the West rather than promote its advancement. Their rediscovery was led by their commitment to uphold tradition, conservatism, and Christianity.

Dawson, Kirk, and Chesterton utilized similar vocabulary in the discussion of the crisis of Western civilization. They share definitions of Christian humanism within the three main ideas involved in their respective works: tradition, conservatism, and liberal learning. The paradigms of character and culture established by tradition and conservatism are conveyed through the pre-modern curriculum of classical liberal learning.[6] For both Dawson and Kirk, the manifestation of Western values and ideas were indicative of the pillars of classical learning infused with Christianity. Over time, Christian culture decreased in the public eye into a largely separate and private issue. The arenas of politics, education, and economics affect culture more significantly than religion in the modern era. Such a dynamic was not always the case; the Church, specifically the Catholic Church, once had a significant influence on culture. Dawson argued that, during the Middle Ages, the majority of Western Europeans identified with Catholic culture: "In Europe it was the peasants who remained most loyal to the Church and who probably provided the greatest number of religious vocations, while in the great cities the Church had to face the growing opposition of the forces of anticlericalism and irreligion."[7] Culture began to take its cues apart from the Church at the end of the Renaissance with the rise of the Protestant Reformation. Kirk and Dawson came to rather similar definitions of tradition, conservatism and humane learning.

Tradition has become an abrasive word in political and educational conversations. It is characterized as "old-fashioned" or stagnant.[8] The modern relationship with progress perpetuates a certain distaste for the things of the past, the place where Kirk found the "permanent things." If the modern world does not see any value in the heritage of the past, then Kirk's definition of tradition ceases to have value for modern society:

> In common usage, tradition implies the spiritual and cultural inheritance which the existing generation has received from previous generations. It implies acceptance, preservation, and passing on. Tradition gives permanence to customs and ideas; it confers upon change the element of continuity, keeping the alteration of society in a regular train. Everything which the living possess has roots in the spiritual and intellectual achievements of the past.[9]

This is all well and good unless the current generation wants nothing to do with their inheritance. If tradition is a tool for understanding culture, does a culture lack insight if it ignores or devalues its past? Kirk points out that tradition is not opposed to changes that avoid constant alteration with no reference to the past.[10] Tradition preserves the permanent things to provide a level of continuity for culture. From where Kirk sat, when a society begins to break down and remove portions of tradition for the sake of progress it removes elements of meaning and purpose as well.

The elements of culture most susceptible to constant alteration, for both Dawson and Kirk, are education, politics and economics. The systematic approach to crafting a perfect society most likely came out of the combination of English empiricism and French rationalism, one realized in the birth of the Age of Enlightenment.[11] The Enlightenment sought to eradicate metaphysics from humane learning and politics; thus, faith would take a back seat to reason.[12] For the *encyclopédistes*,[13] a reordering of the Tree of Knowledge would create a new order and system of value that put the catalysts of progress directly in the hands of human progress while denying any influence from faith and the Church, or as Dawson expressed it: "Science and industry were two wings of the army of progress which were to be coordinated and united by a reformed system of rational education."[14]

Conservatism underwent similar effects when society reordered its priorities. The effects on conservatism appear in economic and educational reform even if, as a belief system, it has nothing to do with socioeconomic status. The ideas brought forth by modern liberalism were fixated on creating equality and wider sociability through progress—at first equal opportunity, but in some cases moved toward equal outcome. Traditionalists hold that modern conservatism was a levelheaded response to this idealism. Conservatism is a doctrine or faith in beliefs intent on understanding the story of humanity and human nature.[15] It is not focused on fiscal spending by government or small-government policies. Liberalism promotes the idea of economic equality as a possible cure for societal problems and disparity. For example, if utility and profitability are taught in institutions of learning, then their graduates through their vocational choices and economic activity will feed consumerism. In short, a liberal ideology will support the practical and democratic needs of modern society "instead of perpetuating an outdated system that favours an educated aristocracy steeped in the humanities."[16] The reality, as Dawson sees it, points to a different outcome. It is an outcome that is not in line with human nature and in fact becomes "so divorced from its foundations that the [participants] become physically exhausted and spiritually depressed by the structure they have to bear. For it is an abnormally expensive economy which uses up both human and natural resources more rapidly than anything hitherto known."[17] Dawson is not alone in this assessment. About fifty years later, Nussbaum's argument as to why democracy needs the humanities serves many of the same concerns, albeit with different means in mind.

For modernity, the epitome of progress is evidenced through educational and economic reform that promotes liberty, equality, and justice. Economically, it means closing the gap in the class system and eliminating disparity. In education, this is done through a broad definition of achievement that makes success in education accessible to a greater portion of the population. These endeavors are not malicious, but seek to enhance the lives of those within the society. Traditionalists did wish to point out that some endeavors came with specific effects; not only does education become more accessible, it also becomes more pragmatic and secularized—certainly less conservative.[18] For Dawson and Kirk, the key to rediscovering the permanent things, in this case tradition and conservatism, is the ability to cultivate culture through liberal studies. It is through humane learning that one learns to be a free-thinking citizen who can discern the foundation from the decoration. The allure of economic and educational equality can be presented through ideals promoting certainty through empirical means. As we have shown, both Christian and secular humanists are aware of certain pitfalls. The importance of humane learning has declined throughout the modern era. For most of these authors, rediscovery of permanent characteristics of humanity, according to tradition and conservatism, begins in the university.

From the inception of the university system, the Church has been involved in the foundation and development of the curriculum and culture of higher learning. Beginning with the French Revolution, the attempt to rid the university of Catholic and Protestant influence, for the most part, has seen a great deal of success.[19] Many universities maintain their religious affiliation, but it is generally not reflected in the curriculum or campus culture. Slowly, but surely, the humanities become less of a focus, and the natural and social sciences are advertised as more lucrative and useful to society, thus fulfilling modernity's movement away from tradition and conservatism. Kirk and Dawson discuss the consequences of the blatant attack on humane learning as nearly irreparable.

Kirk and Dawson each point out that modernity's definition of a democratic community is not the definition attached to tradition and conservatism, and it certainly does not incorporate humane learning in the traditional sense. These authors believe that the new modern community is better defined as collectivism[20] (Kirk) or national education[21] (Dawson). Historically, the Catholic Church has been the most efficient institution at keeping education anchored in Christian humanism at a regional level through parochial schools. Dawson actually sees it as a mark of a "higher culture" to focus on intellectual and spiritual elements within similar settings.[22] Kirk maintains a similar sentiment, in that liberal learning disciplines free minds and trains them in the meaning of things by challenging the higher faculties of the intellect and the imagination.[23] Reconciling the concepts of natural tradition and natural law are especially troublesome in the twentieth-century because of abundant resistance of the Modern Age to adhere to already determined definitions.[24] Even though the future seems bleak, both authors believe that the rediscovery of tradition and conservatism can save Western culture. Its realization lives within the halls of secular and non-secular institutions alike.

The reconciliation of tradition does not mean the return to dominance, but it does call for a new discussion between seemingly disparate voices. Russell Kirk and John Dewey had very different views on education. Kirk believed: "University and college were founded to develop right reason and imagination, for the sake of the person and the sake of the republic."[25] Yet he was distinct that this should not be defined by education focused on global citizenship because of the deluge of available information in a computer age, stating: "What we need is not more information; what we require, as a public, is the ability to discriminate and integrate that mass of information, and to reflect upon it."[26] Dewey's pragmatic approach directed education to a more measurable outcome. As Nussbaum points out, "Dewey always emphasized that history and geography should be taught in ways that promoted an adequate confrontation with the practical problems of the present."[27] The point of reconciliation can be found in the desire to construct a holistic curriculum—both approaches are concerned with obtuseness. The university should develop citizens of the world, but not citizens ignorant of their own history as well. Twentieth-century shifts in topical study and pedagogy has allowed for a broadening of curriculum.[28] The beneficial tenets of tradition and progressivism should be defined through a dialogue with the state of humanity—current and historical. This is a task for the philosophers committed to rediscovering the traditional definition of a holistic state of humanity.

BABBITT AND BELLOC

Two conservative authors, the British essayist Hilaire Belloc and the American critic and professor Irving Babbitt, analyzed what they called "the crisis of Western civilization" with the hope to reform education in order to influence Western culture in the face of modern ideologies. Belloc and Babbitt desire similar outcomes, but possess different insights into the process of restoration. Both saw Western civilization in a state of crisis and needed to be saved from itself. Restoration or rediscovery of the permanent things through conservatism, tradition, and classical liberal learning inform their respective ideas. While Belloc sees the Church, specifically as a Roman Catholic, as the center of the rediscovery, due to its foundation to Western civilization, Babbitt puts the university at the center of rediscovery and restoration. Both authors maintain a critically harsh tone. They justify their tone based on the argument that it is for the sake of saving Western civilization from what they see as its rapid downfall. Both disdain the Modern Age, yet their solutions are inherently different as one depends on the transcendent (Belloc) and the other on the human (Babbitt).

In his book *The Crisis of Civilization* (1937), Belloc implies the greatest fault came from the Protestant Reformation of the Catholic Church. The spirit of Reformation, as he argues in chapter 2, did not come from the sixteenth century, but rather had its roots in the later Middle Ages: "The end of the Middle Ages you have a material advance, an increasing knowledge of the world. . . . There was something creative about the air in which the Middle Ages came to an end; but the forces at work produced nothing permanent."[29] An increased knowledge of the world provided a substitute for the tools of the mechanical superstitions of what was seen as an oppressive theocracy—myth and transcendence. The modern systems of politics, economics, and social interaction have their roots in the reactive portion of the Middle Ages.

Belloc's argument points to the possibility that feudalism, a system based largely on status, and the structure of the Catholic Church enhanced people's lives on a grand scale rather than catered to a sense of individualism. In *Hilaire Belloc: The Man and His Work*, C. Creighton Mandell further defines the effects of the feudal system as one that caused a level of security unique to a pre-modern era.[30] For Belloc, the awareness of the community defines Christendom and is an organic concern of the Middle Ages, especially its high period:

> In the first generation of the 11th century—say about 1020 to 1030—when, the siege having been successfully raised, Christendom began to go forward sure of itself, burgeoning and putting forth its freshest powers, then was the beginning of the period during which our people, our culture, were most themselves,

> when the effect of the religion which made us was wholly mature, complete, and victorious . . . it covers the great 300 years of the 11th, 12th, and 13th centuries, that is, until after the date 1300.³¹

For most authors who claim an allegiance to traditional thought, the interests of the community are of greater concern than those of the individual. Individualism provides an outlet for self-interest and, more importantly, the justification to challenge authority. Belloc condemns the Reformation for this very thing and attributes the decline of Western culture, perhaps a bit extremely, to the protestant nature of the Reformation. One could make the argument that Europeans were finally liberated from the yoke of the Church and Crown. They were free to interpret scripture or possibly deny God if they so wished. The argument of the Reformation claims that it made Christianity less institutional and more accessible to the common believer. For Belloc, this personalization of God diluted the place of institutional authority in society. Due to the strong influence of religion on human beings, a similar dissolution in politics and economics would follow, unaccompanied even by the faith of the reformers.

Belloc gives so much credence to the influential nature of the Church because he believes "that religion is the main determining element in the formation of a culture or civilization."³² A culture without religion would then be a fallacy, and this is why he concludes that a modern ideology such as Communism has no chance of success. It is a form of collectivism, not community built on the mind of the Maker, but rather one built on the self-interested individual. For Belloc, this leads to a wide gamut of concerns for both traditionalists and progressives—unchecked capitalism, political cronyism, and a society devoid of truly caring for community. Interestingly enough, the issue of religion is where Babbitt's process no longer parallels Belloc.

Babbitt was not an orthodox Christian by any reckoning, but drew instead on literature and the discipline of criticism to form his critique on the tenets of modernity. His opponents were slightly different than those who animated Belloc. For Babbitt, the crisis of Western civilization had two parties to blame, specifically scientists and theologians. The excessive empiricism of the Modern Age, in tandem with the excessive divinity enshrined by the Church, led to the lack of exceptionalism and the fall of the West. Babbitt is hesitant to put all of his trust in something transcendent as well as the empirical. Instead he saw the best path through humane learning, one that did not submit itself to something like the Renaissance version of the Church, nor did it promote the modern system of learning focused on utility and profitability.

Babbitt's thesis in *Literature and the American College* declares that the Modern Age became more focused on humanitarianism than humanism. For someone like Belloc, humanism was an innate characteristic of the Church which had seen learning and faith side-by-side from the very beginning. Babbitt, however, points out that this arrangement changed and therefore an idea of wider sociability usurped the advancement of Western culture:

> A person who has sympathy for mankind in the lump, faith in its future progress, and desire to serve the great cause of this progress, should be called not a humanist, but a humanitarian. . . . The humanist is more selective in his caresses [and is] opposed to the humanitarian [due to his interest] in the perfecting of the individual rather than in schemes for the elevation of mankind as a whole; and although he allows largely for sympathy, he insists that it be disciplined and tempered by judgment.[33]

Babbitt contends that the intellectual superiority found through classical liberal learning was replaced by democratic sensibilities. The education system lost its ability to promote genius and high standards for the sake of greater numbers being exposed to an accessible level of education. This was based on the idea that the lower school system conditions young people to expect colleges to give everyone a chance and the faculty to "waste their energies in trying to elevate youths above the level to which they belong, not only by their birth, but by their capacity."[34] He was concerned with the standard of Western education, not the religious culture. This falls in line with his ethos because he sought to reinstitute a high quality of objective standards—the key word being objective. This is something religion is not often found to provide as many see it as subjective.

For Babbitt, science and contemporary theology commit the same crimes against the humanities. The only "religion" Babbitt seemed willing to entertain as benevolent and in line with true humanism is Buddhism: "The Buddhists are perhaps nearer the facts as we know them in putting at the very basis of their belief the doctrine, not of the original depravity, but of the original laziness, of human nature . . . like the man of the Far East, calls it his higher Self, or simply the Law."[35] Buddhism is focused on the ability and will of the individual, not a connection to a transcendent being. The individual needs an inner compass to maintain restraint and discipline of the self. Babbitt, unlike Belloc, attributes such ideas to secular humanism. The ancient humanist committed to virtue and the cultivation of a gentleman scholar are ideals shared by the likes of other traditional Catholic conservatives such as Christopher Dawson, Russell Kirk, and G. K. Chesterton.[36] Babbitt was aware of what he called the "barbarous extremes" of excessive pluralism or monism.[37] To avoid the pendulum of extremity, the preservation of humane learning, especially at the university level, represents a crucial pillar of tradition. According to the traditionalist model, the university better serves students if it commits to excellence in humane learning rather than the fads and specialisms of the present culture.

The physical sciences are anchored in materialism and create a society directed toward the comforts, material wares, and empirical truth of the Modern Age. Traditionalists in the university feared students conditioned under the scientific materialist mind-set will know the price of everything, but the value of nothing.[38] How can educators teach the tenets of the humanities, when students are daydreaming about early retirement and luxury automobiles? Babbitt draws the parallel "that science aspires to be all in all, somewhat after the fashion of theology in the Middle Ages."[39] Given his conclusions about science and divinity, it was only logical for Babbitt to gravitate toward the humanism of the Renaissance as it freed itself from the clutches of the medieval mind, focused on the capability of the individual, and checked itself through the attempt to rediscover ancient values through humane learning. It is here that Russell Kirk felt Babbitt's philosophy possessed flaws because of his unwillingness to incorporate theism into his understanding of tradition. Nonetheless, Kirk still saw Babbitt's response to "the clutch of ideology" in the American university as an important component in the preservation of conservatism, an alternative to a servility of the mind, and a plea for the permanent things in civilization: "If intellectually we linger smug and apathetic in a bent world, leaving the works of the mind to molder, as a people we will come to know the consequences of personal and public decadence."[40]

The principles espoused in the liberal arts provide the solutions for Belloc and Babbitt, but their methodologies hinge on different interpretations of humanity. For Belloc, the Catholic Church and its effects on culture, along with the influence of the university, will restore Western culture. For Babbitt, it is only the humanism preserved by the university that can save Western culture from its immediate problem of the advent of what Kirk and others labeled as scientism—along with other progressive ideologies. Granted, there are those who mean to place Babbitt, at times, within close proximity to the camp of pragmatism. Individuals committed to tradition, who question whether Babbitt is a conservative or a progressive, need only to look for clarification from Claes Ryn:

> Other philosophical concepts from Babbitt are "a oneness that is always changing," "multiplicity," "immediate experience," and, for that matter, "analytic reason." In spite of impressions left from time to time, Babbitt does not really regard these as merely temporary, provisional, pragmatic "truths." They refer to ultimates of human life that always and everywhere constitute experience.[41]

The authors do agree wholeheartedly on the need for a select or aristocratic group that would elevate the standards of education, society, and culture in general. Belloc and Babbitt both reflected the idea that true humanism succeeds at producing an intellectual elite whereas science provides the illusion of betterment: "There is no logical connection between the expansion of temporal knowledge and the loss of spiritual certitude; but the expansion of knowledge interferes with fixed habits of mind, and among these are the forms which spiritual certitude takes."[42] "Our lapse into moral impressionism is also hidden from us by the rapid advance of physical science. We assume that because we are advancing rapidly in one direction we are advancing in all directions[.]"[43] The Church and the university can be influential in the lives of Western people. Both institutions were founded in characteristics of Western culture, specifically humane learning and God. It is a recent development to divorce these characteristics from one another. Each of these authors, in their recognition of a common enemy and state of the Modern Age, saw to it that more than one solution was presented to solve the crisis of Western civilization.

The feeling existed that modern secularists portrayed traditional conservatism as one that promoted a more homogenous campaign toward justice, liberty, and equality and in the eyes of conservatives, this led to the modern trampling of conservative ideals.[44] If examined closely, the conservative movement of the twentieth century and its diatribe against the Modern Age of Western civilization did not seek destruction, but elevation. It was concerned with the elevation of traditional standards and beliefs in order to ground society during the rapid progress of the Modern Age. The conservative camp was not opposed to progress, change, or the evolution of society. It was opposed to the modern definition of progress and the sentiment that change is always for the best and the past is irrelevant and old-fashioned. Russell Kirk warned the Modern Age of an inevitable outcome: "Without men who take long views, we are in a pathless wilderness."[45] Traditionalists were concerned with an ever-changing civilization devoid of Western foundational principles. The rub is often the attachment of Christianity to the perspective of traditional Western heritage.

The ideas of Paul Elmer More in *Aristocracy and Justice* (1904) in conjunction with the ideas of John Henry Newman in *The Idea of a University* (1852) draw out another dialogue of traditionalists' response to modernity. Although More had written on Christian apologetics[46] he wrote with an agnostic, more specifically, a unique Christian tone whereas Newman was unapologetically Catholic in his leanings. Ian Ker, in *John Henry Newman: A Biography*, points out the unique disposition possessed by Newman to incorporate all disciplines to the cultivation of the mind, while subjecting all disciplines to the central element and principle of Christianity.[47] As shown within the other examples in this chapter, the juxtaposition of the two reveal their alliance through tradition, classical liberal learning, and the higher things despite their religious differences. The fact that they both commit to addressing the issues of the Modern Age through the importance of the liberal arts, the place of intellectuals, and the purpose of education reveals that the permanent things transcend intellectual movements, yet are communicated and translated through similar methods. Much like Babbitt and Belloc, More and Newman desired similar outcomes, yet exhibited differences in their overall identity when contemplating the crisis of Western civilization.

MORE AND NEWMAN

One aspect that both authors agree on is the importance of the liberal arts as a saving grace of Western civilization. They embody the disciplines of human knowledge in a variety of different ways, which allow their subjects to cross the barriers often erected by cultural and religious idiosyncrasies. Regardless of their subjects of study, they call for a well-structured set of standards in order to inform and educate those involved in the education process. Even though More professes Christianity, he does not see the necessity of grounding liberal education in the medieval Catholic mind-set. With the exception of Babbitt, most of the traditional conservatives addressed in this discussion equate their ideas with the influence of Catholicism and Anglicanism on culture and education. More appears agnostic at times because of his altogether different perspective on Christianity and education.

Newman thought the Modern Age spoke a language based on empiricism; what can actually be known across all disciplines comes through experimental evidence: "Let us then put aside the scientific use of words, when we are to speak of language and literature. Literature is the personal use or exercise of language. That this is so further proved from the fact that one author uses it so differently from another."[48] The spirit of the age was not overly concerned with the abstract, but rather the tangibles. Due to this specific language spoken more eloquently by the systems of science and mathematics, the humanities were construed as alien because its subjects were not concerned with contributing to the ideas of modern progress. The next chapter participates in a more in-depth discussion of the place and function of the liberal arts for the sake of tradition and its preservation. Newman points out that the liberal arts are concerned with something beyond the practical: "But [liberal] education is a higher word; it implies an action upon our mental nature, and the formation of a character; it is something individual and permanent, and is commonly spoken of in connexion with religion and virtue."[49] Newman and More were not on a witch hunt against science and mathematics. In fact, Newman studied mathematics himself at Oxford and spoke fondly of the contributions to the knowledge and understanding of the physical world.[50] More's opposition referenced a concern for the aims of society as a world made perfect by administering a calculated and crafted system that sought to level the differences in society for the sake of wider sociability:

"What is the true aim of society? Does justice consist primarily in levelling the distribution of powers and benefits, or in proportioning them to the scale of character and intelligence?"[51] If this was the aim of society, did higher standards of intellectualism become obsolete or did they become demonized for the sake of the growing amount of indifference toward the environment associated with traditional liberal learning? Traditionalists and secular humanists lament the sharp decline in students who major in the humanities for the alternative pre-professional majors. This shift concerns both parties because it conditions new generations toward a lack of skepticism, too much trust in the State (politically/economically), and a decrease in contemplation of the soul. Western civilization, for most of its history, committed to providing a system of education that allowed individuals the opportunity to be freethinkers and active members in society. However, the culture of Western society did not always provide opportunities to all walks of life—one of its more damnable qualities and an accelerant in the move away from tradition.

Conservative intellectuals dealt with different possible paths: endeavor to create an isolated Voltaire-esque El Dorado or remain in modern society (if there was still a place for them). The humanism of the West advocated the aspect of civic duty. It is not enough to exclusively live a life of contemplation and introspection. These are important components, but both secular and Christian humanism incorporate a need for intellectual activity that affects the greater community as well. The polis of Greek civilization incorporated the development of an intellectual culture that valued civic responsibility.[52] Christian humanism, on the other hand, takes its cues from Christ's encouragement to go and do things in order to know God.[53] Politics is concerned with pragmatic policies and the service of constituents. Realistically, legislation of policy slows to a crawl in order to accommodate the multitude of agendas. Conservatism values an imaginative component in the democratic process. According to More, those trained to implement their imagination into all areas of human interactions must mask their level of comprehension: "The college man must forget—or never let it creep into his head—that he's a highbrow. If it does creep in, he is out of politics . . . there is no place in politics for the intellectual aristocrat."[54] The term *aristocracy* carried economic baggage unfit for the modern vision of democracy. Taking his cue from Cicero, Newman proposes the idea that freedom through a liberal education would actually realign the individual's priorities when considering Knowledge versus physical wants: "The great Orator [Cicero] implies, that it is only after our physical and political needs are supplied, and when we are 'free from necessary duties and cares,' that we are in a condition for 'desiring to see, to hear, and to learn.'"[55]

Both Newman and More describe a type of political environment aimed at the freedom of the individual. Even if Christianity is an influential part of the desired conservative culture, none of the authors here call for a theocracy.

The stigma of intellectuals is parallel to the stigma of the religious, namely exclusivity and privilege. Frequently, tradition is tied to eras of religious and political persecution typically at the hands of white European males. The rhetoric is anachronistically associated with the traditional conservative movement as a whole, one not devoted to nineteenth and twentieth-century socioeconomic arguments. The tradition that Newman and others spoke of had its roots in pre-modern culture. This is one of the key issues that More maintains with Newman. More recognizes the humanism and love of antiquity from Newman, but he cautions the medieval mind-set that is suspicious of secular learning, as it borders on the ineffectual and superstitious: "At this day the 'gentleman' is the creation, not of Christianity, but of civilization."[56] More echoes this sentiment by saying: "Indeed, as I have said, the medieval tradition, so far as our schools are concerned, has come to have little vital force, it is so much a mere *cadaver* for the seminar, that in advocating its elimination from the common curriculum, we shall scarcely be doing violence to anything useful or sacred."[57] Despite More's apparent distaste for the medieval, he does recognize that tradition possesses something larger and more important than the contribution of one particular age. Whether or not the most pressing concern is religion and superstition or politics and culture, all of these authors agree on the importance of the university as the training ground for the rediscovery of the permanent principles of tradition.

The humanities embody the potential achievements of civilization and the university is a place of exposure and freedom. The origins of the university are linked to the tenets of tradition and humanism. The university carries with it the responsibility to cultivate young minds in order to develop a natural aristocracy. The more elite the institution, the more responsibility it has to set aside utility and profitability for the sake of knowledge itself. The universities of the Western world were originally founded by the Church, but have become more and more secularized in response to the spirit of the age. Nonetheless, Newman was not completely uncomfortable with the secular studies of the university if they reflected the values of antiquity, but More was still wary of Newman's position on the combination of a strictly Catholic cultural influence on Western society and humanism as this may cause a dilemma of traditions, saying, "If we think of his great struggle as a hesitation between the Anglican and Roman Churches, it was, in a deeper sense, the agony of an intuitive soul caught in the dilemma of two traditions."[58]

Regardless of preference in religious tradition, conservative intellectuals want the university to remain a place dedicated to the cultivation of the key component to traditional conservatism—imagination. For traditionalists, the imagination is essential in the face of a civilization that desires to function based on a formula. If people are only a formula, then a scientific explanation and understanding of them would place them within such a paradigm. Due to the complexity of human nature, these authors point out that a modern conservative must be able to innovate and improvise because of the unexpected tendencies of human nature. A cultivated imagination allows for the opportunity of such things. If the university does not provide an environment of cultivation, it surrenders to the fate of utility. Although their respective causes were different, the outcome remains the same; the fear of this fate was present in both More and Newman who both saw evidence of a growing trend at Oxford, respectively: "[The university] will inevitably degenerate into a school for mechanical apprentices or into a pleasure resort."[59] "Certainly it is specious to contend that nothing is worth pursuing but what is useful; and that life is not long enough to expend upon interesting, or curious, or brilliant trifles."[60] They believe the university has a duty to remain committed to the liberal arts rather than the servile arts. It should not cater to the desires of modern society—one that wishes all to have the same level of comprehension as opposed to varying levels or even the existence of an intellectual aristocracy.

More and Newman recognize the natural tendency of individuals to seek out ways in which to order their minds. Traditionalists relied on the liberal arts to provide opportunities to exercise the mind, as well as prompt good "habits of mind." It is difficult to understand and even more difficult to convey that the formation of the mind is more important than the specific knowledge that fills it. According to Newman, cultivation allows the individual to dialogue and work through the "intellectual matters" accessed through good habits.[61] The pure humanist recognizes the natural relationship between tradition and the mind's desire for nourishment and order. More claims, "It is the classic tradition carried in a mind fitted by nature and by long training to live in the clear air of the antique world."[62] More and Newman each saw the benefits to the unique characteristics of the ancient and medieval worlds because of their tendency to submit to authorities outside of the self.

"Habits of the mind" conjure feelings of submission. The spirit of the Modern Age was not one that promoted the idea of submission to an "other," especially in the sense through which Christianity claims its authority originated in the transcendent. Newman and others recognize certain faults within the history of the Catholic Church, but believe that the Church does more good than harm.[63] The resistance of the Modern Age to religious principles and authority bolsters the relevance of Babbitt and More's ideas of reform. Instead of harping on religious topics, they focus primarily on the idea of secular virtues. Ironically, Newman and the others embraced similar ideas, yet maintained their dedication to the Church. An intellectual aristocracy, or upper echelon, is formed through discipline and cultivation, not in the sense of power or money, but by the superiority of the habitual mind.[64] Newman believes an elevation brought about by the intellect allows an individual to embrace the capabilities of humanity while maintaining a level of discipline: "Here I think is the important aid which intellectual cultivation furnishes to us in rescuing the victims of passion and self-will."[65] Such discipline of the passions and will is viewed as "condescension" by the modern world rather than an act of humility. To the traditionalist, submission and discipline to a standard outside of oneself are acts of humility and recognition because the standards are set by something outside of the self. The university originated as a place where these habits could be taught, cultivated, challenged, and grown in order to create a natural aristocracy of free and virtuous thinkers. The respective insights of Newman and More exhibit their commitment to the cultivation of traditional habits of mind: "This is true humility, to feel and behave as if we were low; not, to cherish a notion of our importance, while we affect a low position."[66] "[W]e forget that it is not ours to determine the fundamental relation of things, or to define justice, but to make rules of action in accordance with the decrees, immutable so far as we can see, of a superior power."[67] The university is an environment that houses numerous disciplines and perspectives. By nature, it asks heterogeneous thought to dialogue in hopes of better understanding humanity and the natural world. If the university becomes an employment agency or vocational school it loses its original purpose. These traditionalists see the university as one of the few salvageable components of Western civilization because it was the most adept at providing the platform for multiple theories to interact with one another in a humanistic sense.

Christopher Dawson, Russell Kirk, Irving Babbitt, Hilaire Belloc, Paul Elmer More, and John Henry Newman were not carbon copies of one another. They each had individual tastes and ideas that characterized their unique qualities. Each author practiced this humility differently whether through Catholicism, Protestantism, or Agnosticism. Nonetheless their commitment to humanism never waned. The uniqueness of the Western world prompted many to defend its principles.[68] First, in its connection to the religion of Christianity, and after, its ability to undergo metamorphic changes within its systems of discourse and values as a culture. Twentieth-century conservatives held that the doctrines of tradition and conservatism aid progress through discernment and recognition of the necessary principles inherent in what it means to be human.

They basked in the possibilities created by the light of Christian humanism. They shared an affinity for the discovery of what it means to be human through the active and contemplative life. The crisis of Western civilization is not merely apathy in the classroom or the celebration of achievement at the expense of complex ideas. They felt the crisis affects the core of what it means to be human. For much of its history, the Western world was characterized by the Christian Church. It is within the last few hundred years that the Church's voice was consciously dimmed from public forum for the sake of secular discourse toward a universal humanitarianism. Progress is not the enemy of the likes of Dawson and Kirk. They saw the enemy as the thoughtless secularization of the definition of human beings. This is not to say that secular humanism does not have a place in the definition of humanity, but it is perceived as incomplete. The intent to preserve the conviction that humanity cannot possess a complete definition of itself without the transcendent truth found in Christianity characterizes the discourse of Christian humanism. This is not the case for all conservatives, for example the New Humanists, but they still maintain a foundational value in the tradition of Western civilization. Conservatives often draw on both Belloc and Babbitt in the diagnosis of modernity and prescription of solutions. Both the Church and the university are traditional characteristics of Western culture. The separation of these two spheres of influence surely has its benefits, but traditionalists wished to question whether or not benefits outweighed the consequences. Each of these authors, in their recognition of common problems and the state of the Modern Age, see to it that more than one solution is presented to solve the crisis of Western civilization.

The similar goals and rhetoric of these authors provide evidence for the connection between multiple perspectives toward the goal of reconciliation. The ability of discernment originates from a commitment to humane learning. Habits of the mind are formed through a discourse with the great ideas and great minds of Western history. A four-year degree is not the completion of a cultivated mind. The undergraduate degree is in place to introduce, inspire, and provide students with a skill set worthy of maintaining learned habits for a lifetime. Babbitt says: "The ambition of the true college teacher is not to 'distribute' knowledge to his students, not 'to lodge it with them,' as Montaigne says, 'but to marry it to them and make it part of their very minds and souls.'"[69] This is the definition of what Newman referred to as the advantages of the possession of Knowledge for the sake of itself: "Knowledge, as one of the principal of these, is valuable for what its very presence in us does for us after the manner of a habit, even though it be turned to no further account, nor subserve any direct end."[70] Traditionalists argued that humanism was the best tool for understanding humanity, and they saw Christian humanism as the most complete because of its recognition of Christianity's unique understanding of the Incarnation and how it solely affected humanity. According to conservatism, there are certain insights into humanity that the West internalizes that should not be trifled with, and the institutions responsible for the promotion of these insights should not be abandoned. Despite their individualism, they were bound by service to something higher than themselves, which gave them the strength to swim against the current of modernity. Their goal was the rediscovery of the permanent concepts of Western tradition; their greatest asset was humane learning found in the education possible at the university level; and their belief in the higher things provided a life raft of hope amid the shifting tides of the Modern Age.

NOTES

1. Pieper, *Tradition*, p. 35.
2. R. William Franklin and Joseph M. Shaw, *The Case for Christian Humanism* (Grand Rapids: Eerdmans, 1991), p. 24.
3. Zimmerman, p. 83–84.
4. Benjamin G. Lockerd, "Beyond Politics: T.S Eliot and Christopher Dawson on Religion and Culture," eds. Benjamin G. Lockerd and Anderson D. Araujo, *T.S. Eliot and Christian Tradition* (Plymouth, UK: Rowman & Littlefield, 2014), p. 221.
5. Babbitt resisted any dogmatic religion, while Belloc was a staunch Catholic. Likewise, More eventually converted to an unorthodox form of Christianity, while Newman died a Catholic Cardinal.
6. For further reading see Peter Lawler, "Libertarians vs. Liberal Learning," *Modern Age* 56, no. 1 (Winter 2014), pp. 7–17.
7. Christopher Dawson, *The Crisis of Western Education* (Washington, D.C.: Catholic University Press, 1961), p. 71.
8. For discussions on the different social, political, and economic arenas that make reference to tradition and "old-fashioned" thinking, see: "History in a Democratic Age" in John Lukacs, *Historical Consciousness:* 50–97; "Embracing Diversity: Shopping in the Spiritual Marketplace" in Robert Wuthnow, *America and the Challenges of Religious Diversity* (Princeton: Princeton University Press, 2005): 106–29. Kirk, "The Idea of Conservatism" in *The Essential Russell Kirk*, pp. 4–49.
9. Russell Kirk, *Prospects for Conservatives: A Compass for Rediscovering the Permanent Things* (Houston: Imaginative Conservative Books, 2013), p. 215.
10. *Ibid.*, p. 217.
11. Dawson, *The Crisis of Western Education*, p. 40.
12. See Ira O. Wade, *The Intellectual Origins of the French Enlightenment* (Princeton: Princeton University Press, 1971), pp. 169–205.
13. Denis Diderot and Jean d'Alembert, editors of *L'Encyclopédie: Dictionnaire raisonée des sciences, des arts et de métiers* (1751–1772).
14. Dawson, *The Crisis of Western Education*, p. 42.
15. Kirk, *Prospects for Conservatives*, p. 20.
16. Kirk, *Prospects for Conservatives*, p. 49; Dawson, *The Crisis of Western Education*, p. 64.
17. Dawson, *The Crisis of Western Education*, p. 65.
18. Dawson, *The Crisis of Western Education*, p. 135; Kirk, *Prospects for Conservatives*, p. 19.
19. Dawson, *The Crisis of Western Education*, p. 43.
20. Kirk, *Prospects for Conservatives*, p. 106.
21. Dawson, *The Crisis of Western Education*, p. 78.
22. *Ibid.*, p. 115.
23. Kirk, *Prospects for Conservatives*, pp. 44–45.
24. Garrett Ward Sheldon, "Natural Rights," *Encyclopedia of Political Thought* (New York: Facts on File, Inc., 2001), pp. 117–18.
25. Russell Kirk, "Humane Learning in the Age of the Computer," p. 1. Reprinted with permission from Russell Kirk, "Humane Learning in the Age of the Computer" in *The Wise Men Know What Wicked Things are Written on the Sky* (Washington, D.C.: Regnery Gateway, 1987), pp. 90–100.
26. *Ibid.*, p. 4.
27. Nussbaum, *Not for Profit*, p. 85.
28. *Ibid.*, p. 122.
29. Hilaire Belloc, *The Crisis of Civilization* (Rockford: Tan Publishers, 1992), pp. 77 and 79, respectively.
30. C. Creighton Mandell and Edwards Shanks, *Hilaire Belloc: A Man and His Work* (London: Metheun & Co., LTD., 1916), p. 81.
31. *Ibid.*, p. 64.

32. *Ibid.*, p. 11.
33. Irving Babbitt, *Literature and the American College* (Washington, D.C.: National Humanities Institute, 1986), pp. 74–75.
34. *Ibid.*, p. 111.
35. *Ibid.*, p. 99 and 103, respectively.
36. *Ibid.*, p. 77.
37. *Ibid.*, p. 83.
38. *Ibid.*, p. 10.
39. *Ibid.*, p. 119.
40. Russell Kirk, "A Conservative Purpose to a Liberal Education," *The Imaginative Conservative*, March 12, 2012. http://www.theimaginativeconservative.org/2012/03/conservative-purpose-of-liberal.html.
41. Claes Ryn, "Irving Babbitt and Philosophical Reason," *The Imaginative Conservative*, September 14, 2014. http://www.theimaginativeconservative.org/2014/09/irving-babbitt-philosophical-reason.html.
42. Belloc, *Crisis*, p. 88.
43. Babbitt, p. 104.
44. See Nicole Mellow, *The State of Disunion: Reasons for Modern American Partisanship* (Baltimore: The Johns Hopkins University Press, 2008).
45. Kirk, *Prospects*, p. 15.
46. *The Christ of the New Testament* (1924), *Christ the Word* (1927), and *The Catholic Faith* (1931).
47. Ian Ker, *John Henry Newman: A Biography* (Oxford: Oxford University Press, 1988), pp. 209–10.
48. John Henry Newman, *The Idea of a University* (Notre Dame: University of Notre Dame Press, 1982), p. 207.
49. *Ibid.*, p. 86.
50. See Ian Ker, "Newman's Idea of the University and Its Relevance for the 21st Century," *Australian eJournal of Theology* 18.1 (April 2011): 19–31.
51. Paul Elmer More, *Aristocracy and Justice: Shelburne Essays, Ninth Series* (New York: Houghton Mifflin, 1915), pp, 30–31.
52. Newman, p. 199.
53. Thomas Howard and J. I. Packer, *Christianity: The True Humanism* (Vancouver: Regent College Publishing, 1999), p. 218.
54. More, pp. 45 and 53, respectively.
55. Newman, p. 79.
56. *Ibid.*, p. 154
57. More, p. 88 and 86, respectively.
58. *Ibid.*, p. 82.
59. *Ibid.*, p. 45
60. Newman, p. 122.
61. *Ibid.*, p. 378.
62. More, p. 83.
63. See John Henry Newman, "History of my Religious Opinions from 1833–1839" in *Apologia Pro Vita Sua*, ed. Ian Ker (New York: Penguin Books, 1994).
64. See Edward Short, "The Certainty of Vocation: Newman and the Froudes" in *Newman and His Contemporaries* (New York: T&T Clark International, 2011).
65. Newman, p. 141.
66. *Ibid.*, p. 156
67. More, p. 136.
68. For further suggested reading see Ricardo Duchesne, *The Uniqueness of the Western World* (Boston: Brill Publishers, 2011).
69. Babbitt, p. 125.
70. Newman, p. 78.

Chapter Seven

Not All Books Are Created Equal

Amid the different descriptions and perspectives surrounding the twentieth century, a constant remained—the desire for knowledge. Whether or not the 1900s poisoned Western society is debated at a number of different levels. Regardless of the outcome, Western society never abandoned the pursuit of higher learning, but merely augmented it. Traditionalists were unified in their pursuit of a life of the mind; the university, classical liberal learning, and the *Great Books* were all part of the pursuit. This chapter may feel like a departure from our discussion, but it provides an insight into the medium used to articulate tradition. It is full of esoteric ideas, and yet examines the imaginative discourse utilized by traditionalists to serve their interests of preservation and re-enchantment. The authors throughout these chapters were convinced of tradition's place in the canon of Western thought. They believed certain ideas needed to be preserved alongside the current discussions of their respective ages. Chesterton, Pieper, the New Humanists, the Inklings et al., possessed various backgrounds and faiths, but believed the task to be timeless, namely, the reconciliation, or even the fusion, of the sacred and the secular in all times and places.[1] It is through the liberal arts they expressed themselves as a humanizing body of disciplines both in the traditional universities and the so-called *Great Books* that populated their syllabi. They worked tirelessly to deliver a compelling answer to the popularity of the modern scientific age.

In the face of all that transpired in the twentieth century, traditionalists went about the preservation of permanent ideas integral to their definition of humanity. They did more than just revolt against modernity, and accuse moderns of effecting dehumanization and secularization. They wished to prevent, through the translation and preservation of tradition, the destruction of the past, so that it could convey timeless pursuits, for example a life of the mind. A life of the mind is not something defined by vocation or the mere accumulation of knowledge. It is focused on the idea that there is an ongoing conversation between the ages on the topic of humanity's comprehension of both the material and immaterial realities of the universe. There existed obvious additions and subtractions to this idea, but traditionalists made an effort to preserve the worthwhile components, while flawed by their own age in some ways and shaped in virtue by others. Their commitment—unpopular as it was—to the idea that not all books are created equal generated a platform in support of the tenets of tradition. At times, they found camaraderie with one another and their common ground was the humanities and classical liberal learning represented through the *Great Books*. In an effort to tie these individuals together, one finds their love of learning, the humanities, the significance of the past, and tradition as the foremost adhesives. In reading the numerous works by the individuals discussed here, it is evident that the liberal arts are the heart behind their uphill battles—one that can see its lifeblood in the practice of leisure, the defense of the liberal arts, and the application of a traditional mind.

Twentieth-century traditional intellectuals saw firsthand the shifting value from a liberal education to a more scientific education. Patrick Deneen attributes the decline of the liberal arts to modern ideologies that eventually extended to the present day through postmodern reactions:

> When conservative critics of our universities nowadays lament the decline of liberal education, they usually decry its replacement by a left-leaning politicized agenda. But the deeper truth is that liberal education has been more fundamentally displaced by scientific education buttressed by the demands of global competition. While conservatives might wish to apportion blame to those increasingly irrelevant faculty whose postmodernism has become a form of stale institutional orthodoxy, the truth is that the rise of this sort of faculty was a response to conditions that were already making liberal education irrelevant, a self-destructive effort to make the humanities "up to date." These purported radicals—mostly bourgeois former children of the 1960s—were not agents of liberation, but rather symptoms of the neglect of the liberal arts in a dawning new age of science reinforced by global competition.[2]

Many progressives associated liberal arts education with the ways of the past. Whether by accident or intentionally, the defense of tradition paralleled the defense of the liberal arts. Traditionalists believed that value toward democracy, free thought, and the humane still remained in a solid classical education, rather than one solely based on a knowledge of utility. If education only focused on the utility of "preparing students for life," then education would refocus itself on the presumptions that, as Jacques Barzun puts it, "make dating and 'driver education' part of the curriculum in place of Latin and trigonometry, because 'preparing for life' means giving information that is of everyday use [and] fraught with social consequence."[3] With all of the new empirical information at hand, is there still value and benefit in some of the more immaterial or esoteric aspects of the liberal arts? Traditionalists certainly thought so.

LEISURE

Two of Josef Pieper's works, *In Tune with the World: A Theory of Festivity* (1963) and *Leisure: The Basis of Culture* (1947), address the idea that something is missing in the modern mind-set. For Pieper, the modern individual lost a valuable aspect of being human: "But if celebration is the core of leisure, than leisure can only be made possible and justifiable on the same basis as the celebration of a festival."[4] The loss of leisure is related to the redefinition and the limits of the modern "worker" (*artes serviles*); "(useful or utilitarian) . . . servile work is by nature dependent on something else. It cannot be thought of apart from its purpose; a deep-seated lack of calm which makes leisure impossible."[5] Traditionalists' hope in Western society rests on the idea that the liberal studies are distinct because they are immeasurable pursuits dependent on nothing else, thus embodying the definition of leisure. The modern definition for such pursuits is a "waste of time" because they do not reflect the new basis for Western civilization, namely empirical knowledge.[6] Kronman echoes this sentiment when he describes the historical figures of Socrates and Jesus and their ability to question the meaning of life consistently: "We are drawn to them for this reason, quite apart from the substance of their teachings. We are fascinated by their ability to pursue the question of life's meaning with such unflagging seriousness, and divided between our admiration for them and our wonder at their inhuman remoteness (a source both of pathos and humor)."[7]

In Lewis's eyes, leisure is the desired end, not vocation: "Vocational training, on the other hand, prepares the pupil not for leisure, but for work; it aims at making not a good man but a good banker, a good electrician, a good scavenger, or a good surgeon. You see at once that education is essentially for freemen and vocational training for slaves."[8] Leisure does not mean rest, relaxation, or recreation, but is seen as a time devoted to study and thought—a welcome relief from life's mandatory activities. Traditionalists rely heavily on the heritage and tradition of Western thought as a guide to a contemplative life. Seeking a life of the mind is their means to experience and internalize leisure. The liberal arts can bring the pupil in tune with the quiet inwardness, away from industrialized busyness, so it may serve as a silent and divine reflection. Using Pieper's definition of "festival," the liberal arts embody festivity because "[t]he festival is the origin of leisure, and the inward and ever-present meaning of leisure. And because leisure is thus by its nature a celebration, it is more than effortless; it is the direct opposite of effort."[9]

Pieper challenges those who wish to find leisure and festivity again with the fact that it is not enough to return to "tradition" or "humanism."[10] The one weakness of all study is that it may be simultaneously the best course for tradition and humanism, and yet, "it cannot get to the root of leisure due to the fact that leisure is not susceptible to the human will . . . it cannot be sought voluntarily as a means to an end."[11] Pieper's criticism claims modernity has gone to great lengths to destroy festivity and bring forth the totalitarian state of the worker—especially to the intellectual activity of liberal studies.[12] Work that is practical and characteristically "utilitarian" conveys little concern with interaction of the higher things. The traditionalists' sense of joy of what it is to be human is not defined by labor, but by leisure. Automation provides opportunities for convenience and "less" work. However, the modern scientific age also promotes the wonders of technology to a point where leisure time is no longer a contemplative period of evaluation and reflection, but an absence of busyness and activity. It would seem that Western society, when given the chance, became afraid of stillness and even more fearful of boredom (*ennui*). Traditionalists saw this as a symptom of an unreflective age or as American historian George McCartney suggests through his critique of German historian Oswald Spengler (1880–1936): "Working in the tradition that passes from Kant through Nietzsche, he naturally assumes a culture that is best understood in terms of its own special epistemology. Whether in the arts or sciences, a culture's thought reflects the largely unconscious assumptions of its peculiar worldview."[13] Modernity's new view of festivity marks a sense of loss from the traditional perspective. For Pieper, the redemption is in the fact that leisure and festivity originate in the transcendent and come from outside of the self when one participates in divine worship.[14] These ideas of leisure and festivity, "even if dimmed" are not "without gods."[15] Divine worship may be hidden and blurred by artificial festivity, but the veil of indifference is torn by liberal studies. An acute reaction to issues such as injustice is one of many ideas carried on through the ages by liberal studies in order to conserve a traditional vision of leisure and festivity—"the origin of the arts in worship, and of leisure derived from its celebration, is given in the form of a magnificent mythical image: man attains his true form and his upright attitude in festive companionship with the gods."[16] Hence the subject matter of many traditionalists and at times non-traditionalists who still see value in the West's contribution.

The pursuit of the higher things is navigated through the liberal arts, but it also can preserve a particular relationship between creation and Creator. The relationship is grounded in the examples of what modernity constituted as wasted time, the higher things, and the notion of leisure and festivity. One of the strengths of the liberal arts is that they are not focused merely on the here and now, but deal with the concept of truth as it exists in the past, present, and future. Tradition recognizes this throughout the process of liberal learning, while modern thought and education often categorize this course as too ethnocentric. Kronman points out one of the paradoxical issues in looking to the humanities and liberal arts lies within the modern interpretation of the humanities: "Only in the humanities has the anti-Western animus which these judgments reflect been translated into educational practice, further degrading their authority by undermining values central to the integrity and purpose of the humanities themselves."[17] No matter the means, C. S. Lewis intimated that the hope (quite possibly the reality) is that sacred and secular will eventually have to deal with the same end:

> They must have, or their book (being purely practical in intention) is written to no purpose. And this end must have real value in their eyes. To abstain from calling it good and to use, instead, such predicates as "necessary" or "progressive" or "efficient" would be a subterfuge ... in the last resort they would have to admit that some state of affairs was in their opinion good for its own sake. And this time they could not maintain that "good" simply described their own emotion about it.[18]

In some cases, the trends of modern thought affected higher institutions of learning to the point of altering the purpose of a college degree into utility and profitability—a tradeable commodity in the new marketplace.

The abandonment of knowledge for its own sake is a significant separation from one of the original (traditional) intentions of the university. As the academy became more and more secularized and progressive, it departed from John Henry Newman's definition of liberal learning: "I am asked what is the end of University Education, and of the Liberal or Philosophical Knowledge.... Knowledge is capable of being its own end. Such is the constitution of the human mind, that any kind of knowledge is capable of being its own end."[19] This does not vilify vocational training or secularization, but it does create a distinction between what labors are useful and what are liberating. Nussbaum asks, "Has the market model become the fundamental and defining identity of higher education?"[20] One of the tenets of modernity is the denial of the higher things which characterized human understanding for most of Western history. The replacement was seen by its discontents as an ethos of meaninglessness and pessimism for the sake of empirical description which manifests itself in utility.

Renaissance humanist Leon Battista Alberti (1404–1472) claimed there was another option: "What they are taught by good books is modesty, magnanimity, virtue, and wisdom."[21] Catholic priest and philosopher James V. Schall (1928–2019) echoes this sentiment when he points out that one has to be willing to trust the intentions of the traditional liberal arts and rest in the idea that "something is true" beyond description.[22] A historical tradition exists where there is a resonating agreement that the liberal arts provide the opportunity for human beings to restore their gift of sight for its purpose. The trait of permanence is in opposition to nineteenth and twentieth-century ideologies because of its association with tradition. For most traditionalists, humanity's purpose was to see the glory of God. This is not always the conscious end of humanism as evidenced by the secular humanists included in this discussion, but hope in reconciliation asks if it would not be avoided completely. The paradox is a difficult one to maneuver. Kronman states: "Only in the humanities has the politically inspired belief in the equality of Western and non-Western cultures been adopted as a pedagogical principle and made the basis for a range of educational judgments, including the hiring of faculty and the design of courses and curricula."[23] There are those in the academy who are convinced that religion and classical virtue distort the dialogue meant to be had in the university setting. The contingent of Oxford dons, who began the movement in Lewis's day, enjoyed the popularity of modernity's supreme value of change behind the leadership of British philosopher T. D. ("Harry") Weldon, making the Christian camp just another constituent, rather than the abundant norm.[24] A present-day example, Peter Conn, professor of English at the University of Pennsylvania, has called for the removal of accreditation of "religious colleges." For Conn, the contradiction of a religious institution and academic higher learning is obvious: [T]hey "systematically undermine the most fundamental purposes of higher education. . . . Skeptical and unfettered inquiry is the hallmark of American teaching and research. However, such inquiry cannot flourish—in many cases, cannot even survive—inside institutions that erect religious tests for truth. The contradiction is obvious."[25]

There are those who would disagree with Professor Conn. A 2013 Convocation speech given by the Templeton Honors College Dean, at Eastern University, was dedicated to promoting a life of the mind. Professor Jonathan Yonan's words articulate the hope traditionalists place in the higher things; the hope given by classical liberal learning; the hope that men and women can achieve such heights:

> The university has always kept a place for the useless things, though less so in recent years—for the arts, literature, philosophy, the sciences (especially when we study them just to behold the wonder of this world), for dead and dying languages and dead people, for pure (and not just applied) mathematics. . . . This is the kind of sight which is proper and natural in the presence of God's good creation, which is full of his glory—that we can't see enough. Not that the eye flits from one object to another, distracted again and again, but that the eye must look, it almost seems, endlessly into each part of what God has done.[26]

These are the sentiments of a Christian university. Be that as it may, it does not eliminate the benefits for those who do not adhere to the Christian tradition. The juxtaposition of Conn and Yonan give credence to efforts of traditionalists speaking to the present in Professor Yonan despite popular sentiments of modernity in Professor Conn. The history of the relationship between Christianity and liberal learning is one of record through Christian humanism. Nonetheless, the *Great Books* tradition challenges readers to engage both sides of the discussion within the proper context and idiom of its authors.

The modern mode of thinking demands evidence and application of knowledge, and traditionalists respond to empirical inquiry, but without abandoning the lifeblood of the liberal arts argument. A main focus of the liberal arts, eloquence, is derived from the core fundamentals of the trivium.[27] In order to employ an eloquent defense, one must provide working definitions that bring context and substance to the more argumentative and persuasive aspects of the debate. Traditionalists were concerned that modern thought was often focused on individual perspectives and applications as a form of validation—leading to a more subjective origin of truth and cultural relativism. They used the liberal arts to challenge the individual to take care of one's own intellect as well as align oneself to something greater or as St. Thomas Aquinas and James Boswell state respectively: "The proper operation of man as man is to understand."[28] "Every man is to take care of his own wisdom."[29]

A more traditional liberal arts education focuses on the ability to recognize the necessity of discernment and the responsibility of the individual to yearn for knowledge and wisdom. Often the complaint about the liberal arts is its inaccessibility or lack of universality. These characteristics do not fit with the modern effort toward a "wider success" in learning. Barzun, reticent to agree with modern education, saw it as a step back: "The American atmosphere requires that everybody present shall participate, have a good time, share the good things, and help maintain the universal good fellowship."[30] To enter into a life of the mind is to realize Alberti's idea that "the study of books is not the way to personal advantage. . . . For the life men of learning live is necessarily hard and harsh . . . there is not freedom from striving at any age."[31] The Inklings, especially, saw themselves as translators and educators who needed to promote a broader syllabus. A liberal arts education has distinct characteristics which survived from as early as the classical Greeks.

DEFINING A TRADITIONAL LIBERAL ARTS EDUCATION

In keeping with liberal learning, traditionalists are also concerned with passing on the ideas of the past. They felt their modes of learning suit the desire to teach and live a life of the mind. Much like the philosophers in Plato's cave, it is the responsibility of those who understand how to live a life of the mind to instruct others onto the same path; or as Jeffrey Davis and Philip Ryken put it, "to baptize the imagination and intellect."[32] It is not as simple as teachers instructing students, but there is a mind-set and methodology that provides structure for such an endeavor. The characteristics needed for going about this process, and an example of those who stand as champions for said process, will aid the pursuant to define what it means to be an educator in the life of the mind.

Educators and students alike share some of the same characteristics allowing one to make this a lifelong journey in multiple capacities. It is not the sole responsibility of the educator to produce the desire to learn. Instead, students should approach the subject matter with "an intense desire to know the truth of things 'with gusto,'" that is indicative of an intellectual curiosity that Augustine says, "yearns for an immortality of wisdom."[33] A structure or methodology can be implemented to guide a student, but ultimately the desire must be adopted and expressed by individual wills. Students and educators heed the warning of vexation and exhaustion regarding the life of the mind's pursuit of wisdom. It is a path fraught with those who seem blissfully ignorant while the student and educator struggle with the deepest of questions (such as the "why behind the what").[34] As with Voltaire's Good Brahman, those in pursuit of the life of the mind cannot be enticed by simplistic facades of happiness, because they respond to a deeper calling—a tool fashioned by those discontented with their contemporary age. The end of this pursuit is not one of gold or accolades, but of the intangible joy of learning felt by both educator and student. This pursuit is one that Davis and Ryken claim promotes an "education that transmits and reflects on the highest things."[35]

These pursuits are distinctly part of a traditional liberal arts education centered on the *Great Books* and its authors. Because the great thinkers are few and far between, it is necessary to keep in mind that one lifetime is inadequate to plumb the depths of even one of these thinkers, let alone all of them.[36] The compendium of Western thought created lists of works read and taught by traditionalists. Twentieth-century traditionalists viewed the approach as one of humility and a healthy skepticism born from the ideals of the likes of Socrates and Montaigne: "the only thing I know is that I know nothing" and "*Que sais je?*" (What do I know?). Contra the traditionalists' desire for humility, the twentieth-century scientism desired mastery under the presumption that all indeed could be known. Humility grants to its pursuers the wisdom to withstand the vexation as well as come to terms with the fact that even though there is nothing new under the sun, there is still a lifetime of learning to be had by anyone who is willing to brave the rigors of a life of the mind.

The most effective method toward the liberal arts as a vocation is one that recognizes the authority of the *Great Books* and thinkers from Socrates to Dante and beyond. It allowed traditionalists to reconcile the sacred and the secular due to the nature of conversation within the Western canon. For instance, Voltaire is one of the most biting, sarcastic forefathers of modernity, but he embodies the life of the mind in many ways. The tension is that Voltaire despairs tradition in favor of progress and was a stark Deist. He does, however, embody a life of the mind in his intellectual pursuits. The misconception that traditionalists only value conservative Christian authors is unfortunate. Instead, they thought *Great Books* curricula in universities and colleges reflected the desire to maintain traditional liberal studies in the face of positivist specialization—a worthy syllabus for the likes of Tolkien and Lewis. The "progress" of the West, since the Scientific Revolution, stunted and in some cases halted the process of a classical liberal arts education. A key factor involves the push for modernity to focus on an individualization that disregarded the authority of books, thinkers, and institutions representative of traditional status quo. Why should anyone seek the truth or read these works if they believe that there is nothing to be found or gained by doing so? David Lyle Jeffrey perceives modernity's desire to question and interrogate any source that claims authority with the skeptical intent "concerning in part the possibility of reliable (i.e., verifiable) answers to the other questions."[37] Those seeking a life of the mind do not thoughtlessly berate the authority of the *Great Books* and thinkers of Western tradition; instead they measure all that they have to offer with discernment against the realities of their own age. Reliability and issues of authority largely cloud the judgment surrounding the *Great Books*; something that Robert Woods is keenly aware of:

> Not all the enemies of liberal learning are managers of middle-class America. There are those in the academy, who have been "educated" in modern day "wisdom" to have a posture of disdain toward the Great Tradition. In fact, much of the attack begins there. We should recognize these enemies of the permanent things as anti-traditionalists. I once had an exchange with an individual who claimed there was no great tradition or Western intellectual heritage. I assured him that the Great Tradition is as real as Narnia and my birth city of Rochester, NY. All real in different ways, but real, nonetheless. These are all places we can inhabit and that, in turn, inhabit us. Unfortunately, there are those who would state that since they have never been to Rochester or Narnia they do not exist. This is modern narcissistic folly.[38]

As Woods points out, the disdain for the "Great Tradition" does not emanate from one camp or another, but has a number of skeptics who wish to see it removed from both cultural and academic circles.

During a time when modern modes of thought dominated universities worldwide, the Inklings and others strove to postpone the slow death of the vocation of the liberal arts.[39] Chesterton thought modern society had created a "new man, meaning a man with none of the old illusions about human beings, society, or God."[40] The new growth stemmed from Western society's redefinition of education and knowledge into matters of utility and possession or knowledge as a commodity to compete in the ever-changing world of industry and technology. Those who recognized the success of modernity's influence remained in partial opposition. C. S. Lewis and G. K. Chesterton held to the traditional modes of defining education through the liberal arts: "Education is tradition. . . . It is quaint that people talk of separating dogma from education. Dogma is actually the only thing that cannot be separated from education. It is education. A teacher who is not dogmatic is simply a teacher who is not teaching."[41] Chesterton did not associate dogma with a lack of freedom, as was the contention of his progressive contemporaries. Rather, he saw the freedom of humanity reflected in the divine will and the will of humanity enslaved to itself through appetites and passions.[42] For Lewis, it was one simple principle: "*liberal* comes from the Latin, *liber*, and means free."[43] Freedom shares a similar root for the word "book" (*liber, libri*) and therefore this connection transforms the student from "an unregenerate little bundle of appetites" into "the good man and the good citizen."[44] They saw a relevant value in the necessity of a liberal arts education amid the tide of change. They felt modernity did not value imagination or intellectual curiosity unless there was a direct correlation to utility, which by nature is in opposition to a traditional liberal arts education. Universities began to resemble employment agencies in the modern world, and by extension students diluted the atmosphere primed for the ability to teach successfully. Friction ensued in defining education; is it something that directly corresponds to utility or is it a foundation for a lifelong vocation? Modernity appeared to choose the former. However, there were those invested in the life of the mind who saw the forest for the trees and chose the long and arduous road of the latter while recognizing the growing trend set forth by modern perspectives: "Too often ours is an insipid education consisting of details about supposedly humane, though modestly lethal, legislation, about technological change confused with wisps of environmentalist madness—nothing to move souls, no real causes, no real romance."[45]

Donald Kagan and James Schall recognize that this reevaluation brought about distinct definitions as to what is a traditional liberal education versus the redefined modern liberal education:

> [Liberal education] has included the ideas 1) that knowledge is its own purpose, an end in itself, that it is good to know, 2) that liberty means having the virtues whereby we can rule ourselves, 3) that knowledge includes something

useful, some worthy way of making one's way in the world, and 4) that this liberal learning has a political component, the ideal of living in a free society, of participating in ruling and being ruled.[46]

"Finally, modern educators were more interested in what was not yet known. The 'scientific method' stressed not what was revealed or what was previously learned or even what was useful for the city, but 'new things'. . .with its implication of 'progress.'"[47] A traditional liberal education adheres to the ideas set forth by those who founded the heritage of Western thought. The modern version of this is altered to better reflect, not the needs of the modern West, but the progressive turn. Through this metamorphosis, notions of utility trump ideas regarding the joy of learning.

The traditional liberal arts are lifelong endeavors that pursue freedom of the mind for the sake of knowledge in and of itself—quite fitting for immaterial and metaphysical paradigms. When the individual benefits, the hope is that the community at large benefits as well. If these pursuits are not valued, Schall says intelligence and imagination are shackled and enslaved to the drudgery of purposeless labor—they are made servile rather than liberating.[48] Although she disagrees with his assessment of classical learning, Nussbaum echoes Schall's concern about servile and passive pedagogy.[49] The discourse of a liberal arts education provides an individual with the tools to examine the self which lead to a better understanding of others as well as the universe and, if desired, God. Concepts of justice, freedom, and virtue are but a few of the ideas that elude human beings. These are concepts that often seem beyond humanity, and therefore the drive of a traditional education is to bring men and women closer to the definition of these complex ideas—something not found in the lab. The systematic understanding implemented by traditional modes of thinking guides humanity in the attempt to seek truth in the explanation of self as well as understand the arguments against the "truth of things."[50] This is by no means a measurable or tangible result—one of many difficulties. The structures of study of the liberal arts have the tendency to conflict with the modern conceptions of education. As Weaver puts it: "It is in this reliance upon science and scientism that modern education shows its tendency to hitch itself to cultural fashion, as Gnosticism showed its disposition to adjust Christianity to a contemporary sophistical world view."[51] Traditionalists maintained a hierarchy of knowledge. For example, Cicero found that wisdom and eloquence went hand in hand. The art of eloquent speaking and writing is a necessary focus of a liberal education: "And indeed in my opinion, no man can be an orator complete in all pints of merit, who has not attained a knowledge of all important subjects and arts."[52] The recognition of this hierarchy allows for the structure to pursue things not simply for the sake of being new but because they are worthy of study.

A traditional liberal education correlates to the individual's acceptance of a definition that involves activity and contemplation. The combination of these ideas becomes not merely a discourse of study, but a lifestyle of thought and focused activity instead. Traditionalists want to make sure that the nature of this lifestyle is one that affects the individual in all facets of being rather than in a compartmentalized model beholden to occupation, education, and government as separate influences of identity. The modern mind-set values a divided system of knowing because pursuits of utility find difficulty in crossing defined boundaries. They do serve the designated uses of said knowledge, but traditionalists were in search of a more interdisciplinary relationship. Traditional liberal arts answer with the view of education as an interdisciplinary journey through all facets of life. Jeffrey explains it as a higher code, claiming "the study of the humanities [as] something almost sacramental."[53]

For traditionalists, the sacred seeks virtue and wisdom above all else.[54] For the great minds, whose ideas cultivate these concepts, there is a level of morality and ethics inherent within the pursuit, structure, and value of the higher things. Traditionalists feared a drastic shift in spirit and perspective due to the advancements in Western civilization. Many were convinced it may fall prey to what Richard Gamble sees as "the folly of being distracted by the *how* of the universe to the exclusion of the *why*."[55] The natural curiosity of human nature leaves the individual to his or her own devices, and therefore virtue intertwined with knowledge often encourages healthy attitudes of wonder and humility. Twentieth-century traditionalists foresaw the trajectory of the West drastically shifting from an ethos that once valued the immaterial to one that saw no use for anything beyond material reality. The modern systems were often uncomfortable with the definition of ideas beyond human comprehension, and categorized them as either superstition or lacking in utility.[56] An argument can be made that modernity's recasting of Western civilization was constructed as a secular substitute for Christianity. It invests all the religious purpose and sense of progress and salvation into the idea of faith in the progress of Western disciplines and it values the creative endeavors of Western civilization. According to Schall, the refusal of the modern system "to be open to something that is not ourselves, and not made by ourselves"[57] distinguishes the uniqueness of a traditional liberal arts education and its ability to pursue what is greater than the self.

The study of the higher things and *what is* presents the individual with an arduous task. It does not allow the value of all things to be determined by whim or prejudice. The liberal arts envision an openness of the mind, but one that also has parameters necessary for discerning a proper waste of time. It is not enough to simply read for the sake of reading, but to read wisely. The skill of good reading comes from a relationship with the liberal arts. By using the skills imparted by liberal learning one can argue for and persuade others to focus on discernment, and understand what it means to read wisely in pursuit of human wisdom.

A TRADITIONAL APPLICATION

There are many reasons why traditionalists took up a defense of the liberal arts. All of these reasons can be reduced to a few simple tenets. Tradition converses with permanent truths as simple as the Aristotelian ideas that intellectual curiosity is related to being. Quoting Schall, "We begin our intellectual lives with minds that we did not give ourselves, with minds that have nothing in them until we begin to wonder, begin to know."[58] It is this simple idea that produces the need for the study of liberal arts. A liberal arts education breathes life into rational beings because of its subject matter. For Socrates, the "unexamined life was not worth living" and this sentiment was carried throughout the liberal arts from ancient Greece to the present. There are both secular and Christian implications in living a life of the mind that are anchored in the liberal arts (some of which were seen in chapter 6 with Babbitt and More). Addressing these implications may allow us to see more clearly the liberal arts in the traditional light of a gateway to freedom versus the modern sense of pragmatism.

James Schall's notion that the liberal arts are "those studies, those disciplines which, on-going through them, enable us better to see what is there . . . enabling us to be free enough to know the truth of things."[59] The notion of the liberal arts as an exercise of freedom holds true as the discourse causes reflection on definitions, structures of morality, justice, et cetera. In a Christian sense, St. Clement of Alexandria (150–215) saw study as indicative of one "who yearns to touch the fringes of God's power [and] must of necessity become a philosopher to have a proper conception about intellectual objects."[60] In any case, the liberal arts appeal to both perspectives as they are ultimately concerned with the reduction of ignorance so that an individual may pursue the knowledge of "everything under the sun."

The authors who argued to preserve liberal studies undertook an uphill climb. The argument from moderns regarding the liberal arts posits an idea of utility and function in its determination of value. For instance, Veblen's idea that higher learning needs to reflect new, more practical, economic realities, such that elites are not the only groups attending universities.[61] Thus, the liberal arts are a luxury of a leisure class who can afford lives of study rather than vocation. Reflected in the modern marketplace of ideas, the redefinition of education as a tradable commodity coupled with the allowance of all knowledge without discretion allows for a wide array of possible tracts of study befitting of one's place in the line of a production and consumption-based society.[62] Presumably, modern methods seek a tailored education to fit the individual, rather than ask the individual to mold him or herself with the guidance of traditional education. A traditional perspective encourages contemplation alongside the functional aspects of utility. The non-functional factors into the higher things as they contain value in and of themselves. The functional is concerned with a strictly material knowledge of the physical universe. Tradition's distinction is one that directly correlates to "the end of our pursuit is knowledge of that Being," as stated by David Lyle Jeffrey.[63]

With the increased speed and accessibility of the digital age, the availability of an abundance of knowledge from the scientific to the philosophical also increased. It is only natural that the individual yearn to know, but given the abundance of new information, traditionalists wanted that yearning paired with instruction so that the possession of the tools to continue for a lifetime exist as well.[64] If one is to take up the charge of studying the liberal arts, then one must be ready, as are traditionalists, to answer criticisms of "wasting time" in lieu of study leading to employment. Schall reflects Aristotelian ideas that state it is only fitting that the liberal arts, an insight to the higher things, lead one to the promised land one book at a time.[65] Not all books are created equal; therefore, discernment and reading wisely are crucial components to lifelong learning.

A common thread throughout the vocation of the liberal arts has to do with the importance of discernment of what one reads. The overall notion that the liberal arts are a waste of time since they are studied for the sake of themselves still challenges the reader to "waste" his or her time on higher and worthwhile subjects (e.g., the soul). Traditionalists did believe in the need for other pursuits, but not at the expense of the classical model.[66] Schall challenges the late-modern world not just to read within the liberal arts, but to cultivate the right words, that extract the meaning of human life and how to be alone with the higher things.[67] A hierarchy exists within knowledge. Some forms of knowledge are higher because they serve a higher purpose. Other forms are more practical because they are geared to more functional components of life. The traditional view of the liberal arts shares in the endeavor to pursue a life of the mind within a paradigm that best fulfills the needs of human beings—one that combines the higher and the practical. The argument from modernity stems from the idea that a traditional liberal arts vocation fails to produce measurable products birthed through activity. Both traditionalists and progressives fail to see that to some extent they desire a number of similar outcomes. These similarities can be used to persuade modernity into accepting traditional liberal arts as another regimen to add to its culture of self-improvement and vice versa. The key difference would be to reveal the depth and importance of knowing the higher things and what they can unlock for humanity as a whole and not always on an individual level. However, the clocks cannot be turned back and Paul Johnson's critique of Freudianism speaks to "emergent trends" and a "fundamental revolution" within the worlds of culture that led to the explosion of modern times.[68] The traditionalists in this book held onto the hope that there must be a way to incorporate both perspectives.

Even though there is a distinction between the different modes of thinking, how to rate or recognize what is fruitful immediately becomes problematic. The liberal arts come to the individual during times of quiet reflection and privacy, thus proving difficult to chart its effects. The gauge of modern success is tied to the public life of the crowd, hence more witnesses and evidence. The value of the modern world is anchored in the empirical, so the measure of success rests heavily on quantity.[69] The masters of the liberal arts attempted to open the eyes of those looking to live more efficient lives.

A long line of traditional thinkers existed from St. Augustine to James Schall who proposed that most roads lead to the use of the liberal arts for a complete understanding of humanity. Ultimately, the discourse of the liberal arts is something to be learned and then taught to others. It becomes imperative to exercise discernment because of the mysterious nature and knowledge that surrounds the intangible subjects. If discernment is not practiced, the reader can easily settle for pathways toward shallow doctrines. Alan Bloom claims modern education hopes that "almost every student entering the university believes, or says he believes, that truth is relative."[70] If modern education's wish is granted, then the task of discernment is null and void and therefore delegitimizes the argument of the traditional thinker. St. Basil of Caesarea (330–379) believes in the necessity of training to form the proper habits needed to develop self-restraint and wisdom.[71] Discernment is a learned behavior; one that is taught in order to achieve specific ends and maintain opinions instead of the vanity of learning (i.e., knowledge without understanding). Educators who upheld tradition often saw themselves as mediators—rather than oracles—who transmitted ideas from one age to the next.

The benefit of the liberal arts is that these educators do not have to be alive. There are many fine tutors whose ideas are still relevant to the conversation even though they have since passed, something the Inklings saw in the medieval mind.[72] The twentieth century did possess those fine tutors as well. The willingness, to listen, however, is the responsibility of the reader. The past is persuasive in pointing out worthwhile labors and their attachment to such principles as virtue. For example, John Chrysostom (349–407) alludes to the worthwhile labor of wisdom: "Let us go to the master principle which keeps everything under control. To what do I allude? I mean wisdom. Here great labor is needed to render him sagacious and to banish all folly. This is the great and wondrous function of philosophy."[73] Wisdom, self-discipline, and banishment of folly are attractive virtues and ideals to any thoughtful individual. The liberal arts can be introduced to the majority as such and not necessarily tied to the subject of God, unless the audience is appropriate. In either case, discernment is still a necessity. St. Jerome (347–420) sees discernment as the use of secular wisdom "to make it [his] captive, [his] handmaid, and a matron of the true Israel."[74] One only needs to look at the suspicion of Jerome to realize that a traditional education in the liberal arts is not only about God, but about the masters of philosophy and eloquence alike. Lastly, Augustine speaks of the importance of discernment so that the pupil is not misled or enticed by the wrong ideas or emotions—as in his reference to weeping for Aeneas over his own soul.[75]

This particular excerpt reveals to the modern and traditional alike that the one can see Augustine weeping over the pagan character of Aeneas; while the other can read further when Augustine points out his folly and remorse for doing so. Augustine was lamenting that he was reading the story for its own sake, and missed its deeper meaning. From the letter one ascends, from the page one reads, but one must go upward from the page toward the contemplation of truth. In the case of Aeneas, Augustine was moved by a story, the meaning of which escaped him, for he could not see how he himself had wandered from home. The passage is also about his youthful folly, and the need for God's help via books like the life of St. Anthony to cut through the "mists of concupiscence" while growing up. This is the very reason why Lewis suggests the reading of old books: "If you join at eleven o'clock a conversation which began at eight you will often not see the real bearing of what is said . . . the reason, of course, being that the earlier stages of the conversation have given them a special point."[76]

The liberal arts possess an abundance of evidence in favor of their ability to fuse the sacred and the secular—a reconciliation in any age. They allow for insight into the secular, if that is all one wishes to investigate, but it can also prove to be knowledge for the soul with discernment and guidance. However, once individuals enter into a serious study of the liberal arts, they will find many of their preconceived notions dashed against the rocks, and will find themselves reading *Great Books* and asking insightful questions.[77]

To immerse oneself in the activity of reading books is simply not enough. There are two kinds of readers: those who read poorly and those who read wisely. If a life of the mind is to be led properly then wisdom is a crucial element in reading. Tolkien and Lewis argued specifically for an English syllabus that reflected such virtues. There was significant pushback from those who wished to "modernize" Oxford's curriculum. The lessons within the volumes of the Western canon faced extinction in the face of modern progressivism.[78] Unfortunately for those who sought amendment, a *Great Books* category pointed to a distinction that not all books are created equal.

The awareness and recognition of one's own abilities in reading wisely is helpful. The masters of the liberal arts claimed that these great ideas were accessible to all who were willing to receive them and pursue them with discipline, even if one's education was perhaps unequal to the task of fully comprehending the higher things. Hugh of St. Victor (1096–1141) admonished the unlearned to pursue what studies they could, regardless of how educated or uneducated they might be:

> Others, however, because they know that they are in no way able to compass the highest things, neglect even the least, and, as it were, carelessly at rest in their own sluggishness, they all the more lose the light of truth in the greatest matters for their refusal to learn those smallest of which they are capable. It is of such that the Psalmist declares, "They were unwilling to understand how they might do well."[79]

Such a recognition of self requires honesty, and suggests that inability is often wrongly cited as an impediment for one's studies. On the contrary, Hugh validates the ability of all to comprehend at least some, if not most, of what they read, and encourages every reader to pursue such instruction as may further reveal what Alcuin calls the "hidden things of wisdom."[80] Traditionalists were often perceived as elitists because they desired a focused and accurate comprehension of especially those truths which humbled them and reminded them of their relatively small position in the grand scheme of things. A traditional liberal arts structure of learning naturally employs tools of revelation. A significant pedagogical structure for learning comes from the use of the trivium and quadrivium. Although the seven classical disciplines were standards of medieval education, traditionalists urged that their goals and methods were still applicable to the twentieth century. One of the complaints surrounding the use of the trivium and quadrivium was that it was often exclusively a white male, often Christian, and lamentably colonial, dialogue. At their worst, traditional universities and places of classical learning are guilty of being all of the above and more. Nonetheless, traditionalists saw no fault in the liberal arts themselves, as they believe the classical corpus addresses, even if adulterated by racism, colonialism, and the like, universal and fundamentally human concepts, such that any human could access the pearls of wisdom therein.[81]

Given traditional skepticism about utilitarianism, it is almost ironic that reading wisely can bring forth such significant results. It provides the individual with what he or she needs, beyond material comforts. Modern education promotes an acceptable version of mechanical literacy—a literacy that involves the actual ability to read, but not necessarily wisdom.[82] It is a way of reading that typically does not remove the present individual from the meaning or understanding. This egocentric reading promotes knowledge for the sake of utility and application because the "bad reader" never sees value or insight beyond the self and the use of the information to benefit the self. Jeffrey points out in *Houses of the Interpreter* that "Good reading," is a recognition "that there is an abundant reality which transcends our own ego and that reality is not, after all, merely self-referential."[83] C. S. Lewis applied this to education by claiming: "In coming to understand anything we are rejecting the facts *as they are for us* in favor of the *facts as they are*."[84] Egocentric reading is often leads to irreverent attitudes toward the authority of the author. There are many reasons to study the liberal arts, but reading wisely is one of the more important because of what it does for the individual and community alike. Traditionalists want individuals to strive to read wisely and acquire two elements of mature reading; in doing so, the higher things are closer at hand: "The first is that self-forgetful and submissive abandonment to the authority of the text which one sees in an intelligent child. The second comes later: that disciplined, informed, and discerning questioning of the text which is the work of an educated mind."[85] The ideas and arguments for the application of a traditional education mean nothing if there is no context or scope. Traditionalists believe modern education is in a state of crisis. As soon as Westerners began to question their predecessors for the sake of divorce, they made knowledge about themselves, rather than *what is*. The authority of tradition began to dissipate from its position with the ancients to its modern condition.

To be a good person and a good citizen one should be aware of the current condition of education in reference to its scope. Lewis challenged his own age to see how traditional education deals with pupils versus the way the modern perspectives proceeded to educate:

> [T]he difference between the old and the new education will be an important one. Where the old initiated, the new merely "conditions". The old dealt with its pupils as grown birds deal with young birds when they teach them to fly; the new deals with them more as the poultry-keeper deals with young birds—making them thus or thus for purposes of which the birds know nothing. In a word, the old was a kind of propagation—men transmitting manhood to men; the new is merely propaganda.[86]

Modernity saw itself as a bastion of originality that ushered in progress, as if to say that in looking to the future one must abandon the past. Chesterton took a dim view of the emphasis on innovation, writing: "Nine out of ten of what we call new ideas are simply old mistakes."[87] Chesterton's influence was alive and well in Lewis's words. The criticism from moderns that Chesterton remained a grumpy old reactionary, held down by tradition, fits Lewis as well. Unfortunately for modernity, it was a criticism that neither found offensive:

> Let none say that I am scoffing at uneducated people; it is not their uneducation but their education that I scoff at. Let none mistake this for a sneer at the half-educated; what I dislike is the educated half. But I dislike it, not because I dislike education, but because, given the modern philosophy or absence of

philosophy, education is turned against itself, destroying that very sense of variety and proportion which it is the object of education to give.[88]

Lewis presents a similar response in his 1939 sermon titled, "Learning in War Time": "If all the world were Christian, it might not matter if all the world were uneducated. But, as it is, a cultural life will exist outside the Church whether it exists inside or not. . . . Good philosophy must exist, if for no other reason, because bad philosophy needs to be answered."[89] It is tradition's unwillingness to pluralize to the point of "all-inclusiveness" that caused modernity to shun the Old West.

Pluralization aided in modernity's resistance to exceptionalism. The wider the scope of inclusion, alongside a more accessible standard of education, the greater the number who "felt" served and valued. Statistically speaking, there was no way around this as education became more accessible to more diverse populations in the modern West.[90] As evidenced by the long conversation of tradition, the process of cultivation and maturity is not a race, but a duration of time and attention. Barzun claims that modern education's concern is concentrated around the ideal that all students "make it": "[t]he teacher's response to any liveliness of mind, any curiosity and imagination, has become so respectful that it generally excludes criticism; and often omits any demand for accuracy and logic as too likely to chill ardor."[91] The standards of modern education were lowered to praising the slightest bit of interest rather than the quality of the interest and procession. The tone from traditionalists spoke of the worship of uncritiqued youth while wisdom was sacrificed. Traditionalists desired educated citizens who evaluated themselves against an established dialogue on the character of humanity. They believed modernity abandoned the marathon of cultivating minds for the sprint of making the grade and other measured standards of achievement.[92] The dilemma created the need for those who wished to live a life of the mind, those who did not merely bury their noses in books, but strove to convey the wisdom found within their pages. Traditionalists maintained the exhibition of timeless characteristics in order to evaluate new perspectives.

NOTES

1. Lewis, *Image and Imagination*, p. 22.
2. Deneen, p. 61.
3. Jacques Barzun, *The House of Intellect* (New York: Harper & Bros., 1959), p. 90–91.
4. Josef Pieper, *Leisure: The Basis of Culture* (San Francisco: Ignatius Press, 2009), p. 65.
5. Josef Pieper, *In Tune with the World: A Theory of Festivity* (South Bend, IN: St. Augustine's Press, 1999), p. 8 and Pieper, *Leisure*, p. 45, respectively.
6. See Robert Bud, "Biotechnology in the Twentieth Century," *Social Studies of Science* 21, no. 3 (August 1991): 415–57. Ronald Beiner, "Is Social Democracy Dead?" in *Governing Modern Societies*, eds. Richard V. Ericson and Nico Stehr (Toronto: University of Toronto Press, 2000): 225–41.

7. Kronman, *Education's End*, p. 17.
8. Lewis, *Image and Imagination*, p. 22.
9. Pieper, *Leisure*, p. 49.
10. Ibid., p. 54.
11. Ibid., p. 72.
12. Pieper, *In Tune with the World*, pp. 5, 9, 19–20, and 75 and *Leisure*, p. 25–41, respectively.
13. George McCartney, *Evelyn Waugh and the Modernist Tradition* (New Brunswick, NJ: Transaction Publishers, 2004), p. 18.
14. Pieper, *Leisure*, p. 65.
15. Ibid.
16. Ibid., p. 71.
17. Kronman, *Education's End*, p. 167.
18. Lewis, *Abolition*, p. 28.
19. John Henry Newman, *The Idea of a University*, ed. Martin J. Svaglic (Notre Dame: University of Notre Dame Press, 1982), p. 77.
20. Nussbaum, *Not for Profit*, p. 124.
21. Leon Battista Alberti, *The Use and Abuse of Books*, trans. Reneé Neu Watkins (Illinois: Waveland Press, 1999), p. 27.
22. James V. Schall, *The Life of the Mind: On the Joys and Travails of Thinking* (Wilmington: ISI Books, 2006), p. 111.
23. Kronman, *Education's End*, p. 167.
24. Carpenter, p. 18; Duriez, *Oxford Inklings*, p. 90; F. M. Turner, "Religion," in *The History of the University of Oxford: Volume VIII: The Twentieth Century*, ed. Brian Harrison (Oxford: Oxford University Press, 1994), p. 295.
25. Peter Conn, "The Accreditation Farce," *The Chronicle of Higher Education*. Last modified June 30, 2014. www.chronicle.com/article/The-Great-Accreditation-Farce/147425.
26. Jonathan Yonan, "In Defense of God's Glory" (Fall Convocation Speech, Eastern University, St. David's, PA, 30 August, 2013.
27. The trivium ("place where three roads meet") is traditionally defined as the disciplines of Grammar, Logic, and Rhetoric.
28. St. Thomas Aquinas, *Summa Theologica Vol. I*, "Part I" (New York: Cosimo Classics, 2007), p. 372.
29. James Boswell, *Life of Johnson Vol. 1* (London: Oxford, 1931), pp. 131–32.
30. Barzun, *House of Intellect*, p. 95.
31. Alberti, p. 18.
32. Jeffrey Davis and Philip Ryken, interviewed by Ken Myers. *Mars Hill Audio* 117, MHT-117. 2013.
33. As quoted in James V. Schall, *On the Unseriousness of Human Affairs: Teaching Writing Playing Believing* (Wilmington: ISI Books, 2012), pp. 19 and 26, respectively.
34. Schall, *On the Unseriousness of Human Affairs*, p. 16.
35. Ibid., p. 20.
36. Jeffrey Davis and Philip Ryken.
37. Jeffrey, *Houses of the Interpreter*, pp. 20–21.
38. Robert Woods, "Thinking Christianly about the Liberal Arts," *Classis* XXII, no. 3 (October 2015), p. 17.
39. For two insightful reads on the importance of the liberal arts from a non-traditionalist perspective, read: Michael Roth, *Beyond the University: Why Liberal Education Matters* (New Haven: Yale University Press, 2014) and Fareed Zakaria, *In Defense of a Liberal Education* (New York: W.W. Norton, 2015).
40. As quoted in Schall, *On the Unseriousness of Human Affairs*, p. 20.
41. Chesterton, *What's Wrong with the World*, p. 196.
42. Alison Milbank explains Chesterton's theological perspectives through the use of the "grotesque" in his literary work in *Chesterton and Tolkien as Theologians: The Fantasy of the Real* (New York: T&T Clark, 2009), pp. 56–58.

43. Gregory Dunn, "C.S. Lewis on Liberal Arts Education from *On Principle*," Ashbrook Ashland Scholar Program (April 1999): p.1. Accessed Sept. 9, 2016, http://www.ashbrook.org/publications/onprin-v7n2-dunn/.

44. Ibid., p. 1.

45. Schall, *On the Unseriousness of Human Affairs*, p. 21.

46. Donald Kagan, "What is a Liberal Education?" *The McDermott Papers* (Irving: Univ. of Dallas, 2001).

47. Schall, *Life of the Mind*, p. 38.

48. Ibid., p. 28.

49. Nussbaum, *Not for Profit*, p. 141.

50. Schall, *Life of the Mind*, p. 24.

51. Weaver, *Visions of Order*, p. 121.

52. *The Great Tradition*, p. 70. Selection reprinted from Cicero, "Book I," *De Oratore* (Cambridge: Harvard University Press, 1948).

53. David Lyle Jeffrey, "The Pearl of Great Wisdom: The Deep & Abiding Biblical Roots of Western Liberal Education," *Touchstone Archives*, p. 3, accessed September 5, 2013, http://www.touchstonemag.com/archives.

54. See C. S. Lewis, *The Abolition of Man* and Peter Kreeft, "Missing: A Virtuous People" in *Back to Virtue: Traditional Moral Wisdom for Modern Moral Confusion* (San Francisco: Ignatius Press, 1992): 19–58.

55. *Great Tradition*, p. 92.

56. See Edwin Mims, "Modern Education and Religion," *Christian Education* 14, no. 7 (April 1931): 703–14 and Chilton Latham Powell, "Education and Religion" *The Sewanee Review* 28, no. 4 (October 1920): 558–72.

57. Schall, *Life of the Mind*, p. 42.

58. Ibid., p. 19.

59. Ibid., p. 24.

60. *The Great Tradition*, p. 171. Selection reprinted from the *Stromateis* reprinted from *Clement of Alexandria: Stromateis Books One to Three*, translated by John Ferguson (Washington, D.C.: Catholic University Press, 1991).

61. For further reading see: *Education for Democracy: The Debate over the report of the Presidential Commission on Higher Ed.*, ed. Gail Kennedy (Boston: D.C. Hearth, 1952). Jim Barrett and Diane P. Koenker, "The Saga of History 492: The Transformation of Working Class History," *Labour/Le Travail*, Vol. 61, 2008: 181–214. Bethany Kilcrease, "'The Mass and the Masses': Nineteenth Century Anglo-Catholic Socialism," *Michigan Academician*, Vol. 41, no. 2, Spring 2013.

62. See "Educational Movements Particularly Affecting Working People" and "The Demand Made by Workpeople for University Education" in University of Oxford, Workers' Educational Association, *Oxford and Working Class Education* (Charleston: Bibliobazaar, 2008): 1–10 and 41–54, respectively.

63. Jeffrey, "The Pearl of Great Wisdom, p. 3.

64. Schall, *Life of the Mind*, pp. 9–10.

65. Ibid., p. 25.

66. The other component to the classical model (trivium) included the quadrivium—arithmetic, geometry, music, and astronomy.

67. Schall, *On the Unseriousness of Human Affairs*, p. 139–41.

68. Johnson, *Modern* Times, p. 8.

69. *Stanford Encyclopedia of Philosophy*, "The Social Dimensions of Scientific Knowledge." Last Modified Feb. 9, 2015. http://plato.stanford.edu/entries/scientific-knowledge-social/.

70. Bloom, *The Closing of the American Mind*, p. 25.

71. *Great Tradition*, pp. 183, 191–2. Selection reprinted from St. Basil the Great, *Address to Young Men on Reading Greek Literature* (Cambridge: Harvard University Press, 1970), Vol. I–IV.

72. See Sean Connolly, "The Images of Heaven in Christian Tradition," "Resisting the Move Towards a Modern Minimalism," and "The Mythopoeic in Lewisian Echatology," in *Inklings of Heaven* (Herefordshire: Gracewing, 2007): 187–221.

73. *Great Tradition*, p. 205. Selection reprinted from M. L. W. Laistner, *Christianity and Pagan Culture in the Later Roman Empire* (Ithaca: Cornell University Press, 1951).

74. *Ibid.*, p. 209. Selection reprinted from Philip Schaff and Henry Wace, eds., *A Select Library of Nicene and Post-Nicene Fathers of the Christian Church*, second series, Vol. VI (Grand Rapids: Eerdmans, 1989), pp. 149–51.

75. St. Augustine, *Confessions* (New York: Penguin Classics, 1961), p. 34.

76. Lewis, "On the Reading of Old Books," *God in the Dock*, p. 201.

77. See William Haarlow, "Developments at Virginia, Chicago, and St. John's" in *Great Books, Honors Programs, and Hidden Origins: The Virginia Plan and University of Virginia in the Liberal Arts Movement* (New York: Routledge Falmer, 2003): 101–34.

78. See Jose Harris, "The Arts and Social Sciences, 1939–1970" in *The History of Oxford University, Vol. VIII: The Twentieth Century*, ed. Brian Harrison (Oxford: Oxford University Press, 1994): 217–50.

79. *The Great Tradition*, p. 256. Selection reprinted from *The Didascalicon of Hugh St. Victor: A Medieval Guide to the Arts*, ed. Jerome Taylor (New York: Columbia University Press, 1991).

80. *Ibid.*, p. 245. Selection reprinted from Alcuin's letters from Arthur F. Leach, *Educational Charter and Documents 598 to 1909* (Cambridge: Cambridge University Press, 1911), pp. 11–21.

81. See Tim Lacy, "The *Great Books* Movement, 1920–1948" in *The Dream of a Democratic Culture: Mortimer J. Adler and the Great Books Idea* (New York: Palgrave MacMillan, 2013), Kindle.

82. Jeffrey, *Houses of the Interpreter*, p. 175.

83. *Ibid.*, p. 176.

84. C. S. Lewis, *An Experiment in Literary Criticism* (Cambridge: Cambridge University Press, 1961), p. 23.

85. Jeffrey, *Houses of the Interpreter*, p. 175.

86. C. S. Lewis, *Abolition*, p. 23.

87. As quoted in Schall, *Life of the Mind*, p. 182.

88. G. K. Chesterton, "The Worship of Education," *The Collected Works of G.K. Chesterton: The Illustrated London News 1929–1931*, ed. Lawrence J. Clipper (San Francisco: Ignatius Press, 199), p. 298.

89. C. S. Lewis, *The Weight of Glory* (New York: HarperCollins, 1980), p. 58.

90. See Mary J. Hickman, "Integration or Segregation? The Education of the Irish in Britain in Roman Catholic Voluntary-aided Schools," *British Journal of Sociology of Education* 14, no. 3 (1993): 285–300. Evan Schofer and Wesley Longhofer, "The Structural Sources of Association," *American Journal of Sociology* 117, no. 2 (September 2011): 539–85.

91. Barzun, *House of Intellect*, p. 98.

92. See James V. Schall, "Grades" in *Another Sort of Learning* (San Francisco: Ignatius Press, 1988): 38–44.

Epilogue

Passing the Torch

The twentieth century shows the allure of progress as something that transcends socioeconomic status and political identity. Granted, there are often patterns and consistencies within these structures in regard to the perspectives and advantages of the participating individuals, but progress, for the most part, is a universal yearning. The majority of Westerners—rich, poor, black, white—let it wash over them, and they were swept up in the promises of a new modern scientific age, a better world. The idea of "newness" attracts individuals and communities. "Newness" can be seen as a seductress that begs to be chased. Pieper explains the fixation of newness as a form of distrust of tradition: "Respect for tradition produces a distrust of that zero-point radicalism that fancies it always possible to start again from scratch with a *tabula rasa*, as well as distrust of the inclination to treat each new moment as a 'completely new situation,' and so forth."[1] People go to great lengths and, at times, at great sacrifice, for the opportunity to possess or develop something "new." Science and technology in the twentieth century proved to be a catalyst for the justification of changing beliefs and progress. People generally seemed comfortable with a level of change that jeopardized the remaining vestiges of the traditional West. The reality is that it was not seen as destruction, but improvement. C. P. Snow pointed out the optimism of scientists is often questioned or condemned by nonscientists and vice versa, stating: "The nonscientists have a rooted impression that the scientists are shallowly optimistic, unaware of man's condition. On the other hand, the scientists believe that the literary intellectuals are totally lacking in foresight, peculiarly unconcerned with their brother men, in a deep sense anti-intellectual, anxious to restrict both art and thought to the existential moment."[2]

Is scientific progress the empirical response to prophetic salvation? Literature and film are obsessed with the possibilities of a dystopian future and the question of what causes such a society to emerge. The incendiaries discussed previously touched on a number of the different themes prevalent in dystopian stories—callous mechanization, dehumanization, promise of disease- and crime-free societies, planned societies, and State regulation. These ideas were not relegated to pages of fiction, but were a real possibility if the proper care and evaluation of all things "new" were abandoned. Ironically, the responses of Western tradition, Christian and non-Christian alike, addressed these very same issues. The pre–Modern Age had relied heavily on the past and the dialogue of the liberal arts and humanities. The present age also addresses the human concerns of the Modern Age, but it is done with a privatized spiritual element. Humanism and Christian humanism are very similar, with the exception of the metaphysical or spiritual component to human nature. If modernity's claim that religion was made up and had finally failed was accepted, it meant science was the new religion. What if science failed? There was no talk of returning to a mind-set that re-incorporated the metaphysical way of thinking. If there was nowhere else to turn, the anthem of despair would begin to play and the fear of uncertainty would come to life.

C. S. Lewis, offered anecdotal evidence of the rise of what might be called "vulgar scientism" when recounting his own experiences interacting with working-class Englishmen who were skeptical of history in general but accepted what the T. H. Huxleys of the world told them about "Primitive Man": "He is 'Science,' not 'history,' and is therefore felt to be much more real than The Old Days. In other words, the Prehistoric is much more believed in than the Historic."[3] The place of science in the hearts and minds of moderns experienced a greater popularity over the course of roughly one hundred and fifty years. It redirected humanity's faith in the unseen and unknowable into something that allowed for an unprecedented level of control and understanding. Scientists and secularists create a narrative difficult to unseat as they are concerned with the betterment of humanity. An understanding of the laws of nature could very well lead to a mastery of nature and a type of secular salvation. Mastery aside, there still existed a palpable awareness, even from those in support of science and technology. Ray Bradbury (1920–2012) and other science fiction authors kept a guarded relationship with much of technology. Bradbury recognized that human technologies carried with them blessing and curse. For instance, the automobile possesses clear intended benefits along with unintended consequences. The car allows for quick transportation, but also contributes to a faster pace of life and impacts the environment negatively. According to its adherents, scientism could lead humanity to correct all that is wrong in nature, self, and society. For moderns, the cost of such an endeavor has become irrelevant to the march of progress. One could even make the argument that despite the warnings and writing on the wall, scientism, in some ways, triumphed.

Despite the triumph, the Inklings and fellow traditionalists embodied a real movement, one that did not necessitate immediate success or popular acceptance in order to succeed. Indeed, in many ways, they had failed before they even had begun. Perhaps, without their influence, secularization and progressivism would have a more concrete presence in Western civilization. Some sects of Christianity would call it God's providence, but God has historically let his followers succumb, suffer, and even perish at their own hands. It appears that twentieth-century traditionalists feared a dehumanized modern scientific age as another form of suffering, exile, or enslavement—one that Western society did not recognize because of its focus on progress and newness. The romanticism of the "Oxford Circle" may have understood this, even more so than their allies in tradition because of their ability to converse with and translate the language of the past, specifically the medieval. It is not a far stretch of the imagination to claim that the Inklings, specifically, saw themselves as something akin to the living stones, of whom God's temple was composed, and of whom the Venerable Bede (c. 673–735) wrote in his joint commentary on Ezra-Nehemiah: "So too, we can properly take the successor of this same empire, Artaxerxes, who with the same devotion ordered that the city of Jerusalem be rebuilt, as a type of the Lord, who builds a city for himself from living stones (that is, the one Church made from all the elect) through service of preachers."[4] They certainly were familiar with Bede's commentaries within their scholarly work and its place within their theological perspectives fits nicely. They would not have shied away from the idea that living stones were necessary to build the temple of God on Earth. It seems rather mystical to explain the purpose of all of history as the story of building the temple of God. Most of the traditionalists examined here would not disagree. Their commitment to tradition and the Church influenced their writing and the purpose of their lives. The Inklings were constant teachers; whether in their tutorials at Oxford, their scholarly work, or their popular fictional endeavors, a Scriptural understanding of teaching defined their careers: "For in the same way today too, not only do bishops and priests have a duty to build the congregation of the faithful (namely, God's house) by teaching, and, by taking counsel, to appoint teachers for them able diligently to fulfill the most holy work of the word, but it is also necessary that the people themselves, called from the captivity of the vices to the *vision of true peace*."[5]

The mark they left was received with mixed reviews. The idea that the Church is antiquated (some sects more than others) and does not relate to the modern world is widespread. It is a given that tradition lost its foothold in both secular and religious culture. Does this mean twentieth-century traditionalists failed in their quest? Perhaps not. Instead, one could say they created a bridge between the past and present—the Old West and the Modern Age—in order to translate permanent values for all men and women in any age. It appears though, that their point of view was mainly in the minority. The call for a more progressive Christianity (social gospel) had won out alongside a more progressive ethos for Western society.

Secular culture will be whatever it wants and it will change from age to age. It has the ability to change rapidly to keep up with technological advances—even complete automation seems an inevitability.[6] Christianity was supposed to be a haven for tradition, but even it carries the torch of progress in step with the current age. It did, however, survive despite the expanding trust in science, which may or may not be more important. There are approximately 2.2 billion Christians worldwide, about half of them claiming to be Catholic, 12 percent Greek or Russian Orthodox, and the remainder Protestant.[7] Perhaps the summation from German philosopher and 1908 Nobel Laureate Rudolf Eucken's *Can We Still Be Christians?* (1914) was correct in its assessment—in order to remain Christians in the Modern Age, Christianity had to change.[8] Christianity saw its fair share of updates since the early twentieth century—issues on birth control, Vatican II, female ordination, gay ordination, and gay marriage to name a few. There is a growing presence of polarizing non-traditional views across numerous sects and Christian institutions of learning. The place for traditional perspectives, secular and religious, is caught in the middle.

All of this, in Britain especially, may be a reaction to the rigid principles of the Victorian era, progressive Christianity, or the focus on Empire (nationalism and colonialism). As the world changed certain ideas and perspectives did not seem to fit the new, modern world. The more restrictive and customary practices and ideas were viciously attacked in order to move forward. Instead of the rigidity of convention, the modern scientific era embraced a secularization of the Western mind in order to promote equality, freedom, and undeniable fact. Western society made leaps and bounds with the abolition movement, feminism, environmentalism, and civil rights, but has it been able to usher in utopian societies? The twenty-first century has seen all-time highs in the presence of tolerance, economic opportunities, education, and the like—still no utopias. Postmodernism and tradition share a distaste for the failures of modernity. Traditional and progressive perspectives of meaning and purpose for human beings are often drastically different—one being created by the individual and the other received.

There is more awareness now than ever, but the issues remain. Is "awareness" a satisfactory goal? Traditionalists perceived a need for something more foundational; something that spoke to the nature of human beings; something that Western tradition does not need in order to dominate, but may possess as insight not found in other cultures or traditions. Lukacs offers up this startling, yet thought-provoking possibility: "Discernment can be shown in a number of ways, but the ability to craft a narrative of history that speaks to the value of the past is one of the more important skills. The West possesses a unique ability to keep from repeating the past because the West has the ability to think historically."[9] For Lukacs, this idea was evident at a very young age: "I knew, at a very early age, that 'the West' was better than 'the East'—especially better than Russia and Communism. I had read Spengler: but I believed that the Anglo-American victory over the Third Reich (and over Japan) was, at least in some ways, a refutation of the categorical German proposition of the inevitable and imminent Decline of the West."[10] Cultural relativism would have society believe that all beliefs are paths to truth. This may be the case, but what if Western tradition contains the codex for the meaning and purpose of humanity? Through dialogue and discussion (humanities), these ideas could be accessible and reconciled (obviously not seamlessly) with other religions and cultures through the tradition of the *Great Books*. While Christian humanists sought to preserve the common mind, secular humanists sought to challenge the authority of tradition in one age with doubt and provide what Kronman calls, a "solvent of our certainties" in another.[11] It is the language and ideas contained within the *Great Books* that inspired humanists to defend the voice being silenced by the hum of secularization and the whir of progress.

Whether it comes from the *Great Books* of the Western World, the New Humanists, or the Inklings, the voice of tradition occupies a place at the table. For the Inklings and other imaginative conservatives, survival of the humane relied heavily on imagination. In the modern, empirical world, imagination serves as the first step toward actualization. The imagination of the pre-moderns did not require actualization, thus, for modernity, it was difficult to adhere to the ways of the past. The Inklings, specifically, made an argument that imagination anchored in concrete realization was not imagination in the truest sense. The hope of traditionalists can be heard in the prophetic words from Joseph Cardinal Ratzinger's *Faith and the Future* (1970). On discussing what the Church would look like in the year 2000, he said:

> And so it seems certain to me that the Church is facing very hard times. The real crisis has scarcely begun. We will have to count on terrific upheavals. But I am equally certain about what will remain at the end: not the Church of the political cult, which is dead already with Gobel,[12] but the Church of faith. She may well no longer be the dominant social power to the extent that she was until recently; but she will enjoy a fresh blossoming and be seen as man's home, where he will find life and hope beyond death.[13]

Traditionalists believe that without a pre-modern understanding of imagination, Western society runs the risk of losing its humanity. Issues of mechanization pale in comparison to what many of these authors feared the most—the reduction of humanity to material and its systematic functions. They did not believe that enlightenment would come from modern ideologies, planned economies, and the like. The character of the Modern Age was one that found little value in the past (i.e., tradition). As Chesterton points out in his article "Are the Artists Going Mad?" (1922): "The notion that every generation proves worthless the last generation, and is in its turn proved worthless by the next generation, is an everlasting vista and vision of worthlessness which is fortunately itself worthless."[14] The present generation claims no responsibility to anyone prior or subsequent.

The introduction stated that the discussion would focus on a real interdisciplinary connection between British and American intellectuals who possessed self-consciousness and reflection of the twentieth century through the defense of tradition in a number of capacities. The definition innately transcends time and indeed speaks to different generations because of those who took the time to study and transmit the permanent things. The metaphor of the modern marketplace reveals distinct attitudes, values, and so forth of both pre-modern and modern concepts of reality, such as Christianity, the metaphysical, and scientism. It is evident traditionalists desired to carry what they saw as the light of truth in service to their fellow travelers, even if humanity was unwilling to accept the gift. Intellectually, they made a concerted effort to answer what Isaiah Berlin defines as a radical change in the Western outlook:

> [A] radical change in the conceptual framework within which the questions had been posed; new ideas, new words, new relationships in terms of which the old problems are not so much solved as made to look remote, obsolete and, at times, unintelligible, so that the agonising problems and doubts of the past seem queer ways of thought, or confusions that belong to a world which has gone.[15]

Traditionalists did not see themselves as another competitive commodity on the marketplace of ideas, but harbingers of tradition's permanence.

The interdisciplinary nature of the Western canon, or *Great Books*, and classical liberal learning prove a stable vessel of tradition. Ultimately for most traditionalists, the worthiest of vessels is that of the Incarnate God, but short of that the humane letters envisage humanity in its unique glory. The conversation of tradition within the different disciplines of the Western academy reflects a dignity of Knowledge worthy of human endeavor, while adhering to an authority-based relationship. Traditionalists see progressivism and the modern scientific age as attempts to restructure the authority of tradition in hopes of arresting it for the sake of power and mastery without resistance. The defenders of tradition in the twentieth century from Chesterton, to Lewis, to Kirk were fully aware of the reality that modernity had already internalized what Berlin eventually saw defined as a "new outlook."

The recognition of traditionalists' responsibility to others allowed them to maintain an awareness of the secular identity of their time. It was an age on the brink of replacing the Christian religion, one that had characterized the West for centuries, with a material (and often scientific) understanding of the universe. Even authors like Babbitt and More did not openly profess the need for spirituality. Nonetheless, they did see something amiss in the nineteenth and twentieth centuries. Most of the New Humanists, the Inklings, and other traditionalists (e.g., Dawson and Chesterton) viewed the removal of Christianity from Western culture as the catalyst of crisis—affecting all aspects from economics to education. The extent of the effects requires a more interdisciplinary approach to this subject. An idea not devised by twentieth-century traditionalists alone, but one learned through a humanistic education. Fifteenth-century Pope Pius II (Aeneas Sylvius Piccolomini) instructs in *The Education of Boys* (1450): "The disciplines are interconnected, and a person cannot master one unless he seeks light from another. Indeed, no one possesses the art of correct speaking who has not looked at the poets and read the historians and orators."[16] If they saw themselves as carriers of the light of truth in an age of darkness, there is certainly something saintly about them. As Bede says in *On the Temple*, "The throne of God is the saints, over whom and in whom God forever dwells."[17] It is possible, certainly traditionalists were open to the idea, that the throne of God needed to be carried from age to age. With the exception of a few, the importance of tradition was more than custom or ideas of the past, it was tied directly to the purpose and meaning of humanity, something that reflected the image of God. The responsibility taken on by traditionalists set them apart from mainstream, twentieth-century ideologues. Even if some fans have called for their canonization, they themselves would never make such claims.[18] Subsequent traditionalists owe a debt of gratitude to those of the twentieth century who stood to preserve the link between past and present. The eloquent dance between tradition and progress is nothing new. The twentieth century passed the torch of tradition with the goal of renewed reconciliation and persistent presence regardless of the contemporary spirit.

NOTES

1. Pieper, *Tradition*, p. 58.
2. Snow, *Two Cultures*, p. 5.
3. Lewis, "Christian Apologetics," *God in the Dock*, p. 95.
4. Bede, *On Ezra-Nehemiah*, Translated Texts for Historians 47, trans. Scott DeGregorio (Liverpool: Liverpool University Press, 2006), p. 158. Bede's mystical ideas about the different ages of time would place the Inklings and other Christian traditionalists within the sixth age, linking them to the direct priesthood of Christ.
5. *Ibid.*, p. 62.
6. For just one of countless articles on technological breakthroughs with ethical implications, see: Andy Campbell, "Soon Your Sex Doll Will Have an Intelligent Conversation With

You," *The Huffington Post: Weird News*, last modified June 12, 2015, http://www.huffingtonpost.com/2015/06/11/sex-doll-talks-back-real-doll_n_7563764.html?utm_hp_ref=mostpopular.

7. Jennifer Harper, "84 Percent of the World Population has Faith; a Third are Christian," *The Washington Times* (blog), December 23, 2012 (11:05am), http://www.washingtontimes.com/blog/watercooler/2012/dec/23/84-percent-world-population-has-faith-third-are-ch/.

8. Rudolf Eucken, *Can We Still Be Christians?* (New York: Macmillan Co., 1914), 188–89.

9. Lukacs, *Historical Consciousness*, pp. 23–25.

10. John Lukacs, *At the End of an Age* (New Haven: Yale University Press, 2002), p. 3.

11. Kronman, *Education's End*, p. 255.

12. Jean-Baptiste-Joseph Gobel was a Catholic priest who took the oath of the Civil Constitution of Clergy (1790), which called for the subordination of the Roman Catholic Church in France to the French government during the French Revolution.

13. Thomas L. McDonald, "Ratzinger on What the Church Will Look Like," *Patheos* (blog), January 5, 2014 (1:34pm), http://www.patheos.com/blogs/godandthemachine/2014/01/ratzinger-on-what-the-church-will-look-like/.

14. G. K. Chesterton, "Are the Artists Going Mad?" *The Century Magazine* 105, no. 2 (December 1922), p. 273.

15. Isaiah Berlin, *The Sense of Reality: Studies in Ideas and their History* (New York: Farrar, Straus, and Giroux, 1996), p. 168.

16. Aeneas Sylvius Piccolomini, "The Education of Boys," in *Humanist Educational Treatises*, trans. By Craig W. Kallendorf (Cambridge: Harvard University Press, 2002), p. 105.

17. Bede, *On the Temple*, Translated Texts for Historians 21, trans. Seán Conolly (Liverpool: Liverpool University Press, 1995), p. 158.

18. Although it may be tongue in cheek, the following article calls for the canonization of Chesterton: James Parker, "A Most Unlikely Saint," *The Atlantic* (April 2015), http://www.theatlantic.com/magazine/archive/2015/04/a-most-unlikely-saint/386243/.

Bibliography

Adler, Mortimer J. "Chapter 14: Custom and Convention." *The Great Ideas: A Syntopicon of Great Books of the Western World*, 2 vols. 268–77. Chicago: William Benton, 1952.
Aichele, George, Jr. "Literary Fantasy and Postmodern Theology." *Journal of the American Academy of Religion* 59, no. 2 (Summer 1991): 323–37.
Alberti, Leon Battista. *The Use and Abuse of Books*. Translated by Reneé Neu Watkins. Long Grove: Waveland Press, 1999.
Alhasani, Nadia M. "Tradition vs. Modernity: The Quest for a Cultural Identity." *Traditional Dwellings and Settlements Review* 7, no. 2 (Spring 1996): 35–41.
Allitt, Patrick. *Catholic Intellectuals and Conservative Politics in America, 1950–85*. Ithaca: Cornell University Press, 1993.
———. *Catholic Converts: British and American Intellectuals Turn to Rome*. Ithaca: Cornell University Press, 1997.
Anderson, Sherwood. "I'm a Fool." *The Gateway to the Great Books, Vol. 2*. Edited by Robert M. Hutchens and Mortimer J. Adler, 511–20. Chicago: Encyclopedia Britannica, Inc., 1990.
Aquinas, St. Thomas. *Summa Theologica Vol. I*. New York: Cosimo Classics, 2007.
Aristotle. *Politics*. Translated by Benjamin Jowett and H. W. Carless Davis. Oxford: Clarendon Press, 1920.
———. *Nicomachean Ethics*. Translated by Joe Sachs. Newbury: Focus Pub./R. Pullins, 2002.
———. *On Metaphysics*. Edited by Stephen M. Cahn. *Classics of Western Philosophy*. Cambridge: Hackett Publishing, 2006.
Ashenden, Gavin. *Charles Williams: Alchemy and Integration*. Kent: Kent State University Press, 2007.
Augustine. *Confessions*. New York: Penguin Classics, 1961.
Ayer, A. J. *The Concept of a Person and Other Essays*. New York: St. Martin's Press, 1964.
Babbitt, Irving. *Literature and the American College*. Washington, D.C.: National Humanities Institute, 1986.
Bacon, Francis. "The Sphinx." *The Gateway to the Great Books, Vol. 8*. Edited by Robert M. Hutchens and Mortimer J. Adler, 2–4. Chicago: Encyclopedia Britannica, Inc., 1990.
———. "Of Custom and Education." *The Gateway to the Great Books, Vol. 7*. Edited by Robert M. Hutchens and Mortimer J. Adler, 18–19. Chicago: Encyclopedia Britannica, Inc., 1990.
———. *The Advancement of Learning*. Edited by Mortimer Adler, *Great Books of the Western World, Vol. 30*. Chicago: Encyclopedia Britannica, 1990.
Ball, Terence. *Reappraising Political Theory: Revisionist Studies in the History of Political Thought*. Oxford: Clarendon Press, 1995.

Barfield, Owen. *Worlds Apart: A Dialogue of the 1960s*. Middletown: Wesleyan University Press, 1963.
———. *Romanticism Comes of Age*. Middletown: Wesleyan University Press, 1966.
———. *Speaker's Meaning*. London: Rudolf Steiner Press, 1967.
———. *Poetic Diction: A Study in Meaning*. Middletown: Wesleyan University Press, 1973.
———. "The Evolution Complex." *Towards* 2.2 (1982): 6–12, 14–16.
———. *Saving the Appearances: A Study in Idolatry*. Middletown: Wesleyan University Press, 1988.
Barker, Ernest. *The Character of England*. Oxford: Oxford University Press, 1947.
Barzun, Jacques. *The House of Intellect*. New York: Harper & Bros., 1959.
———. *The Culture We Deserve*. Hanover: Wesleyan University Press, 1989.
"BBC 'The Big Read.'" *BBC*, September 2, 2014. www.bbc.co.uk.
"Beauty." *Stanford Philosophical Dictionary*. http://plato.stanford.edu/entries/beauty.
Bebbington, David. *Evangelicalism and Fundamentalism in the United Kingdom During the Twentieth Century*. Oxford: Oxford University Press, 2013.
Bede. *On the Temple*. Translated Texts for Historians 21. Translated by Seán Conolly. Liverpool: Liverpool University Press, 1995.
———. *On Ezra-Nehemiah*. Translated Texts for Historians 47. Translated by Scott DeGregorio. Liverpool: Liverpool University Press, 2006.
Belloc, Hilaire. *The Crisis of Civilization*. Rockford, IL: Tan Publishers, 1992.
Bendix, Reinhard. "Tradition and Modernity Reconsidered." *Comparative Studies in Society and History* 9, no. 3 (April 1967): 292–346.
Berdyaev, Nicolas. "The Fate of Man in the Modern World." In *Sources in Western Civilization: The Twentieth Century, 1914–1964*. Edited by Arthur P. Mendel. New York: The Free Press, 1965.
Berg, Matthew, James Krukanes, and Marvin Perry. *Sources of Twentieth-Century Europe*. New York: Houghton Mifflin, 2000.
Berger, Peter L. *The Sacred Canopy: Elements of a Sociological Theory of Religion*. Garden City: Anchor Books, 1969.
———. *A Rumor of Angels: Modern Society and the Rediscovery of the Supernatural*. Garden City: Anchor Books, 1970.
———. *The Heretical Imperative: Contemporary Possibilities of Religious Affirmation*. Garden City: Anchor Books, 1979,
Berlin Isaiah. *The Sense of Reality: Studies in Ideas and Their History*. New York: Farrar, Straus, and Giroux, 1996.
Birzer, Bradley J. "Making Modernity Human: Can Christian Humanism Redeem an Age of Ideology?" *The Imaginative Conservative*. November 8, 2012. http://www.theimaginativeconservative.org/2012/11/making-modernity-human-can-christian-html.
———. "How Did Lewis and Tolkien Defend the Old West?" *The Imaginative Conservative*. July 1, 2015. http://www.theimaginativeconservative.org/2015/07/how-did-lewis-and-tolkien-defend-the-old-west.html.
———. *Russell Kirk: American Conservative*. Lexington, KY: University of Kentucky Press, 2015.
Blacker, C. P. *Eugenics, Galton, and After*. London: Duckworth Overlook, 1952.
Bloom, Alan. *The Closing of the American Mind*. New York: Simon & Schuster, 1987.
Boenig, Robert. *C.S. Lewis and the Middle Ages*. Kent: Kent State University Press, 2012.
Bourke, Joanna. "Divine Madness: The Dilemma of Religious Scruples in Twentieth-Century American and Britain." *Journal of Social History* 42, no. 3 (2009): 581–603.
Bowler, Peter J. "Evolution and Eucharist: Bishop E.W. Barnes on Science and Religion in the 1920s and 1930s." *The British Journal for the History of Science* 31, no. 4 (December 1998): 453–67.
Brignell, Victoria. "The Eugenics Movement Britain Wants to Forget." *The New Statesman*. December 9, 2010. http://www.newstatesman.com/society/2010/12/british-eugenics-disabled.
Bronner, Simon J. "The Meaning of Tradition: An Introduction." *Western Folklore* 59, no. 2 (Spring 2000): 87–104.
Bronowski, Jacob. *Science and Human Values*. London: Faber & Faber, 2011.

Boswell, James. *Life of Johnson, Vol. I*. London: Oxford University Press, 1931.
Bowman, Barbara Ann Guthrie. "The Spiritual Quest and Health of C.S. Lewis." PhD dissertation, University of North Texas, 1988.
Bradbury, J. G. "Charles William's Arthuriad: Mythic Vision and the Possibilities of Belief." *Journal of Inklings Studies* 1 (March 2011): 33–46.
Brockelman, Paul. *The Inside Story: A Narrative Approach to Religious Understanding and Truth*. Albany: SUNY Press, 1992.
Brooks, David. "Kicking the Secularist Habit: A Six-step Program." *The Atlantic*. March 3, 2003. http://www.theatlantic.com/magazine/archive/2003/03/kicking-the-secularist-habit/302680.
Brown, Callum. *Religion and Society in Twentieth-Century Britain*. New York: Routledge, 2006.
Brown, Clay. "C.S. Lewis and Postmodernism: Areas of Convergence and Divergence." PhD dissertation, Trinity Theological Seminary, 2005.
Burns, R. M. *The Great Debate on Miracles: From Joseph Glanville to David Hume*. Lewisburg: Bucknell University Press, 1981.
Bury, J. B. *The Idea of Progress*. New York: Dover Publications, Inc., 1955.
Butler, Samuel. "Customs and Opinions of the Erewhonians from *Erewhon*." *The Gateway to the Great Books, Vol. 2*. Edited by Robert M. Hutchens and Mortimer J. Adler, 483–506. Chicago: Encyclopedia Britannica, Inc., 1990.
Butynskyi, Chris. "The Reconciliation of Tradition in the Modern Age." *The Chesterton Review* XLI, no. 1/2 (Spring/Summer 2015): 147–58.
———. "Babbitt and Belloc: Two Peas, Different Pods." *The University Bookmen*. September 29, 2014. http://www.kirkcenter.org/index.php/bookman/article/babbitt-and-belloc-two-peas-different-pods/.
———. "Not All Books Are Created Equal: In Defense of Liberal Studies." *Journal of Faith and the Academy* VII, no. 1 (Spring 2014): 58–74.
Caldecott, Stratford. *The Catholic Imagination of J.R.R. Tolkien*. Boston: Houghton Mifflin Co., 1979.
———. *Beauty for Truth's Sake: On the Re-enchantment of Education*. Grand Rapids: Brazos Press, 2009.
Campbell, Andy. "Soon Your Sex Doll Will Have an Intelligent Conversation With You." *The Huffington Post: Weird News*. http://www.huffingtonpost.com/news/sex-dolls/.
Cantor, Norman F. *Inventing Middle Ages: The Lives, Works, and Ideas of the Great Medievalists of the 20th Century*. New York: Quill, William, Morrow, 1991.
Carey, John. *The Intellectuals and the Masses: Pride and Prejudice among the Literary Intelligentsia, 1880–1939*. London: Faber & Faber, 1992.
Carpenter, Humphrey. *The Inklings: C.S. Lewis, J.R.R. Tolkien, Charles Williams and Their Friends*. London: HarperCollins, 2006.
Cassirer, Ernst. *An Essay on Man: An Introduction to the Philosophy of Human Culture*. New Haven: Yale University Press, 1956.
Chesterton, G. K. "The Seclusion of the Old Lady." *The Club of Queer Trades*. London: Harper & Bros. Publishers, 1905.
———. "Are the Artists Going Mad?" *The Century Magazine* 105, no. 2 (December 1922): 271–78.
———. "The Worship of Education." *The Collected Works of G.K. Chesterton: The Illustrated London News 1929–1931*. Edited by Lawrence J. Clipper. San Francisco: Ignatius Press, 1991: 295–99.
———. *A Short History of England. The Collected Works of G.K. Chesterton Vol. 20*. San Francisco: Ignatius Press, 2001.
———. *Tremendous Trifles*. Create Space Publishing, 2009.
———. *In Defense of Sanity: The Best Essays of G.K. Chesterton*. Selected by Dale Ahquist, Joseph Pearce, & Aidan Mackey. San Francisco: Ignatius Press, 2011.
———. *Orthodoxy*. Amazon Digital Services, 2012. Kindle.
———. *What's Wrong with the World*. Hollywood: Simon and Brown, 2012. Kindle.

———. *Heretics*. Edited by Jim Manis. Hazleton: Pennsylvania State University. http://www.2hn.psu.edu/faculty/jmanis/gkchesterton/Heretics.pdf.

———. *The Everlasting Man*. Lexington: EMP Books, 2013.

Conn, Peter. "The Accreditation Farce." *The Chronicle of Higher Education*. June 30, 2014. http://www.chronicle.com/article/The-Great-Accreditation-Farce/147425.

Corrin, Jay. *G.K. Chesterton and Hilaire Belloc: The Battle Against Modernity*. Athens: Ohio University Press, 1981.

Curry, Patrick. *Defending Middle-Earth: Tolkien Myth and Modernity*. New York: Houghton Mifflin, 2004.

Davidson, John D. "Tolkien, Lewis, and a World Shot Through with Meaning." *The Washington Free Beacon*. Last updated July 11, 2015. http://freebeacon.com/culture/tolkien-lewis-and-a-world-shot-through-with-meaning/.

Darwin, Charles. "The Descent of Man." *The Great Books of the Western World, Vol. 49*. Edited by Mortimer J. Adler. Chicago: Encyclopedia Britannica, 1990.

"Darwinism: Selection, Adaptation, Teleology." *Stanford Encyclopedia of Philosophy*. January 19, 2010. http://www.plato.stanford.edu/entries/darwinism.

Dawson, Christopher. *Religion and Culture*. New York: Sheed & Ward, 1948.

———. *The Dynamics of World History*. Edited by John J. Mulloy. New York: Sheed & Ward, 1956.

———. *The Crisis of Western Education*. Washington, D.C.: Catholic University Press, 1961.

———. "Enquiries into Religion" in *Sources in Western Civilization: The Twentieth Century, 1914–1964*. Edited by Arthur P. Mendel. New York: The Free Press, 1965.

———. *The Formation of Christendom*. New York: Sheed & Ward, 1967.

———. *Understanding Europe*. Washington, D.C.: The Catholic University of America Press, 2009.

Davis, Jeffry and Philip, interviewed by Ken Myers. *Mars Hill Audio* 117. MHT-117, 2013.

Domitrovic, Brian. "Paul Elmer More: America's Reactionary." *Modern Age* 45, no. 4 (Fall 2003): 343–49.

Drayton, Richard. "Science, Medicine, and the British Empire." *The Oxford History of the British Empire: Vol. V Historiography*. Edited by Robert Winks, 264–76. Oxford: Oxford University Press, 1999.

Drout, Michael D. C., ed. *J.R.R. Tolkien Encyclopedia: Scholarship and Critical Assessment*. New York: Routledge, 2007.

Dunn, Gregory. "C.S. Lewis on Liberal Arts Education from *On Principle*." Ashbrook Ashland Scholar Program (April 1999): 1–3.

Duriez, Colin. *Tolkien and C.S. Lewis: The Gift of Friendship*. Mahwah: Paulist Press, 2003.

———. *The Oxford Inklings: Lewis, Tolkien, and Their Circle*. Oxford: Lion Hudson, 2015.

Einstein, Albert. "The Evolution of Physics." *The Gateway to the Great Books, Vol. 10*. Edited by Robert M. Hutchens and Mortimer J. Adler, 490–560. Chicago: Encyclopedia Britannica Inc., 1990.

Ellis, John M. *Literature Lost: Social Agendas and the Corruption of the Humanities*. New Haven: Yale University Press, 1997.

Eliot, T. S. "Tradition and the Individual Talent." *The Sacred Wood: Essays on Poetry and Criticism*. London: Methuen, 1960.

Elton, G. R. *Return to Essentials: Some Reflections on the Present State of Historical Study*. Cambridge: Cambridge University Press, 1991.

Emerson, Ralph Waldo. "Self-Reliance." *The Gateway to the Great Books, Vol. 10*. Edited by Robert M. Hutchens and Mortimer J. Adler, 525–45. Chicago: Encyclopedia Britannica Inc., 1990.

The Encyclopédia: Selections: Diderot, d'Alembert and a Society of Men of Letters. Translated by Thomas Cassirer and Nelly S. Hoyt. Indianapolis: Bobs-Merrill, 1965.

Erskine, John. "The Moral Obligation to be Intelligent." *The Gateway to the Great Books, Vol. 10*. Edited by Robert M. Hutchens and Mortimer J. Adler, 5–13. Chicago: Encyclopedia Britannica, Inc., 1990.

Etsy Jed. "Insular Time: T.S. Eliot and Modernism's English End." In *A Shrinking Island: Modernism and National Culture in England*. Princeton: Princeton University Press, 2004: 108–62.
Eucken, Rudolf. *Can We Still Be Christians?* New York: Macmillan Co., 1914.
Faraday, Michael. "Observations on Mental Education." *The Gateway to the Great Books, Vol. 7*. Edited by Robert M. Hutchens and Mortimer J. Adler, 208–32. Chicago: Encyclopedia Britannica, Inc., 1990.
Ferguson, Niall. *Civilization: The West and the Rest*. New York: Penguin Books, 2011.
Filmer, Kath. "Out of the Silent Planet: Reconstructing Well with a Few Shots at Shaw." *Inklings Jahrbuch fuer Literatur und Aesthetik* 6 (1988): 43–54.
Flower, B. O. "A Nineteenth Century Prophet of Twentieth Century Civilization." *Twentieth Century Magazine* IV (April–October 1911): 167–70.
Frohnen, Bruce, Jeremy Beer, and Jeffrey O. Nelson, eds. *American Conservatism: An Encyclopedia*. Wilmington: ISI Books, 2006.
Foster, Stephen Paul. *Melancholy Duty: The Hume-Gibbon Attack on Christianity*. Boston: Kluwer Academic Publishers, 1997.
Franklin, R. William and Joseph M. Shaw. *The Case for Christian Humanism*. Grand Rapids: Eerdmans, 1991.
"Francis Herbert Bradley." *Stanford Encyclopedia of Philosophy*. February 19, 2013. http://www.plato.stanford.edu/entries/bradley.
Freud, Sigmund. *The Future of an Illusion*. New York: Classic House Books, 2009.
Gamble, Richard, ed. *The Great Tradition: Classic Readings on What It Means to be an Educated Human Being*. Wilmington: ISI Books, 2007.
Galton, Sir Francis. "Hereditary Genius." *The Gateway to the Great Books, Vol. 8*. Edited by Robert M. Hutchens and Mortimer J. Adler, 227–61. Chicago: Encyclopedia Britannica, Inc., 1990.
Gay Peter. *Modernism: The Lure of Heresy*. New York: W.W. Norton & Co., 2007.
Gilbert, George Holley. "The Hellenization of the Jews Between 334 B.C. and 70 A.D." *The Journal of Theology* 13, no. 4 (1909): 520–40.
Graves, Robert and Alan Hodge. *The Long Week-End: A Social History of Great Britain 1918–1939*. New York: W.W. Norton & Co., 1941, reissued 1994.
Gushurst-Moore, André, *The Common Mind: Politics, Society and Christian Humanism from Thomas More to Russell Kirk*. Tacoma: Angelico Press, 2013.
Haldane, J. B. S. *Daedelus or Science and the Future*. New York: E.P. Dutton & Co., 1924.
———. "Auld Hornie, F.R.S." *Modern Quarterly*, no. 1 (Autumn 1946): 32–40.
———. *The Causes of Evolution*. New York: Longman's, Green & Co., 1932. Reprint Ithaca: Cornell University Press, 1966.
Haldane, John. "Chesterton's Philosophy of Education." *Philosophy* 65, no. 251 (January 1990): 65–80.
Harper, Jennifer. "84 Percent of the World Population Has Faith; a Third are Christian." *The Washington Times* (blog), December 23, 2012 (11:05am), http://www.washingtontimes.com/blog/watercooler/2012/dec/23/84-percent-world-population-has-faith-third-are-ch/.
Hastings, Max. *Catastrophe 1914: Europe Goes to War*. New York: Alfred A. Knopf, 2013.
Heisenberg, Werner. *Physics and Philosophy*. London: Penguin Books, 1958.
Herrick, James. "C.S. Lewis and the Advent of the Posthuman," in *The Magician's Twin: C.S. Lewis on Science, Scientism, and Society*. Edited by John G. West. Seattle: Discovery Institute Press, 2012.
Heyck, Thomas William. "Myths and Meanings of Intellectuals in Twentieth-Century British National Identity." *Journal of British Studies* 37, no. 2 (April 1998): 191–221.
Himmelfarb, Gertrude. *The New History and the Old*. Cambridge: The Belknap Press of Harvard University Press, 2004.
Holyer, Robert. "C.S. Lewis on the Epistemic Significance of the Imagination." *Soundings: An Interdisciplinary Journal* 74, no. 1/2 (Spring/Summer 1991): 215–41.
Honda, Mineko. *The Imaginative World of C.S. Lewis: A Way to Participate in Reality*. Lanham: University of America Press, 2000.

Howard, Thomas and J. I. Packer. *Christianity: The True Humanism*. Vancouver: Regent College Publishing, 1999.

Imbert, Yannick. "From Myth to History and Back Again: Inklings Arthuriana in Historical Context" in *The Inklings & King Arthur: J.R.R. Tolkien, Charles Williams, C.S. Lewis, and Owen Barfield on the Matter of Britain*. Edited by Sørina Higgins. Berkeley: Apocryphile Press, 2017.

Inwagen, Peter van. "C.S. Lewis' Argument Against Naturalism." *Journal of Inklings Studies* 1, no. 2 (October 2011): 25–40.

Irenaeus. *Against the Heresies*. Pickerington: Beloved Publishing, LLC, 2015.

James, William. *The Principles of Psychology, Vol. 1*. Digireads.com Publishing, 2010.

Jaschik, Scott. "Disappearing Liberal Arts Colleges." *Inside Higher Ed*. October 11, 2010. http://www.insidehighered.com/news/2012/10/11/study-finds-liberal-arts-colleges-are-disappearing.

Jeffrey, Lyle David. *Houses of the Interpreter: Reading Scripture, Reading Culture*. Waco: Baylor University Press, 2003.

———. "The Pearl of Great Wisdom: The Deep and Abiding Biblical Roots of Western Liberal Education." *Touchstone Archives* (2007): 1–8.

Jewell, Jason and Chris Butynskyi. "Spiritual Quest in a Scientific Age." In *The Inklings and King Arthur*. Edited by Sørina Higgins. Berkeley: Apocryphile Press, 2018.

Johnson, Paul. *Modern Times: The World from the Twenties to the Eighties*. New York: Harper & Row Publishers, 1983.

Kelley, Donald R. *The Descent of Ideas: The History of Intellectual Ideas*. Burlington: Ashgate, 2002.

Ker, Ian. *John Henry Newman: A Biography*. Oxford: Oxford University Press, 1988.

Kilby, Clyde S. and Douglas R. Gilbert. *C.S. Lewis: Images of His World*. Grand Rapids: Eerdmans, 2005.

Kipling, Rudyard. "Mowgli's Brothers." *The Gateway to the Great Books, Vol. 8*. Edited by Robert M. Hutchens and Mortimer J. Adler, 126–41. Chicago: Encyclopedia Britannica, Inc., 1990.

Kirk, Russell, *Prospects for Conservatives: A Compass for Rediscovering the Permanent Things*. Washington D.C.: Regnery Gateway, 1989.

———. *The Conservative Mind: From Burke to Eliot*. Washington, D.C.: Regnery Publishing Inc., 2001.

———. *The Essential Russell Kirk: Selected Essays*. Edited by George A. Panchias. Wilmington: ISI Books, 2007.

———. "A Conservative Purpose to a Liberal Education." *The Imaginative Conservative*. March 12, 2012. http://www.theimaginativeconservative.org/2012/03/conservative-purpose-of-liberal.html.

Knight, Gareth. *The Magical World of the Inklings: J.R.R. Tolkien, C.S. Lewis, Owen Barfield, Charles Williams*. Cheltenham: Skylight Press, 2010.

Knippenberg, Hans. *The Changing Religious Landscape of Europe*. Amsterdam: Het Spinhuis, 2005.

Kreeft, Peter. *The Philosophy of Tolkien*. San Francisco: Ignatius Press, 2005.

———. "Missing: A Virtuous People" in *Back to Virtue: Traditional Moral Wisdom for Modern Moral Confusion* (San Francisco: Ignatius Press, 1992): 19–58.

Kronman, Anthony. *Education's End: Why Our Colleges and Universities Have Given Up on the Meaning of Life*. New Haven: Yale University Press, 2007.

Kuhl, Rand. "Owen Barfield in Southern California." *Mythlore*, Issue 4 (October 1969): 8–10.

"Letters from Einstein about God (and Toys) Sell for $420, 625." *NBC.com*. June 11, 2015. http://www.nbcnews.com/science/science-new/letters-einstein-about-god-toys-sell.

Lewis, C. S. *Dymer: A Poem*. London: J.M. Dent and Sons, 1953.

———. "*De Descriptione Temporum*." Inaugural Lecture from the Chair of Medieval and Renaissance Literature at Cambridge University, 1954. http://www.archive.org/stream/DeDescriptioneTemporum/DeDescriptioneTemporumByC.S.Lewis.

———. *The Discarded Image: An Introduction to Medieval and Renaissance Literature*. Cambridge: Cambridge University Press, 1964.

———. *God in the Dock*. Grand Rapids: Eerdmans, 1970.

———. *The Weight of Glory*. New York: HarperCollins, 1980.
———. *Surprised By Joy: Inspirational Readings of C.S. Lewis*. New York: Inspirational Press, 1994.
———. *The Collected Poems of C.S. Lewis*. London: HarperCollins, 1994.
———. *Of Other Worlds: Essays and Stories*. New York: Harcourt, 1994.
———. *Mere Christianity*. New York: Simon & Schuster, 1996.
———. *The Abolition of Man*. San Francisco: HarperCollins, 2001.
———. *That Hideous Strength*. New York: Scribner, 2003.
———. *The Collected Letters of C.S. Lewis, Vol. 3: Narnia, Cambridge, and Joy 1950–1963*. San Francisco: HarperOne, 2007.
———. *An Experiment in Criticism*. Cambridge: Cambridge University Press, 2012.
———. *Image and Imagination*. Cambridge: Cambridge University Press, 2013.
———. *The Pilgrim's Regress: An Allegorical Apology for Christianity, Reason, and Romanticism*. Grand Rapids: Eerdmans, 2014.
———. *Miracles: A Preliminary Study*. San Francisco: HarperOne, 2001.
Lockerd, Benjamin G. "Beyond Politics: T.S. Eliot and Christopher Dawson on Religion and Culture." *T.S. Eliot and Christian Tradition*. Edited by Benjamin G. Lockerd and Anderson Dr. Arajuo. Plymouth: Rowman & Littlefield, 2014: 217–38.
Loconte, Joseph. *A Hobbit, A Wardrobe, and Great War*. Nashville: Nelson Books, 2015.
Lothian, James. *The Making and Unmaking of the English Catholic Intellectual Community, 1910–1950*. Notre Dame: University of Notre Dame Press, 2009.
Lovejoy, Arthur O. *The Great Chain of Being*. Cambridge: Harvard University Press, 1936.
Luckhurst, Roger. "In the Zone: Topologies of Genre Weirdness." In *Gothic Science Fiction: 1980–2010*. Edited by Sara Wasson and Emily Alder, 41:21–35. Liverpool: Liverpool University Press, 2011.
Lukacs, John. *Historical Consciousness: The Remembered Past*. New Brunswick: Transaction Publishers, 1994.
———. *At the End of an Age*. New Haven: Yale University Press, 2002.
MacDonald, George. *Phantastes*. East Peoria: Versa Press, 2011.
Macdonald, Greville. *The Religious Sense and its Scientific Aspect*. London: Hodder, and Stoughton, 1904.
Mackenzie, Donald. "Eugenics in Britain." *Social Studies of Science, Special Issue: Aspects of the Sociology of Science: Papers from a Conference, University of York, UK 16–18 September 1975* 6, no. 3/4 (September 1976): 499–532.
Mackenzie, John M. "The Popular Culture of Empire in Britain." *The Oxford History of the British Empire: Vol. IV The Twentieth Century*. Edited by Judith M. Brown and W. M. Roger Louis, 212–31. Oxford: Oxford University Press, 1999.
Magee, Bryan. *Modern British Philosophy*. New York: St. Martin's Press, 1971.
Mandell, C. Creighton and Edward Shanks. *Hilaire Belloc: A Man and His Work*. London: Metheun & Co., LTD., 1916.
Markos Louis. *Lewis Agonistes: How C.S. Lewis Can Train Us to Wrestle with the Modern and Postmodern World*. Nashville: Broadman & Holman, 2003.
Marsden, George. *The Secularization of the Academy*. Oxford: Oxford University Press, 1992.
Martyr, Justin. *The First Apology, the Second Apology, Dialogue with Trypho, Exhortation to the Greeks, Discourse to the Greeks, the Monarchy of the Rule of God*. Translated by Thomas B. Falls. Washington, D.C.: The Catholic University of America Press, 2008.
Mayr, Ernst. "Darwin's Impact on Modern Thought." Proceedings of the *American Philosophical Society* 139, no. 4 (December 1995): 317–25.
McAllister, Ted V. *Revolt Against Modernity: Leo Strauss, Eric Voegelin, and the Search for a Postliberal Order*. Tulsa: University of Kansas Press, 1996.
McCartney, George. *Evelyn Waugh and the Modernist Tradition*. New Brunswick: Transaction Publishers, 2004.
McCleary, Joseph R. *The Historical Imagination of G.K. Chesterton: Locality, Patriotism, and Nationalism*. New York: Routledge, 2009.

McDonald, Thomas L. "Ratzinger on What the Church Will Look Like." *Patheos* (blog), January 5, 2014 (1:34pm), http://www.patheos.com/blogs/godandthemachine/2014/01/ratzinger-on-what-the-church-will-look-like/.
McGrath, Alister. *The Intellectual World of C.S. Lewis*. Oxford: Wiley & Sons, 2014.
Michael, Donald N. "The Problems of Cybernation." In *Sources in Western Civilization: The Twentieth Century, 1914–1964*. Edited by Arthur P. Mendel. New York: The Free Press, 1965.
Milbank, Alison. *Chesterton and Tolkien as Theologians: The Fantasy of the Real*. New York: T&T Clark, 2009.
Mill, J. S. *On Liberty*. Edited by Elizabeth Rapaport. Indianapolis: Hackett Publishing, 1978.
Montaigne, Michel de. "Of Custom," in *The Complete Works*. Translated by Donald M. Frame. New York: Alfred A. Knopf. 2003.
Moorman, Charles. *The Precincts of Felicity: The Augustinian City of the Oxford Christians*. Gainesville: University of Florida Press, 1966.
More, Paul Elmer. *Aristocracy and Justice: Shelbourne Essays, Ninth Series*. New York: Houghton Mifflin, 1915.
Morrisson, Mark S. *Modern Alchemy: Occultism and the Emergence of Atomic Theory*. Oxford: Oxford University Press, 2007.
Mosse, George. *Towards the Final Solution: A History of European Racism*. New York: Howard Fertig, 1985.
Newman, John Henry. *The Idea of a University*. Edited by Martin J. Svaglic. Notre Dame: University of Notre Dame Press, 1982.
Nichols, Aidan. *G.K. Chesterton, Theologian*. Manchester: Sophia Institute Press, 2009.
Novalis, *Philosophical Writings*. Translated by Margaret Mahony Stoljar. Albany: SUNY Press, 1997.
Nugent, Walter. *Progressivism: A Very Short Introduction*. New York: Oxford University-Press, 2010.
Nussbaum, Martha. *Not for Profit: Why Democracy Needs the Humanities*. Princeton: Princeton University Press, 2010.
Oakeshott, Michael. "The Voice of Poetry in the Conversation of Mankind," in *Rationalism and Politics and Other Essays*. Indianapolis: Liberty Fund, 1991.
Ortolano, Guy. "F.R. Leavis, Science, and the Abiding Crisis of Modern Civilization." *History of Science* 43, no. 2 (June 2005): 161–85.
Pacini, David. *The Cunning of Modern Religious Thought*. Philadelphia: Fortress Press, 1987.
Paine, Thomas. *The Age of Reason: Parts I & II*. Edited by Moncure Daniel Conway. New York: Merchant Books, 2010.
Parker, James. "A Most Unlikely Saint." *The Atlantic*. April 2015. http://www.theatlantic.com/magazine/archive/2015/04/a-most-unlikely-saint/386243.
Pearce, Joseph. *Literary Converts: Spiritual Inspiration in an Age of Unbelief*. San Francisco: Ignatius Press, 1999.
Piccolomini, Aeneas Sylvius. "The Education of Boys" in *Humanist Educational Treatises*. Translated by Craig W. Kallendorf. Cambridge: Harvard University Press, 2002.
Pieper, Josef. *In Tune with the World: A Theory of Festivity*. Translated by Richard and Clara Winston. South Bend: St. Augustine's Press, 1999.
———. *Tradition: Concept and Claim*. Wilmington: ISI Books, 2008.
———. *Leisure: The Basis of Culture*. San Francisco: Ignatius Press, 2009.
Pietsch, Tamson. "Rethinking the British World." *Journal of British Studies* 52, no. 2 (April 2013): 441–63.
Plato. *Six Great Dialogues*. Translated by Benjamin Jowett. Mineola: Dover Publications Inc., 2007.
Polyani, Michael. *Science, Faith, and Society*. Chicago: University of Chicago Press, 1964.
Reichenbach, Bruce. "C.S. Lewis and the Desolation of Devalued Science." *Seven* 4 (1983):14–26.
Reilly, Kevin, Charles Steger, James Barker, and James Bernhard Macheve. "Do Humans Still Need to Study the Humanities?" *The New Republic*. March 17, 2015. http://www.newrepublic.com/article/121308/what-purpose-do-humanities-serve.

Reilly, R. J. *Romantic Religion: A Study of Owen Barfield, C.S. Lewis, Charles Williams, and Tolkien*. Great Barrington: Lindisfarne Books, 2006.
Russell, Bertrand. *Why I Am Not a Christian and Other Essays on Religion and Related Subjects*. New York: Simon & Schuster, 1957.
———. "A Free Man's Worship." www.philosophicalsociety.com. 1903.
Ryan, J. S. "Uncouth Innocence: Some links between Chretien de Troyes, Wolfram von Eschenbach, and J.R.R. Tolkien." *Inklings Jahrbuch fuer Literatur und Aesthetik* 2 (1984): 25–41.
Ryn, Claes. "Irving Babbitt and Philosophical Reason." *The Imaginative Conservative*. September 14, 2014. http://www.imaginativeconservative.org/2014/09/irving-babbitt-philosophical-reason.html.
Sarot, Marcel. "The Cardinal Difficulty for Naturalism: C.S. Lewis' Argument Reconsidered in Light of Peter van Inwagen's Critique." *Journal of Inklings Studies* 1, no. 2 (October 2011): 41–53.
Scarborough, Milton. *Myth and Modernity: Postcritical Reflections*. Albany: SUNY Press, 1994.
Schall, James V. "Grades," in *Another Sort of Learning*. San Francisco: Ignatius Press, 1988.
———. *The Life of the Mind: On the Joys and Travails of Thinking*. Wilmington: ISI Books, 2006.
———. *On the Unseriousness of Human Affairs: Teaching Writing Playing Believing*. Wilmington: ISI Books, 2012.
Schiller, F.C.S. *Studies in Humanism*. New York: The Macmillan Co., 1997.
Schopenhauer, Arthur. "On Education." *The Gateway to the Great Books, Vol. 7*. Edited by Robert M. Hutchens and Mortimer J. Adler, 197–203. Chicago: Encyclopedia Britannica, Inc., 1990.
Schwartz, Adam. *The Third Spring: G.K. Chesterton, Graham Greene, Christopher Dawson, David Jones*. Washington, D.C.: The Catholic University of America Press, 2005.
Schwartz, Sanford. *C.S. Lewis on the Final Frontier: Science and the Supernatural in the Space Trilogy*. New York: Oxford University Press, 2009.
Sheldon, Garrett Ward. "Natural Rights." *Encyclopedia of Political Thought*, 17–18. New York: Facts on File, Inc., 2001.
Shils, Edward. *Tradition*. Chicago: University of Chicago Press, 1981.
Shiner, L. E. "Tradition/Modernity: An Ideal Type Gone Astray." *Comparative Studies in Society and History* 17, no. 2 (April 1975): 245–52.
Snow, C. P. *The Two Cultures & A Second Look*. Cambridge: Cambridge University Press, 1965.
Spiegel, Gabrielle. "The Task of Historian." Presidential Address at 123rd Annual American Historical Association, New York City, 2009. http://www.historians.org/about-aha-and-membership/aha-history-and-archives/presidential-addresses/gabrielle-m-spiegel.
Stark, Rodney. *Discovering God: The Origins of the Great Religions and the Evolution of Belief*. New York: HarperCollins, 2007.
Stears, Marc. *Progressives, Pluralists, and the Problems of the State: Ideologies of reform in the United States and Britain, 1909–1926*. Oxford: Oxford University Press, 2002.
Strachey, Lytton. *Eminent Victorians*. London: Penguin Books, 1986.
Strauss, Leo. *Political Philosophy: Six Essays by Leo Strauss*. Edited by Hilail Gildin. Indianapolis: Pegasus, 1975.
Tavener, John. *The Music of Silence: A Composer's Testament*. Edited by Brian Keeble. London: Faber & Faber, 1999.
Taylor, Charles. *A Secular Age*. Cambridge: Harvard University Press, 2007.
"The Social Dimensions of Scientific Knowledge." *Stanford Encyclopedia of Philosophy*. February 9, 2015. http://www.plato.stanford.edu/entries/scientific-knowledge-social/.
Tolkien, J.R.R. *The Lord of the Rings*. Boston: Houghton Mifflin, 1982.
———. *The Letters of J.R.R. Tolkien*. Edited by Humphrey Carpenter with Christopher Tolkien. New York: Houghton Mifflin Co., 2000.
———. *Tree and Leaf*. Boston: Houghton Mifflin, 2001.
———. *The Fall of Arthur*. New York: Houghton Mifflin, 2013.

Townsend, Robert. "The Rise and Decline of History Specialization Over the Past 40 Years." *Perspectives on History: The Newsmagazine of the AHA* (December 2015). http://www.historians.org/publications-and-directories/perspectives-on-history/december-2015/the-rise-and-decline-of-history-specializations-over-the-past-40-years.

Trentmann, Frank. "Civilization and Its Discontents: English Neo-Romanticism and the Transformation of Anti-Modernism in Twentieth-Century Western Culture." *Journal of Contemporary History* 29, no. 4 (October 1994): 583–625.

Turner, F. M. "Religion." *The History of the University of Oxford: Volume VIII: The Twentieth Century*. Edited by Brian Harrison. Oxford: Oxford University Press, 2007.

Veblen, Thorstein. *The Theory of the Leisure Class*. Oxford: Oxford University Press, 2007.

Veldman, Meredith. *Fantasy, the Bomb, and the Greening of Britain: Romantic Protest, 1945–1980*. Cambridge: Cambridge University Press, 1994.

Waddington, C. H. *The Ethical Animal*. Chicago: University of Chicago Press, 1960.

Wain, John. *Sprightly Running: Part of an Autobiography*. New York: St. Martin's Press, 1962.

Waite, A. E. *The Hidden Church of the Holy Graal*. London: Rebman Ltd., 1909.

Watson, James. *The Double Helix: A Personal Account of the Discovery of the Structure of DNA*. New York: Atheneum, 1969.

Weaver, Richard M. *Visions of Order: the Cultural Crisis of Our Time*. Wilmington: ISI Books, 1995.

Weber, Max. *The Sociology of Religion*. Boston: Beacon Press, 1993.

Wells, H.G. *Mr. Belloc Objects to* The Outline of History. New York: George H. Doran Co., 1926.

———. *The Outline of History: Being a Plain History of Life and Mankind*. Revised by Raymond Postgate. Garden City: Garden City Books, 1961.

West, John G., ed. *The Magician's Twin: C.S. Lewis on Science, Scientism, and Society*. Seattle: Discovery Institute Press, 2012.

Whitehead, Alfred North. *Science and the Modern World*. Cambridge: Cambridge University Press, 1953.

Williams, Charles. *War in Heaven*. Grand Rapids: Wm. B. Eerdmans Pub. Co, 1947. Kindle.

———. *Outlines of Romantic Theology*. Edited by Alice M. Hadfield. Berkeley: Apocryphile Press, 2005.

Williams, Peter. *C.S. Lewis vs the New Atheists*. Milton Keynes: Paternoster, 2013.

Williams, Neville, and Philip Waller, eds. *Chronology of the Modern World: 1763–1992*, second edition. New York: Simon & Schuster, 1994.

Wills, Garry. "Catholics and Population." *National Review* (July 1965): 643–48.

Woods, Robert. "Thinking Christianly about the Liberal Arts." *Classis* XXII, no. 3 (October 2015): 16–18.

Yonan, Jonathan. "In Defense of God's Glory." Fall Convocation Speech. August 30, 2013. Eastern University, St. David's, PA.

Zaleski, Philip and Carol. *The Fellowship: The Literary Lives of the Inklings: J.R.R. Tolkien, C.S. Lewis, Owen Barfield, Charles Williams*. New York: Farrar, Straus, & Giroux, 2015.

Zimmerman, Jens. *Incarnational Humanism: A Philosophy of Culture for the Church in the World*. Downers Grove: InterVarsity Press, 2012.

Index

Adler, Mortimer, 55, 60n15
Allitt, Patrick, 18, 25–26, 44–45
Anglican, 68, 89, 122, 146; Anglicanism, 144
Anglo-Catholic, 50, 64, 128; Anglo-Catholicism, 66
anthroposophy, 87, 113
Aristotle, 2, 15n17, 47

Babbitt, Irving, 134, 139–144; non-religious principles, 147; Straussian, 50; traditionally minded, 142, 147
Bacon, Francis, 46, 79, 103n23
Bacon, Roger, 93
Barfield, Owen, 15n20, 30, 33, 127; ancient language, 111–112; discarding the spiritual, 113; evolution of meaning, 124–126; scientific inquiry, 115–116
Barzun, Jacques, 11, 154, 159, 171
Belloc, Hilaire, 139–144; Catholic intellectual, 18, 26; response to Wells, 43–44
Berdyaev, Nikolai, 49
Berger, Peter, 81–83
Berlin, Isaiah, 39–40, 180
Bloom, Allan, 41, 167
Boenig, Robert, 27, 128

Cantor, Norman, 27
Carpenter, Humphrey, 27–30, 68

Catholicism, 17, 26, 66–67, 144, 148; intellectual, 26, 44, 70
Chesterton, G.K., 1, 5, 10, 17, 26; common mind, 63, 69, 72; conservatism, 64, 69, 73; dogma, 66, 68, 70–72; faith, 68, 71, 73, 74n7; influence on Inklings, 126, 128; Middle Ages, 64, 66, 68; on modern society, 65–66, 69–71, 73, 162, 170; orthodoxy, 72–73; reconciliation, 67, 69, 71–73; on science, 78, 86–87; traditionalist, 40, 43–44, 63–65, 180–181; transcendent, 69, 71–73; Western culture, 69, 70, 73
common mind, 1, 2, 4, 22, 83, 117, 128–129, 135. *See also* Chesterton, G.K., common mind
common sense, 22, 56, 64, 66, 72
Comte, Auguste, 22, 79
conservatism, vii–2, 13, 20, 22, 25, 31, 79, 134, 138, 142, 143, 145, 146, 148, 149; and tradition, 37–41. *See also* Chesterton, G.K., conservatism; Dawson, Christopher, conservatism and crisis of western civilization; Kirk, Russell, conservatism and crisis of western civilization
convention, 10, 37, 40, 42–43, 47–49, 51, 52, 54, 57–59
Crick, Francis, 97–99
crisis of Western civilization, 32, 69, 134, 135, 139, 140, 143, 144, 148–149

custom, 10, 128, 181; and tradition, 37–59

Darwin, Charles, 86, 89–90, 94, 95, 99, 100; Darwinian, 64, 94, 116; Darwinism, 94; Darwinism, social, 91, 95
Dawson, Christopher, 1, 26, 66, 73, 93, 94, 134, 141, 148, 181; conservatism and crisis of western civilization, 135–138; on knowledge, 21; on the Modern Age, 18–19; religion in the marketplace, 81, 83–85
dehumanization, 49, 73, 114, 153, 176
developmentalism, 93, 95
Dewey, John, 20, 55, 138
dogma, 6, 43, 58, 93, 94, 96, 122, 134. *See also* Chesterton, G.K., dogma
Duriez, Colin, 22, 28, 30–31

education: liberal, 55, 144–145, 154, 162–164; modern, 50, 131n95, 159, 163, 167, 169–171; traditional, 21, 163, 166, 168, 170
Eliot, T.S., 31, 37, 38
Ellis, John M., 6–7, 17
Elmer More, Paul, 1, 14n8, 50, 143
empiricism, 41, 79, 88, 114, 136, 140, 144
the Enlightenment, 2, 17, 53, 58, 65, 79, 83, 110, 114, 124, 136
Erskine, John, 58–59
eugenics, 89, 90–92, 97, 98
evolution: emergent, 93, 95; human, 94–96, 99–100, 127

Fabian, 54, 92
faith, 9, 20, 23, 58, 136, 140, 141, 176, 179; Inklings', 109, 121–122, 125, 127; and the marketplace, 77, 78, 84, 85, 87, 94; in science, 95. *See also* Chesterton, G.K., faith
fantasy, 2, 23, 26, 27, 107, 111; and myth, 123, 126, 127; use of in imaginative literature, 117–122, 128
Faraday, Michael, 58
fellowship, 107, 112, 159
Ferguson, Niall, 23
festivity, 155–156
Freud, Sigmund, 23, 53, 56–57, 83, 128; Freudian, 28, 89–90

Galton, Sir Francis, 90–91
Gnostic, 72, 113; Gnosticism, 163
Great Books, 6, 8, 11, 14n15, 32, 179, 180; and liberal learning, 153, 159–161, 168; and tradition, 38, 41–42, 47, 55, 57, 58
Gushurst-Moore, André, 22, 64, 110–111

Haldane, J.B.S., 94–97, 108, 111
hermeticism, 87
higher things, 143, 149, 156–158, 164, 166, 169, 170
humanism: Christian, 4, 18, 32, 69–73, 134, 135, 138, 145, 148–149, 159, 176; secular, 4, 6, 117, 141, 149
humanist, 23, 50, 84, 141, 147, 157; New, 4, 13, 15n22, 22, 32, 33, 50, 63, 133, 149, 153, 179, 181
Hutchins, Robert, 55
Huxley, Julian, 90, 99
Huxley, T.H., 90, 99, 176

idealism, 40, 49, 136
ideology, 9, 13, 16n45, 19, 51, 63, 65, 74n7, 128, 137, 140, 142
imagination, 4–6, 28, 29, 49, 69, 85, 120–123, 128, 138, 145–147, 160, 162, 163, 171, 177, 179
imaginative literature, 69, 107, 117–124, 126–128
Imago Dei, 86
individualism, 13, 31, 38, 48, 84, 140, 149

James, William, 53, 55–56
Jeffrey, David Lyle, 121, 127, 161, 164, 166, 169

Kelley, Donald R., 7, 8, 19, 77
Kipling, Rudyard, 59
Kirk, Russell, 1, 38, 65, 134, 141–143, 148, 180; conservatism and crisis of western civilization, 135–138; on tradition, 39, 43, 73, 134
Kronman, Anthony T., 5–6, 9, 51, 88, 155, 157, 158

leisure. *See* Pieper, Josef, on leisure
leisure class, 54–57, 165
Lewis, C.S.: critic of scientific progress, 78, 85–89, 92, 93, 100; imagination,

127, 128; liberal learning, 161, 162, 168–171; as a medieval, 27, 128; myth and fantasy, 117, 118, 121; reaction to scientism, 107–111, 114–117, 176; and tradition, 41, 45, 50, 51, 180
liberal learning, vii, 2, 14, 134, 135, 138, 145, 157, 159, 161, 163, 164; classical, 8, 25, 32, 41, 135, 139, 141, 143, 153–154, 158, 180
liberalism, 18, 64, 66, 136
Lockerd, Benjamin, 4, 134
Loconte, Joseph, 109
Lothian, James, 26, 70
Lukacs, John, 12, 13, 50, 178–179

MacDonald, George, 118–119, 121
materialism, 12, 87, 100, 101, 128, 142; scientific, 111
McAllister, Ted, 44, 48
McGrath, Alister, 22, 26–27
medieval. *See* Middle Ages
metaphysical, 2–3, 15n20, 19, 21, 24, 29, 37, 44, 49, 50–51, 55, 58, 64, 81, 94, 95, 97, 101, 114, 115, 119, 120, 163, 176, 180; metaphysics, 2, 12, 22, 100, 102, 125, 136
Middle Ages: character and principles, 22, 24, 27, 139, 142, 144, 145, 147, 148, 177; and the Inklings, 108, 112, 113–117, 121, 126, 128; and science, 77, 85. *See also* Chesterton, G.K., Middle Ages
Mill, J.S., 42, 47, 51
Montaigne, Michel de, 47, 149, 160
Morrisson, Mark, 24, 87, 112–113
mysticism, 15n20, 25, 124
myth: of progress, 109; use of, 113, 122–129
mythical, 117, 128, 156
mythopoeia, 25, 118

naturalism, 116, 122, 124, 128
Neo-Conservative, 13, 16n45
Newman, John Henry, 18, 26, 134, 157; on the university, 143–149
Nietzsche, Friedrich, 8, 51, 83, 156; Nietzschean, 111
Nussbaum, Martha C., 5–6, 11, 20, 42, 138, 157

Oakeshott, Michael, 6
obtuseness, 5, 138
Old West, 4, 49, 171, 178
Oxford, 4, 63, 168; Christians, 28–30; circle, 28, 177

Pearson, Karl, 90
pedagogy, 5, 42, 55, 138, 163
permanent things, 4, 10, 12, 21, 28, 30, 38, 58, 78, 117, 133–137, 139, 142, 144, 161, 180
Pieper, Josef, 1, 3, 8, 39, 40, 48, 127, 153, 155, 156, 175; on leisure, 155–156
pluralism, 13, 20, 60n11, 82–84, 103n20
positivism, 12, 22, 49, 51, 79, 88, 102
postmodern, 18, 22, 47, 125, 154, 178
pragmatism, 8, 20, 73, 98, 142, 165
pre-modern, 4, 21, 37, 57, 128
progressivism, 2–3, 4, 8–10, 12, 14, 22, 25, 30, 38, 40, 48, 59, 63, 67, 77, 82, 85, 89, 91, 92, 133, 138, 168, 177, 180; progressives, 4, 5, 7, 9, 10, 25, 38, 40, 43, 51, 58, 59, 116, 140, 154, 166

reconciliation, 7, 10, 11, 18, 20, 28, 32, 39, 44, 46, 121, 133–134, 138, 149, 153, 158, 168, 181. *See also* Chesterton, G.K., reconciliation
romantic religion, 30
romanticism, 25, 66, 122, 128, 177
Russell, Bertrand, 40, 45, 80

Schall, James V., 157, 162–167
Schiller, F.C.S., 3
Schwartz, Adam, 19, 26
Schwartz, Sanford, 63, 92
science fiction, 91, 93, 117, 176
scientific: age, 3–4, 6, 8, 9, 12, 23, 37, 39, 40, 45, 47, 51, 57, 58, 77, 88, 100–102, 107, 108, 113–114, 117, 128, 133, 153, 156, 175, 177, 180; knowledge, 88, 92, 95–96, 98, 99, 110, 114, 124, 125; process, 88, 98–99, 124; progress, 24, 38, 39, 79, 88, 91, 97, 176; revolution, 45, 83, 86–87, 93, 96, 102, 161
scientism, 2, 4, 8, 19, 26, 32, 51–52, 142, 160, 163, 176–177, 180; Inklings reaction to, 107–116, 121, 127, 131n95; in the temple of science, 78, 87–89, 92,

94, 125, 126, 128
secularism, 24, 26, 70, 80, 88, 107; secularization, 7, 13, 14, 14n5, 17–20, 24, 44–45, 49, 50, 65, 70, 79, 81–84, 103n21, 149, 153, 157, 177, 178
Shaw, Bernard, 66, 72, 94
skepticism, 8, 46, 145, 160, 169
Snow, C.P., 45–46, 175
socialism, 66
St. Augustine, 58, 160, 167, 168
Stark, Rodney, 78, 80–82
Steiner, Rudolf, 113
Strauss, Leo, 50
superstition, 66, 72, 146, 164

technology, 5, 6, 7, 9, 31, 72, 77, 93, 108–110, 128, 156, 162, 175, 176
temple, 78, 80, 89; of science, 77, 78
theosophy, 87
Tolkien, J.R.R.: anti-modern and anti-scientism, 109, 110, 112; liberal learning, 161, 168; as a medieval, 27; myth and fantasy, 118–121, 126; tradition, 45, 50
transcendent, 2, 3, 39, 48, 53, 54, 95, 114, 124, 127, 134, 139–141, 147, 149, 156. *See also* Chesterton, G.K., transcendent

utilitarian, 50, 65–66, 155, 156; utilitarianism, 66, 169

Veblen, Thorstein, 53–57, 165
Veldman, Meredith, 26, 27, 66, 108
Voltaire, 160, 161

Waddington, C.H., 92, 96, 99–102
Wain, John, 30
Watson, James, 92, 96–99
Wells, H.G., 43–44, 91–94, 96
West, John, 86–87, 89
Western canon, 4, 8, 27, 38, 50, 60n15, 72, 134, 161, 168, 180
Western culture, 2, 6, 8, 10, 11, 14n15, 18–19, 46, 54, 138–143, 149, 181. *See also* Chesterton, G.K., Western culture
what is, 13, 164, 170
Whitehead, Alfred North, 8, 42
Williams, Charles, 1, 14n8, 27–29, 49, 67, 69; and hermeticism, 112–113; relationship with myth, 118, 122–123, 125, 126, 129n32; and science, 89
Woods, Robert, 161

Zaleski, Philip and Carol, 22, 28
zeitgeist, 24, 88

About the Author

Christopher Butynskyi is lecturer of European history at Eastern University in St. Davids, Pennsylvania. He holds a PhD in humanities from Faulkner University's Great Books Honors College. His work on tradition and the Western canon, the Inklings, and other related topics appears in *The Chesterton Review*, *The University Bookman*, *The Journal of Faith and the Academy*, and *The Inklings & King Arthur*, edited by Sørina Higgins.

www.ingramcontent.com/pod-product-compliance
Lightning Source LLC
Chambersburg PA
CBHW050906300426
44111CB00010B/1397